A Continent for the Taking

A Continent for the Taking

THE TRAGEDY AND HOPE OF AFRICA

Howard W. French

ALFRED A. KNOPF   NEW YORK   2004

THIS IS A BORZOI BOOK
PUBLISHED BY ALFRED A. KNOPF

www.aaknopf.com

Photographs © Robert Grossman

Knopf, Borzoi Books and the colophon are registered trademarks of
Random House, Inc.

Library of Congress Cataloging-in-Publication Data
French, Howard W.
A continent for the taking : the tragedy and hope of Africa / Howard W. French.—
1st ed.
p. cm.
Includes bibliographical references (p.) and index.
ISBN 0-375-41461-4 (alk. paper)
1. Africa, Sub-Saharan—Description and travel.   2. Africa, Sub-Saharan—Social
conditions—1960–   3. Africa, Sub-Saharan—Politics and government—1960–
4. United States—Foreign relations—Africa, Sub-Saharan.   5. Africa,
Sub-Saharan—Foreign relations—United States.   I. Title.
DT352.2.F74 2004
967.03'2—dc22   2003058920

Manufactured in the United States of America
First Edition

To my parents, who taught me to ask,
and to Avouka, William and Henry, who understood

There *are* paths. If you can't see them—and why should you see them?—you've only got your own eyes to blame. A white man can't see everything: and he has no need to see everything either, because this land is not a white man's land.

—CAMARA LAYE, *The Radiance of the King*

Not even God is wise enough . . .

—A YORUBA PROVERB

Contents

Contents

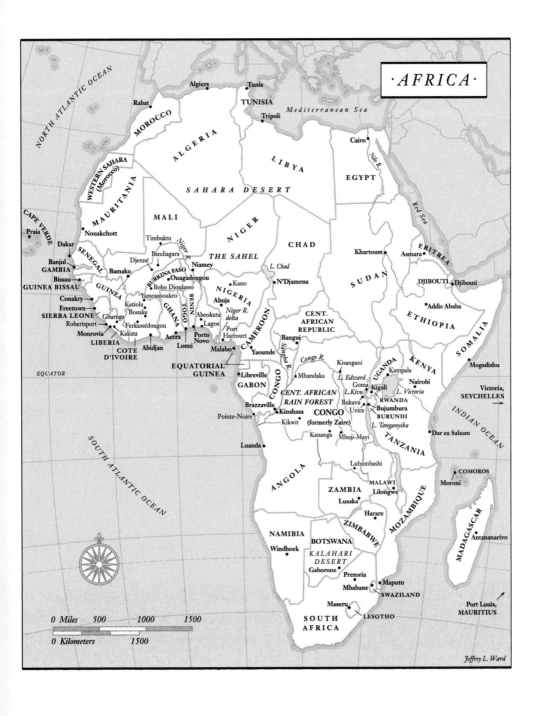

·AFRICA·

NORTH ATLANTIC OCEAN

Algiers
Tunis
TUNISIA
Rabat
Tripoli
Mediterranean Sea

MOROCCO
ALGERIA
LIBYA
Cairo
EGYPT

WESTERN SAHARA
(Morocco)
SAHARA DESERT
Nile R.

MAURITANIA
MALI
NIGER
CHAD
Khartoum
Asmara
ERITREA
Red Sea

CAPE VERDE
Praia
Nouakchott
Timbuktu
Bandiagara
THE SAHEL
Niamey
L. Chad
DJIBOUTI
Djibouti

Dakar
SENEGAL
Djenné
Niger R.
N'Djamena
SUDAN

Banjul
GAMBIA
Bamako
BURKINA FASO
Ouagadougou
Kano
Addis Ababa

Bissau
GUINEA BISSAU
Bobo Dioulasso
NIGERIA
Abuja
CENT.
AFRICAN
REPUBLIC
ETHIOPIA
SOMALIA

Conakry
GUINEA
Yamoussoukro
BENIN
TOGO

Freetown
SIERRA LEONE
Katiola
Bouake
GHANA
Abeokuta
Lagos
Niger R.
delta
Bangui

Gbarnga
Ferkassédougou
Port
Harcourt
CAMEROON

Robertsport
Monrovia
Kakata
Accra
Lomé
Porto
Novo
Malabo
Yaounde
Sangha R.
Mogadishu

LIBERIA
COTE
D'IVOIRE
Abidjan
EQUATORIAL
GUINEA
Libreville
Congo R.
Kisangani
UGANDA
KENYA

EQUATOR
GABON
Mbandaka
L. Edward
Kampala

CONGO
CENT. AFRICAN
RAIN FOREST
Goma
L.Kivu
Kigali
Nairobi
Victoria,
SEYCHELLES

Brazzaville
Bukavu
RWANDA
L. Victoria

Pointe-Noire
Kinshasa
CONGO
(formerly Zaire)
Uvira
Bujumbura
BURUNDI
INDIAN OCEAN

SOUTH ATLANTIC OCEAN
Kikwit
Kananga
Mbuji-Mayi
L. Tanganyika
TANZANIA
Dar es Salaam

Luanda
Lubumbashi
COMOROS
Moroni

ANGOLA
ZAMBIA
MALAWI
Lilongwe
MOZAMBIQUE
MADAGASCAR

Lusaka
Harare
Antananarivo

NAMIBIA
BOTSWANA
ZIMBABWE

Windhoek
KALAHARI
DESERT
Gaborone
Pretoria
Maputo
Port Louis,
MAURITIUS

Mbabane
SWAZILAND

Maseru
LESOTHO

SOUTH
AFRICA

0 Miles   500   1000   1500

0 Kilometers   1500

Jeffrey L. Ward

Introduction

Africa eludes us; it is so clearly outlined on the map, and yet so difficult to define. It is both the great, primordial rain forests at the heart of the continent and the immense deserts of the north and south.

From afar, Westerners have long fancied it to be divided into "black" and "white," in the image of their own societies, and yet observant visitors are more likely to be struck by Africa's diversity, and by the absence of any sharp dividing lines.

The continent is simply too large and too complex to be grasped easily, and only rarely, in fact, have we ever tried. Instead, we categorize and oversimplify, willy-nilly, ignoring that for the continent's inhabitants the very notion of Africanness is an utterly recent abstraction, born of Western subjugation, of racism and exploitation.

Throughout my life, I have roamed and explored the cardinal points of the Africa we see on the map, and a great many places in between. But "my" Africa, the Africa I first discovered in 1976 as a college student on summer vacation visiting my family in Ivory Coast, will forever be the musty, tumultuous world of the continent's west and central regions. As I climbed down the stairway from a jet onto Liberia's steamy, pungent soil for a brief layover on the long flight from New York to Abidjan, where my family then lived, it would be a trite understatement to say that I could not have imagined how my personal discovery of this Africa would change my life.

I would come to master languages and patois from the region. I would marry one of its daughters and the first of my two sons would be born there. The thrill of travel and discovery in this part of Africa—a civil war in Chad, a coup in Guinea, a stolen election in Liberia—would turn me away from an early, passing interest in becoming a lawyer and propel me instead into a career in journalism.

My growing intimacy with the continent, where I discovered that questions of identity were usually far more complex than the stark black-white divide that I had grown up facing as an African-American in Washington, D.C., in the 1960s, would subtly but permanently change my notions of race.

Most important, as a privileged witness to a quarter century–sized slice of history, my understanding of Africa would gradually transform the way I saw the world. It awakened me as nothing else before to the selfishness and shortsightedness of the rich and the dignity of the poor in their suffering, and to the uses and abuses of power.

As important as this transformation has been to me, this book aims to be more than a memoir of Africa and of the impact it has had on my own life. In a much broader sense, it is an extended meditation on the consequences of another encounter, this one centuries old and far more fateful, between Africa and the West.

The personal reportage contained in these pages ranges from my earliest travels on the continent to the end of the century. Cumulatively, I spent nearly a decade living in Ivory Coast, spread out over two decades—the early 1980s and the late 1990s—and from this country, once a prosperous oasis, and now, sadly, a wreck like so much of the rest of the immediate subregion, I roamed far and wide.

The "action" here, as it were, takes place in my home regions of West and Central Africa—places like Nigeria, Africa's most populous country; Liberia, the closest thing America has ever had to an African colony; Mali, home to some of the continent's oldest and most distinctive cultures; and Congo, formerly known as Zaire, whose geographical position astride the equator, in the very center of the continent, and turbulent history give it a strong claim to being Africa's heart, literary clichés aside.

Although this book is full of personal experiences, some of them harrowing, its object is not a mere rehashing of old war stories. In some respects, the dates or details, as narrowly defined, are less important than the broad patterns of treachery and betrayal of Africa by a wealthy and powerful West, often aided and abetted by the continent's own woeful leaders—patterns that are being repeated even now.

Africa is the stage of mankind's greatest tragedies, and yet we remain largely inured to them, all but blind to the deprivation and suffering of one ninth of humanity. We awaken to the place mostly in fits of coarse self-interest and outright greed. Once upon a time, these brief awakenings involved a need for rubber or cotton, gold or diamonds, not to mention the millions of slaves, branded and ferried like cattle across the Atlantic, whose contributions to the wealth of Europe and its coveted New World are scarcely acknowledged.

Today, the pickings are as "exotic" as ever, but have been updated to meet the needs of our modern era. Africa interests us for its offshore oil reserves, which are seen as an alternative to supplies from an explosive and difficult-to-control Middle East, or for rare minerals like coltan, which powers our cellular phones and PlayStations. There is one new twist on our selfishness, however—an interest in Africa driven by fear, of AIDS and Ebola and emigrants.

This book is deeply critical of the Clinton administration's behavior in Africa, which may strike some as unfair, given that President Clinton arguably paid more attention to the continent than any American president before him. But even a rare, high-profile trip by a sitting president cannot obscure America's role in downplaying the Rwandan genocide so as to escape direct involvement.

Nor does Washington's brief but active engagement with the continent after the 1994 genocide, which is explored in detail in these pages, make up for extraordinarily misguided policies, driven more by guilt than by genuine care, that resulted in the largely unheralded deaths of at least 3.3 million Congolese—the largest toll in any conflict since World War II.

The Clinton administration, actually, is no more than a representative sample, because the deplorable fact is that the United States has never had a sound Africa policy, starting from the height of the independence era, when the Central Intelligence Agency helped engineer the overthrow of Patrice Lumumba, Congo's first prime minister, in September 1960, after a mere two months in office. The coup was the first of dozens that would contribute to making Africa the world's least stable and arguably most corrupt continent.

When we pay attention to Africa's contemporary leaders, it is often to lampoon them. How conveniently we forget how this tragic pattern was set in place, in Congo as elsewhere, by what John le Carré once called, with appropriate scorn, "the global architects, the world order men, the political charm-sellers and geopolitical alchemists who in the cold war years managed, collectively and individually, to persuade themselves—and us, too, now and then—that with a secret tuck here, and a secret pull there, and an assassination somewhere else, and a destabilized economy or two, or three, they could not only save democracy from its defects but create a secret stability among the chaos."

President George W. Bush trumpeted his willingness to spend money to fight AIDS on the African continent, but cynically derived the funds for this initiative by robbing the nearly bare cupboard of American economic aid for the poorest region of the world. Meanwhile, the United States was prepared to spend $100 billion or more to overthrow Saddam Hussein, whom Bush denounced as a scourge to mankind.

But in Africa, where genuine scourges exist—plagues of chronic hunger and preventable disease—America remains dumb to the suffering, and indeed often makes things worse. While we push free enterprise to the world, we close our markets to African textiles and subsidize American farmers in ways that make it impossible for the poor of Africa to compete. While preaching democracy, we have nurtured African tyrants, quietly washing our hands of them, as with Mobutu Sese Seko of Zaire and his successor, Laurent Kabila—whose stories are told here in some detail—the moment they become inconvenient.

The United States is by no means alone in this treatment of Africa—indeed, this book is a chronicle of the calamitous continuum in the encounter between Africa and the West. This long-running tragedy began in Congo, where much of my story unfolds, with the destruction by imperial Portugal of well-structured kingdoms in its pursuit of slaves for use as beasts of burden in the Americas.

In its own modest way, this book is intended to help remedy our complaisant forgetfulness and our hypocrisy. My aim is to help remind those who yearn to know and understand the continent better, and indeed Africans themselves, of the continent's many cultural strengths; my own discovery of them kept me going through otherwise depressing times, injecting relief in a tableau of terrible bleakness. Therein lies a genuine source of hope for Africa's nearly 800 million people and for the Africans of the future.

A Continent for the Taking

CHAPTER ONE

Prehistory

I remember clearly, even now, how and when Africa grabbed hold of me, and as is so often the case for people living abroad, my infatuation began with a romance. The lightning struck me in January 1980, in a small, smoke-filled nightclub called the Keur Samba, in Treichville, the densely packed working-class neighborhood and old colonial "indigenous quarter" of the capital of Ivory Coast, Abidjan.

The dance floor was tiny, and as I would quickly learn was commonplace in Africa, when people were moved to dance, they simply jumped up without any other formalities and joined the crowd. The club's African play list was heavy on fast numbers with thumping bass lines, and it did not take long to get swept up in the atmosphere amid all the bumping and swaying. For someone new to the country who had come alone, the discovery that partners were irrelevant was a pleasant surprise.

My father, who is a doctor, had designed and was running a regional primary healthcare program for the World Health Organization, and my parents had been living in Abidjan together with my brothers and sisters for a few years. I had just moved to Ivory Coast after graduating from college to find myself while plotting my next moves in life, and for a young American out on the town by himself, the packed nightclub with its throbbing African sounds and colliding bodies seemed like the very definition of exotic. And then I met Mariam.

With the strobe lights flashing wildly and the club jam-packed, it took me longer than it should have to notice that no matter in which direction I turned I was still bumping into the same lithe, dark-skinned woman. But when a fifties rock-and-roll number came on, changing the mood of the place abruptly, the dance floor cleared momentarily. Damp with sweat and tired of the smoke, I followed a stream of customers outside onto the unpaved street for a breather. When I stopped a few paces from the exit, there she was again.

Under the faint streetlight I could finally fix her features as she smiled. She was a startling beauty, with the form of a ballet dancer and the élan of a gazelle, and an extraordinary head full of fine black tresses that tumbled down her back. There was an ever-so-brief moment of awkwardness, and then, suddenly, we both began talking. We spoke in French for a few minutes, and because of that, when she got around to asking me where I was from, she was a bit surprised to learn that I was American. I, on the other hand, assumed she was from Ivory Coast, and asked her what region of the country her family was from. The question elicited an immediate shock. "Me, from Ivory Coast?" she said, indignantly. "I am not from here. I am from a grand country, Mali; a place with a real history!"

Now it was my turn to be taken aback. Ivory Coast was the economic success story of the region. The people of the country had grown smug over their success, bragging about Abidjan's multiplex cinemas and ice-skating rink, its shopping malls and Miami skyline, and condescending to their much poorer neighbors. By contrast, Mali was one of Africa's poorest countries—a landlocked dust bowl plagued by recurrent droughts and famines that had languished under pseudo-socialist dictatorships since independence in 1960.

Mariam and I ended up leaving the nightclub together for a *maquis*, one of the cheap open-air drinking places that abound in Treichville. Of course I had read plenty about Mali's past greatness, about the fabled empires named Mali and Ghana, whose civilizations had flourished astride the ancient caravan routes across the Sahara between the sixth and fifteenth centuries. I was familiar with Malian sculpture, and that led me to share with my new friend one of my first impressions of her: There was something about her beauty that reminded me of the Chiwara mask, a graceful antelope-like sculpture from Mali that was one of the region's most distinctive forms.

I had grown up in a strong African-American family, where pride and self-respect were passed on daily, and in abundance—together with lots of history. Bowing and scraping were alien to us, and we were reminded of the achievements of blacks at every turn, from people like Charles Drew, the doctor who pioneered blood transfusion and had been my father's professor in medical school, to Ralph Bunche and Paul Robeson. Even so, it seemed that Mariam, whose pride in her culture was boundless, could easily teach us a thing or two when it came to holding our heads up. For Mariam, no matter how much I knew about Mali, it wasn't enough. For her, her homeland was the center of the universe, the cradle of African civilization and the repository of its greatest culture.

Mariam soon became my first African girlfriend, and we saw each other steadily for the next few weeks. She was visiting Abidjan from Paris, where she lived, and I was working as a translator, helping a French writer produce an English edition of her first novel. We would often meet at Mariam's hotel in Adjamé, a cheap but clean little affair where she could spend a couple of months in town without going bankrupt. She was buying West African goods—cloth, clothing, spices and artwork—to take back to Paris for sale there. The trip had far more than a mercantile interest for her, though. For Mariam, Africa would forever be home, the place where she returned to recharge.

As Mariam's stay drew to a close, I announced my decision to visit Mali. She seemed delighted, but as someone who jetted back and forth to Europe, she thought it funny of me to insist on going there overland, perhaps even as far north as Timbuktu. Jamie, my younger brother by seven years, was as determined as I was to see the continent from ground level, much as any ordinary African would, so together we set out by train for the north of Ivory Coast, as the first leg of our journey.

No one could say how much it had cost to build the Régie Abidjan-Niger railway, whose tracks were laid from Abidjan to Ouagadougou, the capital of Burkina Faso (formerly known as Upper Volta), between 1905 and 1954, or how many lives were lost in the process, but these many decades later it was easy to view it as a positive legacy of France's colonialism in the region. The train's cars were packed with migrant workers from the Sahel, the parched, impoverished badlands south of the Sahara Desert, carrying home their savings and cheap manufactured goods—black-and-white TVs, bulky radio-cassette decks and electric fans from China and India—bought with the meager salaries they had earned as laborers on cocoa plantations or as domestics.

Abidjan's fancy, "developed" veneer, all haughty and self-impressed, peeled away instantly as the train chugged along, propelling us through a thick patch of rain forest, then through verdant plantation land, and northward, with the temperature rising steadily, into the savannah.

We were traveling as light and unencumbered as possible, out to discover Africa and searching for ourselves a bit, too, along the way, and we must have made a curious sight for our fellow travelers. For luggage we had nothing more than a couple of changes of clothing stuffed into two goatskin sacks, which we wore slung over our shoulders. I had a wire-bound notebook to write in, and an old Olympus 35mm camera. For reading, I had brought along Freud's *Introduction to Psychoanalysis* and a hefty paperback travel book, Susan Blumenthal's *Bright Continent*, whose brilliant mixture of learned reflection and backpacker's-eye view made it the best African travel guide I have seen before or since.

At each stop along the way, in cities with strangely beautiful names like Katiola and Bouaké, the scenery grew more stark and simple, as did the dress and manners of the people we encountered. Before long, young girls were converging on the train at each station, shouting their sales pitches in Dioula, the commercial lingua franca of the northern half of the country, instead of French, and offering cold water to drink in clear little pouches of plastic. Other girls carried small brown smoked fish, exposed and still baking under the powerful sun, or bread borne on large enamel plates they balanced on their heads. These were not the fancy French baguettes of Abidjan, but big, boxy loaves of white bread with which the vendors rushed forward toward our open windows in a sales competition that was desperate yet always cheerful.

We fell asleep well after dark, at the end of a long and sweaty day, both feeling that the "real" Africa that we were searching for wouldn't reveal itself in earnest until we got off the train and trod the dusty ground, unmarked by man's hand, that stretched to the horizon outside. Later I came to distrust this concept of authenticity deeply.

We were awakened when the train lurched to a stop in the morning to discover that we were in Ferkessédougou, our jumping-off point for Mali, which was still about a hundred miles to the northwest. It had rained overnight and suddenly the air was surprisingly chilly. We took a taxi to the *gare routière*, where Peugeot 504 station wagons left for Bamako, the capital of Mali, and discovered that it was little more than a puddle-filled lot.

Around its circumference sat a bunch of *buvettes*, little tumble-down shacks that passed as restaurants, each with its own hand-painted sign describing the fare. We settled into one, feeling faintly like cow-boys moseying around in an old western. But instead of being served whiskey, a characteristically light-skinned young Fulani man poured thick, heavily sweetened condensed milk into our coffee and whipped up our helpings of bread and fried eggs.

Afterward, we scouted out what looked like the best car, negotiated our fare to Bamako and then waited for a departure we figured was imminent. A two-hour lesson in patience awaited us, as well as a very neat illustration of power. We were in a world of peasants and the poor, and they already understood perfectly well what we were just dis-covering and could never completely accommodate ourselves to: that there is often little more to do in life than sit around and wait until those who are more powerful are ready to budge.

In this case, the more powerful meant the drivers, who seemed to live and work according to an internal calendar whose secrets were known only to themselves and to their coxswains—the boys who helped collect their fares. Although there was a nominal fare between any two points, supply and demand was the ultimate arbiter, and the driver was free to negotiate the cost upward whenever the cars were few and passengers many. Departure times were even more elastic, and seemed governed not just by how many would be occupying the vehi-cle, which counted a great deal, but also by the Muslim obligation to pray five times each day, by the need to eat and, most vexingly of all, by what seemed to my untrained eye to be the reckoning of innumerable omens.

But finally we took off, and it felt great to be moving again, even if the car was filled almost beyond its capacity. Since I am six foot four, I had luckily taken the precaution of paying a little extra so that I could sit in the front seat, where there was a little more leg room and a prime view of the scenery. We were heading north, supposedly toward the Sahara, but oddly the vegetation was getting steadily greener. By the time we reached the border, several hours later, the cramped space and huge potholes in the road had left me feeling like an invalid.

When we climbed out of the car at the crossing, we were introduced to a brand-new waiting game, this one run by the poker-faced customs officers. The border crossing was, in reality, little more than a legally sanctioned stickup spot. And in this racket, if it is true that the driver and the customs agents could not be called friends, they were clearly complicit. Our chauffeur had obviously tithed away a portion of the passengers' fares to pay off the customs agents, and he stood nearby, watching the scene with studied disinterest, as the passengers pleaded poverty so as to surrender as little as possible and the agents gradually escalated their threats to extort whatever they could.

But the agents' ultimate leverage was our driver. After an interval of about forty-five minutes or so—long enough for our driver to eat, drink something and relieve himself, and for Jamie and me to eat a few small wooden skewers of grilled mutton deliciously seasoned with a sprinkling of powdered red pepper and spices—he beckoned us back into the Peugeot and began making ready to leave. His departure would have stranded our fellow travelers, with no question of a refund for the fares they had already paid. As the driver and customs men surely knew, this was enough to get the men to take off their shoes or to fish into secret pockets to retrieve some hidden cash, and the portly market women among them to start undoing the elaborately wrapped cloth they wore to find the crumpled bills they had so carefully hidden in their bras or in secret folds.

The drive from there was our introduction to the savannah. The reddish clay earth stretched infinitely in whichever direction one looked, melding in a blur at the horizon with the low, bright sky. Other than the little circular villages, with their peaked thatch roofs and red walls made of mud and straw, the only relief from the landscape was the incredible termite mounds—huge baroque cathedrals that rose to the height of a tall man.

When night fell, we may as well have been on the moon as on that unlit highway with its deep craters, the location of which the driver seemed to know almost by heart. He slowed down for some of the holes and slalomed to dodge others. Despite his best efforts, though, every now and again he would hit one—perhaps, I thought, he was too tired to give a damn—but as we plummeted to the bottom and were then jolted back out of even the deepest potholes, the passengers scarcely stirred from their deep slumber. The sky was lit brilliantly with stars, and the savannah mimicked them with the fires of villagers, which could be seen twinkling in the distance. Malian music was playing on the driver's radio, and the alembic strumming of the kora, a long, eighteen-stringed harp, and the soaring declamations of the singers were carrying me back to the age of the great empires.

We arrived in Bamako a little before dawn. Trying to be frugal and not knowing the city, we decided to do what so many other travelers at the station had done. We unrolled our little straw mats, clutched our goatskin bags close to us, covered our faces with pieces of clothing and slept right there on the ground. A few hours later, we rose to the sunrise and the sound of heavy traffic to discover Bamako in all of its dusty and smoke-filled glory.

France and the Soviet Union had each taken halfhearted stabs at turning this capital into a city, and the scars were everywhere. Long ago, the streets had been laid out in a tidy grid, including a formal administrative sector. The Russian-built Hôtel de l'Amitié loomed imposingly over the place like the landmark transplanted from another world that it was.

At heart, though, Bamako remained little more than a big, sooty village. Tall women in blue boubous, the regal robes and matching headdresses worn throughout the Sahel, cleaned their teeth with wooden chew sticks, spitting into the dust-choked gutter. Slender men crouched like baseball catchers, only much lower still, pouring water from tin teapots to rinse their faces and clean out their ears, as they performed their Muslim ablutions at street's edge. Cobblers repaired carefully preserved shoes with glues and tacks in their ramshackle sidewalk stands.

People seemed to be sweeping everywhere, kicking up little clouds of dust as they worked at making things neat, but the effort was existential at best, given the milky whiteness of the sky, laden with gritty tidings from the Sahara borne on every breeze. Meanwhile, pubescent girls dressed in tatters raced one another through the cluttered streets hawking their huge mangos and sprays of lettuce to cars that paused in the traffic. Police working from the roadside pulled over taxis for invented infractions in order to take a cut of their receipts. And slender young prostitutes, all with the same tightly plaited hair and dazzling black skin, winked and beckoned at foreigners in every café and restaurant.

To be sure, this was Africa, I thought, but it was still not the Africa I was searching for. Jamie and I had checked into the Grand Hotel, a misnomer these days with its dumpy furnishings and faded paint, although the cavernous rooms and central location hinted at an impressive past. Every few hours we had to return to the room to take refuge from the dirt and clamor, and to slake a constant thirst brought on by the city's dry heat and copious sand. And while an old ceiling fan paddled the room's hot air noisily, in this pre-Walkman era I took solace in tapes of Ornette Coleman and Muddy Waters, which I played on a little cassette machine while we planned our next steps.

Mariam had urged me to visit her mother, whom she described as a grand Bamako personality; a major figure among the Bambara ethnic group, who dominated the city's trade. We searched for her in the huge market, molded in clay with blunt, towering spires in the Sudanese style, and after only a couple of queries quickly found her there the next evening, installed amid the huge stacks of imported cloth that she sold, and somehow looking far simpler than I had imagined. She had never imagined me at all, because Mariam had never mentioned me to her. There was no reason to. And after she recovered from my surprise introduction as "Mariam's friend," in Bambara she explained my presence to the curious market women who had been spying on the scene from their nearby stalls.

Jamie and I needed new clothing. The spare load that we had packed was already proving insufficient; moreover, the jeans and Western-style shirts we had brought tended to cling in the heat, adding to our discomfort. We asked Mariam's mother where we could get some of the lightweight and baggy West African two-piece cotton outfits that so many of the men here wore. "Quickly and cheaply," I added, causing some raised eyebrows. Americans were well known for being pushy and always in a bit of a hurry, but at least they were supposed to be rich. What kind of Americans were we, with our rumpled dress and billowy Afros? She quickly gave us an address, though, and after offering some elaborate thank-yous we were on our way.

Newly outfitted the next day in our Malian clothes, we set out for the north. We were thrilled to be moving on, in another Peugeot sedan, but we were quickly given one more painful lesson about distances. It was 480 miles to Mopti, our next stop. On our Michelin map the road was grandiosely labeled as a national highway, but in reality it was a badly patched, unlit two-lane strip, without relief, without rest stops and with almost no turnoffs or exits. We pulled into Mopti exhausted, just as the day was about to give out, and checked into a little French-style *relais* that had been tastefully designed to blend into its surroundings—or perhaps it had just been built cheaply. The walls were made of banco, a mixture of clay and straw, and though the air conditioner belched and droned furiously, it seemed better suited as a conduit for mosquitoes than a source of cool air.

As tired as we were, we badly needed to stretch our legs, so we set off for the town. Darkness fell quickly, and as we walked the cramped and crooked streets, the muezzin called loudly from the spindly minaret of a nearby mosque, giving us a start. It had been another one of those blistering days when the white sky hangs heavy and blindingly low and sleeping dogs hug the shaded sides of buildings, keeping as still as they know how in order to keep cool. Just about now, though, the streets around us were suddenly coming alive with people, and though most of them were heading out for prayer, some were just luxuriating in the cooler evening air.

The language spoken in Mopti had a strange and mellifluous ring to our ears compared to the sharply clipped rhythms of the Bambara spoken in Bamako, a close cousin of Dioula, which we were used to hearing every day in Abidjan. Everything else, too, seemed to exclaim that this was a different world—ancient, exotic, almost biblical—and it was going to our heads. Tourists were few in these parts, and wandering through a neighborhood built of banco and scrap materials, with our huge Afros we were drawing stares from people curious to know where in the world such odd-looking foreigners came from.

Feeling giddy and playful, Jamie and I decided to have a little fun. Rather than speak English or French and give ourselves away immediately, we invented an ersatz dialect on the spot, suppressing our amusement as best we could as we made our way along the unpaved street talking loudly in our own strange new tongue. Our game was good for a laugh between us, but West Africans are accustomed to living in a linguistic babel, and the gibberish we spoke drew little more than a few double takes.

We hit the road again the next day in a worse-for-the-wear Renault van, larding our goatskins with tins of sardines and sausages, loaves of bread and extra bottles of mineral water. Our destination was Bandiagara, a town that appeared close on the map, but which we were warned could take the better part of a day to reach. Each time someone gave us their estimate of the road time that lay ahead, it ended with a sigh of "Insh'Allah" (God willing). Out here, everything depended on one's vehicle and beyond that God's favor, or simply one's luck.

We had chosen Bandiagara because all of the tour books had described the little town as the gateway to the homeland of the Dogon, a people fabled throughout West Africa for their flinty independence and unusual lifestyle. Their lore had spread so deeply into Europe that Bandiagara and the nearby Dogon cliffs were becoming an obligatory pilgrimage for a certain kind of tourist back then: the bearded and braless northern European tribe who wore tie-dyes and sandals, in homage to what they imagined was a genuinely African lifestyle.

Many Dogon still elected residences on the very face of the steep escarpments that rise from their Sahelian plain. Theirs was an existence in caves. They had deliberately kept their distance from the life-giving Niger River in order to preserve their freedom from slave raids and forcible conversion to Islam, whether at the hands of the Bambara from the south or the Moroccans from the north. Their choice was stark and simple: Life would be harsh, but it would be *their* life, and it has remained that way up to the present.

Across the centuries, the Dogon had developed an extraordinarily sophisticated cosmology, one replete with detailed and precise observations of the heavens, and a particular focus on Sirius, which at 8.6 light-years away is the brightest star in the sky. Without the benefit of modern scientific instruments, somehow they had also divined the existence of a dwarf companion star to Sirius, which they named Po Tolo. Long ago they had accurately described its orbit and said it was composed of a metal that they believed was the densest material in the universe. Although telescopes had first noted this companion star a century ago, until 1970 Western astronomers weren't able to photograph what the Dogon had said was there all along.

When the French anthropologist Marcel Griaule began writing about their cosmology in the 1950s, the Dogon suddenly became a kind of pre-modern freak show, a people whose cultural achievements, like the building of the pyramids or the construction of the monumental statues on Easter Island, knew no simple explanation. Before our trip, I had read Griaule's book, a dizzying work full of talk about the dryness of the moon and the architecture of the Milky Way, but the proto-science that was attracting all the tourists was not what had drawn me to visit the Dogon. It was their rugged, hardheaded independence that intrigued me.

Try as I might, I could not imagine hotter weather as we set out in our lumbering vehicle, which was packed to bursting, like every commercial vehicle in rural Mali, with people, goats and chickens. As Mopti receded in the distance, and finally vanished like an oasis, the town struck me as merely a more rural version of Bamako: less asphalt and concrete, no high-rise buildings and much more of the molasses pace that one associates with tiny, out-of-the-way towns everywhere.

At last, it seemed we were truly abandoning the beaten path and, by the look of things, even traveling back in time. The appearance of our fellow passengers seemed to confirm this impression. The women's faces and hands were stenciled with ceremonial dyes. Their gums, too, had been rendered black from treatment with charcoal-laden needles. Some of them wore huge, gold-leafed hoop earrings that tugged at their pierced earlobes under blazing red and gold headdresses.

Theirs was a way-out concept of beauty, strikingly unaffected by the definitions of attractiveness in the West, whose standards had long ago worked their way into Africa's big cities, conveyed by movies, television shows and the ever-spreading tentacles of commerce and materialism. We had come a long way, and had peeled back many layers, I thought, congratulating myself that we were perhaps finally arriving in the "authentic" Africa I was seeking.

I had been haunted throughout the trip by the affinity between the plaintively shouted choruses in the early, pre-electric Muddy Waters I listened to every day on my tinny little tape player and the wailing kora music of Mali, tinged with woe, that we had heard in every car we had ridden in. The blues had their roots in American slavery, and huge numbers of those slaves had come from West Africa. Surely the resemblance was more than a coincidence.

At Jamie's urging I asked the driver to play my tape, and as we thudded along on the dusty washboard road, he popped it in, setting off a Muddy Waters shout about "rolling and tumbling, and crying the whole night long." But after the driver had heard a minute or two of this, he turned his head quickly to pronounce a dismissive verdict. "Ça c'est la musique des toubabs," he said with a derisive snort, using one of West Africa's few universally understood words, a term that literally means "outsiders" but is typically reserved for whites.

So much for my theories, I concluded a bit dejectedly. But the tape remained in the player and as Muddy continued his rousing calls, the twelve-bar Mississippi blues, with its gut-stirring, soulful repetition, gradually lulled the driver and passengers into mellowed acceptance, just as the Malian kora had slowly hypnotized me.

When we reached Bandiagara, there was no station, not even a dusty parking lot. The road simply came to an end. A narrow footpath was the only way forward, so Jamie and I gathered our things and walked down the gentle incline toward the town. Actually, Bandiagara resembled a settlement: a rocky, unpaved street lined with simple, blocky buildings. We had no idea where we would be staying, or indeed if there was a hotel to be found. But our problem was soon resolved when we were approached by a passel of scuff-kneed boys dressed in plastic sandals and tee shirts. The eldest among them quickly suggested that they act as our guides, offering to take us to see what every foreigner comes to see: the Bandiagara cliff dwellers.

We had long since developed a practiced equanimity in such situations, which was aimed at deflecting the overeager merchants, touts or street urchins who clamorously proposed their services, usually several of the boys at once. Our show of indifference didn't seem to discourage them at all, though. In fact, we soon found ourselves being offered a place to sleep for the night, on the rooftop of the home belonging to one boy's family, who turned out to be town *notables*, or dignitaries.

Over the years, Jamie and I have often marveled at this gesture of hospitality, if that is the right thing to call it. Just imagine, my brother once said, the kind of reception two young African adventurers might receive if they arrived by bus, scruffy and unannounced, in some mountain village in West Virginia.

It was already late in the afternoon, and if the sun's radiation had eased a few notches from the spectral levels of midday, the heat still left us feeling heavy and listless, and drained of all ambition for what remained of the day. After a quick walk around the town, the boys took us to our rooftop sleeping quarters. It was atop a sturdy, two-story affair made of sandy cement, rather than the cheaper banco that most people built with, and its little touches—ironwork railings and wood trimmings—set it apart even further. The view from above was of the vast and desolate Bandiagara plain, and under a hazy sky we could just make out the Dogon cliffs in the distance.

We had become instant celebrities, in the sense that our presence had drawn a small crowd of teenage boys, and they were endlessly curious about us. Why did we speak French if we were Americans? How much did my tape player cost, and why didn't we bring several of them, to trade, or better yet, to give away? Why did people as light-skinned as we insist that we were black Americans every time they called us *blancs*?

All in all, there was nothing to give offense. Indeed, the tone was friendly, and eventually we were offered mint tea. The younger boys were then invited to leave, signaling that a more serious discussion would now begin. As our hosts took turns pouring the thick, sweet tea from a beautifully engraved brass pot, artfully hoisting and lowering its swan's-neck spout as the tiny ceramic cups filled, the older boys took a last swipe at convincing us to hire them as our guides, and then settled into a startling discussion of their own history.

Above all, I wanted to know why they had settled in such inhospitable territory. Outside of the land we had driven through in the south of the country, where greenery abounded and water was plentiful, almost every other people in Mali had clung near to the banks of the Niger River. In times of frequent drought, the river was far more than a mere waterway; it was truly a lifeline.

"From here we could see the enemy coming from far away," one of the youths said immediately, pointing to the black clouds massing in the distance and the swirling dust storms kicking up beneath them. "In this way, we were able to defend ourselves from attack. That worked for a long while, but when it was no longer enough, our people moved onto the cliffs."

This was, of course, essentially the same story I had read in my travel books, only now it was no longer potted history. Here was a seventeen-year-old boy explaining to me with unshakable confidence the cultural will to survive that had preserved both his people's lives and their unique identity. In his own simple but straightforward way, he had answered the dilemma posed by the Nigerian novelist Chinua Achebe in his masterpiece about the destruction of his own Igbo culture by Christian missionaries. "How do you think we can fight when our brothers have turned against us? The white man is very clever. He came quietly and peaceably with his religion. We were amused at his foolishness and allowed him to stay. Now he has won our brothers, and our clan can no longer act like one. He has put a knife to the things that held us together and we have fallen apart."

Jamie and I were determined to discover things for ourselves, so we set out the next morning armed with a bit of water and food, and our sturdy straw-peaked Malian hats. But before long we were lost in the rocky, blistering hot plains of Dogon-land, hungry and thirsty and more than a little concerned that we wouldn't be able to find our way back to the settlement. Our stubbornness thus proved to be costly, for we never made it to the cliffs. I have longed to visit them ever since, regretting that we didn't do the simple thing and go with our eager and friendly guides. But the conversation with the boys has proved more important to me over the years than a sight-seeing excursion alone could ever be, because the discourse prompted some what-if questions about Africa that I have pondered one way or the other ever since.

If the Dogon, a smallish ethnic group with modest lands, could win the struggle to keep their culture and identity intact in the midst of persistent encroachment by outsiders, what might Africa have become if larger, even better-organized ethnic groups had been afforded the geographical space or other means to resist foreign domination? I have in mind ancient kingdoms like Kongo in Central Africa, or Dahomey and Ashanti in West Africa, just three out of numerous examples of African peoples who created large, well-structured states, with codified legal systems, diplomats and many other kinds of bureaucrats, and a range of public services from customs to mail delivery. One can easily imagine proto-states like these taking their places among today's modern nation-states, if only they had been given the opportunity to develop. Instead, as we will see, they were willfully and utterly destroyed, as were invaluable cultural resources and much of Africa's self-confidence.

This question that haunts me has also been posed by Basil Davidson, the pioneering British historian of Africa, in *The Black Man's Burden*, a brilliant summing-up of his life's work. Davidson writes that Ashanti, the kingdom that once controlled most of present-day Ghana,

> was manifestly a national state on its way toward becoming a nation-state with every attribute ascribed to a West European state, even if some of these attributes had yet to reach maturity. It possessed known boundaries, a central government with police and army, consequent law and order, and accepted national language. . . . What might have happened if indigenous development could have continued, and pre-colonial structures had remained free to mature into modern struc-

tures, can indeed be anyone's guess. Suppose the sovereignty of Asante [a widely used alternate spelling for Ashanti] had not been hijacked. . . . Could the resultant Asante nation-state have answered to the needs of the twentieth century? Would it have acted as a magnet of progress for its neighbors? Or would it have become a curse and a burden?

Regrettably, history provides no answer. We are left, instead, with a humiliating picture of Africa and Africans, such as the images that endure in popular fiction like *Tarzan*. How many Westerners today realize, or are even capable of imagining, that it took most of the nineteenth century for the mighty British to overcome the Ashanti, after a series of bitter and closely contested wars? Ultimately, the West African kingdom was undone by superior technology, in particular the Enfield rifle, which was accurate at nearly eight hundred yards, and later, machine guns such as the Maxim, which allowed the British to mow down their opponents. But it is important to recall, especially since such things are not taught in schools, that the British-Ashanti wars were struggles between two proud civilizations that shared similar concepts of nobility, courage and duty to the sovereign, but were separated by radically different notions of fair play and ethics.

These differences eerily echo the complaints of the British a century earlier during the American Revolution, when it was they who decried the irregular tactics of George Washington's men as unsporting. The Ashanti, who outdid even the British in gallantry, thought it proper to allow their enemy to beat an orderly retreat after defeating them in battle. And when mounting sieges of British-controlled forts, the Ashanti armies even allowed their mortal enemies to resupply themselves with drinking water.

Britain, on the other hand, unilaterally abrogated its treaties and other diplomatic agreements with the Ashanti, who at several points in the century-long conflict made plain their desire for a peaceful modus vivendi that could accommodate their enemy's commercial interests. When the British army captured the Ashanti capital, Kumase, for the first time, in 1874, its treasures were painstakingly looted, including large stores of gold, sculpture, ivory and royal furniture. Then the city was deliberately burned to the ground.

Henry Morton Stanley wrote at the time that "King Coffee is too rich a neighbor to be left alone with his riches, with his tons of gold dust and accumulations of wealth to himself." But even this humiliation was not enough. When the British came back to Kumase in 1895, it was to declare that Ashanti independence was an "intolerable nuisance," and to force the new king, Prempeh, and the Queen Mother to publicly prostrate themselves, embrace the boots of the colonial governor and two colonels, and swear allegiance to the queen of England.

One pretext for the British action was the practice of human sacrifice by the Ashanti in their religious rituals. The British played up this example of "barbarism" while doing their utmost to annihilate West Africa's most powerful, sophisticated and accomplished political culture. For anyone in possession of these facts, looking back today it is anything but clear that the British conducted themselves in the more "civilized" manner.

In the end, in its inimitably cavalier way, Britain smashed an African state that Basil Davidson said deserved comparison with the contemporaneous, pre-Meiji Japan of the mid-nineteenth century. Amid Europe's great, late-nineteenth-century wave of conquest and colonization in Africa, London chose to govern its new possessions directly, and in the process not only obliterated native memories of indigenous political culture and accomplishment, but also deprived the locals of any significant hand in the new forms of administration. Under direct rule in Africa, a heavy emphasis was placed on doing things cheaply, even by comparison with other colonial territories. The notion that Britain was nobly bearing the white man's burden, doing good works and bringing civilization to a supposedly dark continent, is belied by a simple statistic. At the end of World War II, Britain had a mere 1,200 senior colonial service officials in all of its African possessions combined, meaning that London had assigned a skeleton crew to run more than a dozen colonies covering nearly 2 million square miles, with a population of 43 million.

Then, in 1957, barely a half century after wiping out the Ashanti proto-state and imposing colonial rule, an astoundingly fickle Britain changed its mind and granted Ghana independence under state structures it copied directly from European blueprints. The question that goes unasked in Western news coverage of Africa, and in most of the other ritualized hand-wringing over the continent's plight, is why should anyone be surprised that violent European hijacking of Africa's political development resulted in misery and chaos?

How could it be that in America, a country where 12 percent of the population traces its ancestry to African slaves, the vast majority of the population remains totally unaware of this derailment, except by a deliberate and long-term burial of the truth? Chinua Achebe offers one possible answer when he speaks of "the desire—one might indeed say the need—in Western psychology to set Africa up as a foil to Europe, as a place of negations at once remote and vaguely familiar, in comparison with which Europe's own state of spiritual grace will be manifest." "White racism against Africa," he adds, "is such a normal way of thinking that its manifestations go completely unremarked." Hollywood, however belatedly, has slowly come around to accepting the dignity of Indians and drawing sympathetic pictures for us of what existed in the so-called New World before its conquest and colonization. But where Africa is concerned the great forgetting continues.

What is even worse, people who are ignorant of Africa, or merely hostile to the idea of black achievement, are quick to ridicule anyone who finds anything of merit in the continent's past. In a lucid critique of the nearly identical way in which Western historians have systematically downplayed black Haiti's early-nineteenth-century revolutionary victory over Napoleon's armies, the University of Chicago anthropologist Michel-Rolph Trouillot writes: "The world of the West basks in what François Furet calls the second illusion of truth: what happened is what must have happened. How many of us can think of any non-European population without the background of a global domination that now looks preordained? And how can Haiti, or slavery, or racism be more than distracting footnotes within that narrative order?"

A favorite prop in this endeavor has been to focus on the wildest theories of the so-called Afrocentrics, a mostly black group of scholars who have often painted ludicrously idealized pictures of the African past. At heart, what this ridicule amounts to is a clever game of concealment, whose aim is the erasure or covering up of what should be Europe's own great shame.

From Hegel to Conrad, we have been told time and again that Africa has little history worth recalling, or to believe the late Oxford scholar Hugh Trevor-Roper, no history at all, "only the history of Europe in Africa." "The prehistoric man was cursing us, praying to us, welcoming us—who could tell?" says Marlow, hero of *Heart of Darkness*, as he makes his way up the Congo River. "The earth seemed unearthly. We are accustomed to look upon the shackled form of a conquered monster, but there—there you could look at a thing monstrous and free." Africa was a nearly blank slate when the white man arrived, a dark continent. And yet, since we know that Europeans have been almost obsessive about recording their own history, we would do well to ask, Why does so much amnesia surround Europe's collision with its neighbors to the south?

The first extended contact between Europeans and a major state in sub-Saharan Africa most likely began in 1491, when Portuguese missionaries visited the Central African kingdom of Kongo, a three-hundred-square-mile proto-state comprised of half a dozen provinces. Its capital, Mbanza-Kongo, was situated just on the Angolan side of what is now that country's border with the Democratic Republic of the Congo.

By all accounts, the people of the kingdom were warmly hospitable to the Portuguese, who were the first Europeans they had ever laid eyes upon. Indeed, although no actual event of the sort is recorded, one easily imagines a reception akin to the first American Thanksgiving. As missionaries are wont to do, they set about trying to make converts, and because the Kongolese king, or Mani Kongo, was interested in obtaining European goods—including firearms—in exchange for allowing them to do so, he gave the proselytizers a free hand.

Kongo struggled valiantly with the unanticipated consequences of this fateful decision over the coming decades and, for a supposedly savage culture, fought with extraordinary honor to keep its head above water against what quickly became a Portuguese deluge. But the kingdom would have none of the success of the Dogon, and when the Portuguese embrace became suffocating, there was no way to escape it.

Looking back, one can point to a mere accident of history that sealed Kongo's fate. Portugal's great age of exploration, conquest and finally colonization was launched by the invention of the caravel in the 1440s. And when some of these swift new ships, which were capable of sailing into the wind, were blown off course in 1500, the leader of the expedition, Pedro Alvares Cabral, inadvertently chanced upon the land, previously unknown to Europeans, that we now know as Brazil. The exploitation of Brazil, initially for the cultivation of sugar, created such powerfully compelling economic opportunities for the Portuguese that just nine years after the first missionaries had arrived in Mbanza-Kongo, the soul-saving rationale for the Portuguese presence in Central Africa mutated almost overnight into something quite different: a rush to sell as many Africans as possible into slavery.

Soon, many of those same missionaries were mounting expeditions hundreds of miles from the coast, sowing panic and chaos among the inland peoples who were thrust into deadly competition against one another, and indeed against Kongo, in the capture of slaves for shipment to the New World.

It has become fashionable in discussions of the European slave trade to object that Africans were themselves great slavers long before the white man ever set foot on the continent. But seen against the failure of Western education to give generation after generation of students a clear picture of the horrors of Europe's imperial conquest, this insistence strikes one as little more than an attempt to change the subject. The prior existence of slavery in Africa is undeniable fact, but there can be little comparison between the age-old institution of African slavery, in which captives were typically absorbed and assimilated into the culture that captured them, and the industrial scale of Europe's triangular slave trade, and even less with its dehumanizing impact and brutality.

Where was the humanity of the "civilized" Europeans during the early years of the rush to dehumanize Africans, who were traded just as coolly as one would truck in timber or coal? Indeed, even the Catholic conventions of the day legitimized the inhuman treatment of "pagans."

Where the African practice of slavery hurt most was in helping plant the seed in the European mind for the immense traffic that followed. The first Europeans who traded in African slaves were in reality more interested in acquiring gold. But when the early Portuguese travelers learned of abundant production of gold near places like El Mina (The Mine), in present-day Ghana, they paid for the metal with slaves captured elsewhere along the coast, and discovered that the Fanti people who lived in that coastal area were eager buyers.

Surprisingly, to this day, there has been little willingness to contemplate the true impact of over four centuries of slavery on Africa. Slavery's cost to the continent did not *merely* involve the loss of untold millions of souls who died along the bone-strewn footpaths where captives in chains were driven to the coast, or perished in the horrific Middle Passage. Nor, finally, can it be measured in the ten million or so hardy survivors who ultimately reached the Americas. There was an immense social impact on Africa, too.

As the Portuguese trade in slaves flourished, the English, French, Danes and Swedes were attracted to it as well. Steadily, what had begun as a good business, at least when seen from the narrow perspective of the elite in the African societies who provided slaves, turned into an unmitigated disaster, one that destroyed not only the weaker societies that were preyed upon, but also the stronger kingdoms that were the predators.

By the 1700s, each year sixty thousand slaves on average were being shipped across the Atlantic from West and Central Africa. This figure does not begin to take into account the number of people killed in the violent slaving raids that ripped through the African countryside, disrupting life in all but the most desolate corners of the continent, as far inland as the dry escarpments of Dogon-land. All the while, in a foreshadowing of what, 450 years later, was to befall the feeble commodity-based economies put in place by the Europeans during the colonial era, the terms of trade in Africa's slave business were steadily whittled down until the market price of a slave was essentially zero.

At the outset, Europeans paid for their black captives with horses, then with guns and cheap manufactured goods like copper kettles, cloth and shaving bowls, then with crude metal bars. By the peak of the trade, when the death and destruction had softened up the continent for the colonialism that was soon to come, the Europeans were engaging in outright asset stripping.

Africans were purchased using shovelfuls of shiny, indestructible cowry shells, which the Europeans introduced as a unit of exchange and loaded into their ships as ballast in Indian Ocean ports of call such as the Maldives. Bit by bit, the tonnage in useless shells was replaced by enchained men, women and children as the slavers took on their living cargo along a huge stretch of the African coast, from present-day Angola in the south to Mauritania in the northwest.

The cost of the slave trade in terms of sheer population loss was nothing short of catastrophic. The continent had always been underpopulated because of its poor soils and difficult climate, and because of the endemic diseases that have plagued mankind in Africa ever since the species emerged there. Some demographers calculate that had there not been an Atlantic slave trade, by 1850 the total population of the continent would have been about seventy million, or 40 percent higher than the actual population at the time.

But in the end, what may represent the most damaging legacy of all is that the Western slave industry, like its Arab-run twin, which was concentrated in East Africa, fueled mass migration and generalized warfare among Africans, as neighbor was pitted against neighbor, society against society. Europeans had created a thirst for their goods, and for the quick profit that came from trading in fellow humans, which Africans used to buy them. The ensuing scramble wiped out the intricate and inherently conservative social codes that prevailed in one society after another. In the space of a generation, or even less in many instances, the authority of king or chief, and the respect for communal laws and customs that had kept people finely tuned with their local environment over centuries, was destroyed.

"For Africans, enslavement was a threat that compounded the uncertainties of existence—a fear at the back of the mind, dulled by familiarity perhaps, an ache that induced a lingering fatalism in society as it passed from generation to generation," writes John Reader in his illuminating survey, *Africa: A Biography of the Continent.* "Kidnapping, capture, enslavement threatened villagers in various parts of West Africa for up to 400 years: 20 generations lost some kinsmen to the slavers, or saw their neighbors routed. . . . The pre-existing political economies in which chiefs and elites commanded the respect and occasional material tribute of their subjects were transformed into systems controlled by warlords and powerful merchants who obliged indebted chiefs and elites to collect slaves as payment against forced loans."

In the kingdom of Kongo, this threat was clearly perceived by the first African sovereign to face it. The king when Portugal's slave trade went industrial, Affonso, was an enthusiastic and remarkably flexible modernizer. A fervent convert to Christianity, he quickly learned to read and write, and by reputation came to know the Scriptures better than the monks sent to spread the faith in his land.

Affonso immediately sensed the potential threat to his culture inherent in its collision with expansionist Europe. And although he recognized the disadvantages his people faced against the technologically superior outsiders, as leader of his own well-organized empire of two million, he was no less self-confident.

For Affonso, preserving his empire meant buying time: absorbing as much Western learning as he could, and adapting it in ways that would not destroy Kongolese culture. Sons from his court were sent to be schooled in Portugal, and Affonso constantly begged the missionaries and other envoys from Lisbon to send more teachers in order to fortify his elite. The footrace between slavery and education proved to be no contest in the end, though, and Affonso watched in growing despair as the threads that held his realm together came unstitched. Even his relatives became caught up in the slave trade, if not as slavers, then as slaves themselves.

Among the most pathetic diplomatic exchanges ever between a sub-Saharan African and a European happen to be the oldest surviving documents written by an African in a European language. In a series of letters written in his own hand in 1526, Affonso appealed to the Christian virtue of his Portuguese counterpart, King João III: "Each day the traders are kidnapping our people—children of this country, sons of our nobles and vassals, even people of our own family. . . . Corruption and depravity are so widespread that our land is entirely depopulated. . . . We need in this kingdom only priests and schoolteachers, and no merchandise, unless it is wine and flour for Mass. . . . It is our wish that this kingdom not be a place for the trade or transport of slaves."

Later that year, Affonso wrote João III again to deplore the destabilizing influence of the accelerating Portuguese barter trade of European merchandise for human beings. "These goods exert such a great attraction over simple and ignorant people that they believe in them and forget their belief in God. . . . My Lord, a monstrous greed pushes our subjects, even Christians, to seize members of their own families, and of ours, to do business by selling them as captives."

The king of Portugal's reply was brutal in its simplicity and resounded like a death knell for Affonso's kingdom. Kongo, he said, had nothing else to sell.

Leviathan

Having already done a five-year stint in West Africa as a freelance reporter a decade earlier, in 1994 I accepted a posting to Abidjan as the *New York Times* West Africa bureau chief. West Africa had received hardly any press attention in the United States for years, but I accepted the job as a personal challenge. My marriage to Avouka, whose family is from both Ivory Coast and neighboring Ghana, had given me some extra perspective on the region. So had the many friendships I had developed in Africa and the countless trips around the continent that I had taken during my first six years living in Abidjan, in the early 1980s, when I had worked as a translator, university professor and then as a journalist.

We had barely arrived in Abidjan in August, with our two children in tow, when a big story beckoned from Nigeria. The country had been in an open state of crisis since June, when the true winner of annulled presidential elections, the millionaire-turned-politician Moshood K.O. Abiola, had been jailed. In the hardball world of Nigerian politics, the logic behind the treason charge against him was as simple to understand as it was outrageous: Abiola had had the gall to try to prevent the military from hanging on to power by asserting his legitimate right to the presidency.

My predecessor, Kenneth Noble, had generously left me a list of important contacts. He had also warned me about the airport, stressing that unless a driver or greeter whom you can trust meets you there, you risk being kidnapped, robbed or even killed. Lagos had been plenty dangerous a decade earlier, when I had visited the city often, so I took the warning seriously. I sent a telex to the Eko Hotel where Ken's driver, David, worked, gave him my flight number and arrival time, and asked him to be sure to meet me.

I had far less luck, though, in placing calls to Nigeria to set up interviews with people during the week that I planned to stay. Africa's giant, it was often said, had feet of clay, and one obvious sign of this was a telephone system that barely functioned. What good was it, I wondered, to have the most energetic and self-confident population on the continent, not to mention one of the most generous endowments of natural resources anywhere, if something so basic as the telephone system was allowed to fall into permanent disrepair?

My flight from Abidjan landed at Lagos in the middle of a blazing afternoon, and I began to note the decay even as we deplaned. It had not been so long ago that Murtala Muhammed airport was a marvel of Africa. As recently as the 1980s, Nigeria had been a country that sensed it was going places. The country proudly led the continent in democratization, in the fight against apartheid and in boldly developing heavy industries—oil, steel, automobiles—that no black nation had mastered before.

In the 1980s, the new Lagos airport boasted retractable boarding corridors that allowed passengers to avoid the rainy season's deluges and walk straight from the plane to the terminal. This might seem like a negligible detail to a Westerner, but here the symbolism was important. Landing in Lagos was meant to feel just like arriving at Heathrow or JFK, sending a message to the world that Nigeria was no moldering African backwater, but an emerging power.

As my plane landed at the airport a decade later, however, I had to clamber down the rolling stairway from the aircraft the old-fashioned way and then precariously climb back up a teetering, ladder-style stairway into those fancy boarding bridges, which had long been immobilized by rust and a lack of maintenance. Corruption had eaten away at everything here since that bygone era of pride and optimism. Most would say the rot had started under the elected government of Shehu Shagari, who was overthrown in a military coup in 1983, and things had gotten steadily worse under a succession of bemedaled generals.

Nigeria had become one of Africa's most tragic stories, as if a great family franchise had been run into the ground by decadent nephews prematurely handed the reins of management. The callow nephews in this tale were army generals, and like King Midas in reverse, the officers who had run the country for the last decade had debased everything they had touched, starting, of course, with politics, which they had turned into a contest of self-enrichment.

The leader who ran the country in the mid-1990s, General Sani Abacha, stood out even in this crowd. As an officer who had been involved at a senior level in every coup since the one that overthrew Shagari, he represented the final evolutionary wrinkle of a predatory, runaway institution: a general who offered no explanations for his actions, no smiles and no mercy. With the coup to prevent Abiola from taking office as the elected president in November 1993, Abacha had finally become the man in charge, no longer a power in the shadow of the more respected, more charming or more ostentatiously clever generals he had once served.

In the months before my arrival, Nigerians were discovering to their horror that Abacha was more interested in killing people than in dazzling them. He gladly ruled from the shadows, from behind dark glasses, where he seemed to relish his image as the person his countrymen feared most. Abacha rarely appeared in public, working by night and sleeping well into the day. He reportedly kept long lists of enemies, real and imagined, whom he methodically tracked, executed or jailed. Gradually he came to take on the aura of a motion picture monster, and in a society notable for bold individualism, for a people who were not intimidated easily, Abacha lurked menacingly in the popular imagination, like Jaws, a hidden leviathan that gave people the chills.

I had taken care not to check any bags, and was relieved to get through the immigration formalities without a hitch. My relief was redoubled when I stepped outside and was approached by David, who by way of bona fides showed me the telex that I had sent his boss. A broad, thickset man of medium height and a ready smile, David insisted on carrying my bags, and we began our long walk to the parking area, where he had left his car.

As we descended a stairway, a thin, sinister-looking man wearing an agbada, the loose and flowing three-piece outfits favored by many Nigerians, approached me and asked to see my papers. David, who was walking a few paces ahead, turned to say to me in his guttural English,

"Don't mind that man." I wasn't inclined to show my passport again anyway and merely kept walking. But the thin man stepped up his pace determinedly and approached David, warning him excitedly, "Do you know me?" and waving a wrinkled ID card. "Don't you know that I am a police officer? You just wait. I will show you."

As the man sped off angrily, David laughed. "It is good Mr. Noble told you to have me meet you. It is always like this here. We Nigerian people, we are no good. We are always making trouble. Why?"

As David put my things into the trunk of his Peugeot sedan, I saw the thin man approaching again. This time, though, he had two armed soldiers with him. David told me that no matter what happened I should let him do the talking. His car was slow to start, and before the engine could turn over, the men were upon us. This time the thin man stayed in the background, and while one soldier stood in front of the car with his rifle raised, the other came to my side of the car and demanded my passport.

"Don't give it to him, Mr. French," David insisted. "They have no right. Don't listen to them."

With that, the soldier became furious, and ran around to the driver's side to threaten David. "Why did you tell the man not to obey me?" he asked angrily, raising his gun.

To my amazement, David grew only bolder. "This man already had his passport checked inside. You people are just making trouble for nothing." The soldier then demanded David's papers, and he flashed an ID card, perhaps his driver's license, but refused to hand it over. "Here is my business card," he said, giving it to them. "If you need to see me, you can find me at work. I will wait for you there, but you will leave this man alone."

This made the soldiers only angrier. "Who is this American man to you?" one of them screamed. "Are you willing to die for him?"

David began to start the engine again. It was no longer flooded and turned over smartly. "Stop your car, or I will shoot you," the soldier in the front shouted.

Then, as he put the car in gear, David said, more as a dare than a question, "Can you shoot me? Are you sure?"

I wasn't so sure, but throughout the whole tense standoff I had been a powerless spectator. The car sped off, forcing the soldier who had been standing in front of us to dive out of the way. I held my breath and waited for gunfire, but it never came.

Welcome back to Nigeria, I thought, shaking my head in disbelief. David smiled as he drove toward the highway, and then delivered an important lesson in survival. "You must never fear those people," he said. "If you do, you are finished."

David took me to the Sheraton Hotel in Ikeja, a hotel that was located more than ten miles from the center of Lagos but had the advantages of reliable power, decent telephones—by Lagos standards—and good security. When I checked in, a woman at the reception desk named Bunmi, who had known my predecessor, urged me to stay on the "executive floor."

I must have winced at the seeming extravagance, because she immediately pulled me aside to explain. "There are all kinds of people in this hotel, and the government is watching everybody," she told me. "It is only a matter of time, but one day they will come looking for you. If you are on the executive floor, we can at least warn you without them knowing, and you may be lucky enough to escape arrest."

After the airport experience, I happily accepted the offer and tried to settle in. Like the grease that crackled and spit in the large aluminum bowls that market women used on street corners to deep-fry fish and yams, Nigeria was boiling. With union leaders openly challenging the government with calls for a nationwide strike to force Abacha to relinquish power and install Abiola in his rightful place, and with opposition figures having the run of Lagos and being quoted widely even in the more conservative press, there was a feeling that the country might once again be heading for a calamitous civil war.

For a brief time, Abacha's ministers had attempted conciliation, offering concessions that sounded more generous in the headlines than in the newspaper stories beneath them. One of these was an offer to release Abiola if only he would agree to renounce his mandate, not meet publicly with supporters and forswear overseas travel. Abiola's fiery senior wife, Kudirat, was the first to publicly scoff at the proposal, not even allowing it to get a full run in the afternoon newspapers before announcing that her husband would accept nothing of the sort.

As dangerous as the moment seemed, this kind of defiant spunk filled me with hope for Nigeria, indeed for all of Africa. According to widely held theory, civil society is supposed to flourish only in relatively prosperous countries. Democracy, in turn, is said to survive only in places where there is a vibrant civil society and a large middle class.

The early 1990s had already seen countries like Mali, Benin and Congo-Brazzaville defy this logic, however briefly in Brazzaville's case. They had each "gone democratic" as a result of citizens' uprisings, unsupported and almost unnoticed by the outside world.

Western diplomats had long spoken patronizingly about Africa and about Africans, sometimes doubting aloud, as French president Jacques Chirac often did, if they were "ready" for democracy. But except for South Africa, which caught the world's imagination because of the presence of white people and large Western investments, whenever Africans had attempted to answer in the affirmative, through their actions, the West had remained silent and unmoved. Now it was the turn of Nigeria, Africa's demographic giant, to try to break the mold, but the reactions of the outside world were much the same. Apart from muffled protests about the annulment of Abiola's election, there had been little more than hand-wringing over whether or not to impose sanctions on the Abacha regime.

About half of Nigeria's oil was exported to the United States, where the country's so-called Bonny Crude was prized for its "sweetness," or lack of polluting sulfur, which made it ideal for gasoline production. Washington had long railed against Muammar al-Qaddafi and had waged a war against Saddam Hussein, but as long as oil continued to flow, seriously chastising Abacha for aborting Africa's biggest experiment with democracy was never seriously considered.

After the "Black Hawk Down" debacle in Somalia in 1993, the United States had resolved that helping Africa was not worth another American life. Now, Washington's timid response to the Nigerian military's hijacking of the democratic process was sending the message that Africa wasn't worth a few pennies' rise in the price of American gasoline, either. In fact, for all their gilded rhetoric about democracy and human rights, the actions of the United States, France and Britain had long shown a pronounced preference for the devils they knew well in Africa—Abacha, Mobutu, the apartheid system in South Africa— over the untidiness of their democratic opponents.

In Nigeria, the West was slow to realize the full extent of the evil it had, in effect, endorsed. Western diplomats would often say that Abacha was preferable to some junior officers coming in and taking over, but they had never stopped to ask themselves the right question in the first place: What can we do to help democracy prevail?

I began to realize just how awful things could be under Abacha that first week in Nigeria, and it was hardly a case of prescience. To my amazement, the executive floor of the Sheraton was swarming with pro-democracy activists, some of whom were hiding out there, while others, including the opposition press, merely came to pick up the latest tidbits on opposition strategy. Abiola's top aide, Fred Eno, and I had eaten breakfast together a couple of times that week, but he was constantly interrupted by the gaggle of cellular phones that he carried, which rang busily with calls from the unions, from lawyers and from reporters.

Abacha's government had announced that the venue of Abiola's treason trial was being shifted from Lagos, the huge southern coastal city that was the stronghold of his Yoruba ethnic group and of the democratic opposition, to Nigeria's answer to Brasília, Abuja, a city created in the center of the country in 1976, in large part to neutralize the Yoruba influence over the government. There was no precedent or legal justification for the change of venue, and the opposition was marshaling its forces in a courageous attempt to try to stop it. After a few days of following the street action in Lagos, I decided to fly to Abuja to take the temperature of the military leadership.

My goal, of course, was to land an interview with Abacha. His interviews with Western journalists had been extremely rare, and were always given under the kind of carefully controlled circumstances that reeked of public relations deals. I knew it would be a tough sell, but I had a few contacts in Abuja and was eager to work them.

Nigeria's new capital is situated in the middle of nowhere, and its airport is far away. Closer to the desert, it was much hotter here than it had been in Lagos, but mercifully far less humid. Feeling mugged by the heat, I wanted to doze off, but my driver, a small, talkative Igbo— the country's third-largest ethnic group, and Nigeria's preeminent traders—was eager to hear about life in Ivory Coast, and he plied me with questions.

The highway ran straight and seamless through a savannah of anthills and reddish earth. It was built by European companies at vastly inflated prices, with huge kickbacks for everyone involved, in the same fashion as any public project in Nigeria. We flew through this singed emptiness in the hired car until Abuja announced itself on the horizon with the presence of its grand religious buildings—an otherworldly mosque with a massive gold dome and an equally huge white cathedral whose shapes hovered in the afternoon heat like mirages. Later I learned that the scale of the buildings had been carefully matched, reflecting the ever-delicate balance between Islam and Christianity in the country.

Abuja signaled its political ambitions through buildings like these, and through the dowdy formalism of its other structures, like the huge white gates at the city's edge. Otherwise, it was an oddly unfinished place, an African Oz of immense boulevards and little traffic, of huge hotels and few guests, and of impressive-looking government ministries with no sign of the comings and goings of bureaucrats.

A well-known American academic had previously introduced me to Adamu Mohammed, a senior national security advisor as well as confidant to Abacha, so I called him as soon as I checked into the Abuja Sheraton. He said he would come and pick me up later that evening. In a couple of prior telephone conversations with Mohammed there had been subtle hints that I might get to meet Abacha, but each of these discussions was heavily laden with bitterness about what he called the American press's simpleminded approach to Nigeria. "You people fail to understand the complexities of this place," he told me. "You think that you can simply take the rules of your society and apply them here, but that is a foolish mistake. Nigeria is a country of two hundred fifty ethnic groups. We have our own specific problems, and our own traditions, and people must appreciate and understand that before they can begin lecturing us."

On the surface it seemed like a reasonable enough, if not so original, gripe. The biggest problem with the grievances of this very sophisticated person, however, was that they were being proffered as cover for Abacha, a man whose claims to leadership rested on raw power, and on raw power alone. No amount of sophistry could hide the fact that Abacha's dictatorship was dragging Nigeria ever further from the rule of law, fueling ethnic tensions, gutting the economy, and forcing more and more of the country's talented educated class to choose a life of exile in order to survive.

Mohammed came for me a little after 10 p.m. He has a dark complexion and the somewhat drawn and leathery skin of a heavy smoker. His dress, a simple white boubou, was surprisingly plain, and yet he was possessed of a certain elegance that radiated from a lively intelligence, and an ocean full of Nigerian self-confidence. Soon we were climbing into the black, chauffeured government Peugeot that was awaiting us and driving through the poorly lit streets of the big village that masqueraded as Nigeria's new capital. Mohammed started working me over with sentences that began with phrases like "What you people fail to understand about Nigeria . . ." As I began playing devil's advocate, he launched into an increasingly rabid attack on the southerners and the conversation grew more and more strained.

"They are unruly people, those southerners," he said. "They think that they can just take over the country by sowing disorder, but we will never allow it. Lagos should never be confused with Nigeria. Here we have traditions and order, and we respect authority. All those unruly people know is chaos."

Both Mohammed and I knew that the people he was referring to, who were still leading a boisterous protest movement against Abacha largely in the south, had the firm ground of principle to stand on. I was sympathetic to their cause, and the more hysterical he became, the less I was able to pretend otherwise.

Ray Ekpu, the editor of *Newswatch*, one of Nigeria's major weekly magazines, had confirmed to me just a day or two earlier in Lagos what I had already surmised about the crisis: "When you remove all of the excuses for canceling the elections, and the allegations against Abiola, you come down to one hard fact: The northerners do not want power to go to the south. If Abiola had been someone from a minority ethnic group, perhaps they would have accepted it. But in their minds, the Yoruba already control the civil service and the business of Lagos, and they feel that holding on to power is their only way to survive."

Nigeria had been created by the British as a colonial entity in 1914 and bequeathed to its people as an independent state in 1960. From the very beginning the prize of independence was a booby trap, an eagerly awaited gift that would explode just as it was being unwrapped. The colony's masters in London had done little to prepare the population for the task of running a European-style nation-state. The truly explosive element, however, was the country's very composition. Nigeria was a creation of European imperialists and mapmakers, and it pulled together an amalgam of diverse regions and peoples who spoke mutually unintelligible languages.

The new Federal Republic of Nigeria's three largest groups, the Muslim Hausa-Fulani in the north, the Yoruba in the southwest and the Igbo in the southeast—the last two both predominantly Christian— had been lassoed into one state only by a huge accident of history. Each of these ethnic groups was larger than the population in many African countries. Each had stronger cultural and historic links with peoples in neighboring countries to the north, west and east, and each yearned for self-determination. It is hardly surprising, therefore, that differences in temperament, culture and even training received from the British— who concentrated their educational efforts in the south and encouraged poorer northerners to make careers in the military—quickly set Nigeria on a path toward disintegration.

This ticking bomb exploded in 1967, with the Biafran War, a gruesome civil conflict that, like World War I, had begun in confusion, seemingly by spontaneous combustion, and was egged on by outsiders, most conspicuously by a France anxious to see West Africa's Anglophone behemoth broken into less formidable bits. The Biafran War ended in 1970, but the combustible fuel of ethnicity had never altogether ceased fuming.

Between cigarettes, an exasperated Mohammed made calls on his cellular phone, usually speaking in Hausa, which I do not understand. Perhaps it was my imagination, but I sensed that he was telling associates to call things off, and I felt my chances of landing a meeting with the scar-faced president slipping away. Over the next few hours, what I had hoped would be an evening with the dictator devolved instead into a series of encounters with the regime's dignitaries. To a man, they were people who had played significant roles in their country's history, and they were trotted out, it seemed, to impress upon me that Nigeria's situation wasn't just a matter of Abacha against the world. But like dodgy exhibits in a shoddy court brief, they had produced exactly the opposite effect.

The first character was Chukwuemeka Odumegwu Ojukwu, the Igbo general who had led the Biafran secession. I had once mentioned him briefly to Mohammed as someone I had met in Ivory Coast at a New Year's party at my parents' house years earlier, during his long exile there, and for an uninspired hour or so, the would-be founder of Biafra, as full of ambition and as accomplished at betrayal as ever, tried to convince me that Abacha's efforts to rewrite the constitution and reorganize Nigerian politics along "truly democratic lines" were legitimate.

This was hard enough to believe on the face of it. But hearing it from the man who had confused the fate of Igbo Nigeria with his own ego, unnecessarily prolonging the Biafran War long after it had become hopeless, while reputedly earning himself a fortune in gun-running, was upsetting. This was the man who had instigated the war and then fled Biafra aboard an airplane intended to carry orphaned children to safety. I held my tongue, so as to avoid any incident.

Hours later, though, the evening ended disastrously at the Abuja home of another top Abacha aide, Baba Gana Kingibe, a northern aristocrat who was the regime's foreign minister and later its interior minister, or top cop. Kingibe had run on Abiola's ticket as his vice-presidential candidate, and his treachery arguably put even Ojukwu's to shame.

Kingibe was a classic civilian version of the modern northern elite: impeccably educated in Britain and full of snobby witticisms; insufferably condescending, but also simmering with resentments and insecure as hell. His generation of ambitious northerners, men in their fifties, was driven by an obsession never to be dominated again by their generally better educated, richer peers in the south. The south may have been where Nigeria's oil was, but the north still controlled the army. As long as it continued to do so, people like Kingibe were determined to control the country's resources—particularly the El Dorado of oil revenues aptly referred to by greedy politicians as the national cake.

Over drinks in his sunken living room, stylishly appointed with sleek European furniture, Kingibe probed for ways to establish some rapport with me, and the conversation kept returning to the subject of American blacks. Not quite able to hide his disdain, he hinted strongly that African-American politicians had been receiving payoffs from Nigeria in an effort to build a Nigeria lobby in Washington. With the notable exception of Senator Carol Moseley-Braun of Illinois, who had made a trip to Abuja to meet with General Abacha, and told CNN afterward that the Clinton administration should "treat Africa like any other nation" (*sic*), however, there had been precious little to show for it.

In the insidious language of Nigerian military rule this sort of thing is called "settling people," a term with an oddly colonial ring about it that means "to buy someone's silence or cooperation." With all the money the Abacha regime could offer Jesse Jackson, Kingibe wondered aloud, why did Jackson remain so ill informed about Nigeria, and so obstinate in his criticism of the government? What would it take to get Colin Powell to give Nigeria a fresh look, instead of dismissing the country as "a nation of scammers," as he once had? Nigeria was the world's largest black state, Kingibe said. America depended on Nigeria for its oil supply. Surely there must be a basis there for a good working relationship.

As I grew weary of all the questions about how Nigeria could "settle" black Americans, I began asking some of my own. I couldn't resist. What about Abiola? What about the canceled elections in which you stood on his ticket? Why don't you let the Lagos courts hear the treason charges? Why take the extraordinarily dubious step of changing the venue?

"Let me explain something to you, Mr. French," Kingibe said to me in his effete nasal drawl, equal parts West African privilege and Oxford polish, as his eyes narrowed menacingly. "This Abiola problem has nothing to do with the courts. It has nothing to do with the law. Do you understand now? Is that clear? Now you may leave." My evening had just ended.

Back in Lagos the next day, I looked for Fred Eno, Abiola's chief of staff, hoping to be brought up to date on what was happening in the democracy movement, but he had left the hotel. In fact, all of the opposition types who had been haunting the place had disappeared. I learned later that Eno had been jailed, like countless others who had tried to resist Abacha openly. Others had simply been killed. I would never speak to Eno again.

Nigeria under the generals, I thought, was like a decadent Rome, a place that had unraveled to such an extent that the only hard-and-fast rule that held any longer was the oldest rule of all—might makes right. The country's only greatness was its unrealized potential. To paraphrase Charles de Gaulle's famous, irony-dripping put-down of Brazil, Nigeria was a land whose future would always remain bright. With Abacha at the helm, I wondered whether even this might not be too generous.

The immensity of the problem here started, of course, with the population—more than 100 million people—but could be seen almost anywhere one looked, from the endlessly long bridges in Lagos that choked and froze twice a day with traffic jams, or go-slows, to the scale of thievery and injustice on display every day. Life had hardened people so thoroughly that when a pedestrian is hit by a car along one of the city's major highways, no one even stops to help. I had always thought this was Nigerian urban legend, hyperbole, until I saw for myself the remains of a man run over so many times he had been reduced to the thickness and consistency of wallpaper paste.

Just as there are places I love to visit, there have always been

African cities it gives me great pleasure to leave, and Lagos under Abacha was at the top of the list. On this trip, the first of my tour, after I boarded an Air Afrique jet for Abidjan, and the pilot waited for permission to pull back from the gate, Nigeria reserved one final unpleasant surprise for me. A soldier climbed aboard with rifle in hand to demand a few bottles of champagne from a French-speaking crew member. With this kind of example being set by the military, I thought, how could this sort of lawlessness ever be stopped? The soldier got his champagne.

Visas to Nigeria had always been hard to come by during my stay in the region, and over the next year, they became even harder to obtain. The Abacha dictatorship was steadily tightening its grip, growing more isolated and more paranoid by the week, and the best proof that the dictatorship's shock treatment was working was that usually dauntless Nigerians were becoming scared.

Habeas corpus was suspended. Union leaders were rounded up. Leading newspapers were closed. Even the army's officer corps faced constant purges. Without producing the least evidence, in June 1995, Abacha arrested Olusegun Obasanjo, a former military leader and the only Nigerian general who had ever surrendered power to an elected government (in 1979). Obasanjo was charged with treason, for supposedly plotting to overthrow the Abacha government, and was tried in secret that year and sentenced to death.*

Almost simultaneously, Abacha's agents jailed Shehu Musa Yar'Adua, Obasanjo's former vice president, and a leading delegate to the constitutional conference created by Abacha. Yar'Adua's principal offense was introducing a motion at the conference demanding a quick return to democratic rule. He, too, was charged with treason and sentenced to death. Yar'Adua was murdered in jail not long afterward through lethal injection—some said it was battery acid—by Abacha's security agents.

Most shocking of all, though, was the arrest and execution of Kenule Beeson "Ken" Saro-Wiwa, a playwright and environmental activist who had given prominence to his Ogoni ethnic group's demands for a cleaner environment and a share of the wealth from

---

*After Abacha's sudden death, in June 1998, Obasanjo was released from detention. In February 1999 he was elected president.

their region's rich oil production. His arrest had shone the harshest spotlight on Nigeria.

Abacha was not known for his taste in literature, but his handling of Saro-Wiwa played itself out like an ode to Kafka. A peaceable, pipe-smoking man who had made his reputation in the country as a writer of biting satirical fiction and of popular television comedies, Saro-Wiwa had gradually become an impassioned, and increasingly bold, activist on behalf of the 500,000 or so Ogoni people. Abacha and Saro-Wiwa had known each other for years, meeting in the aftermath of the Biafran War, in the 1970s, when they were friendly neighbors in Port Harcourt. Their children had even once played together in the same government flats. But amid the savage repression that followed Abacha's seizure of power in November 1993, Saro-Wiwa became an ineluctable target.

From the very start of the regime's crackdown on dissent, it is clear that the diminutive writer and his Movement for the Survival of the Ogoni People, or MOSOP, were not considered to be just any rabble-rousing opposition group. Unlike Abacha's hijacking of the country's democracy, MOSOP's campaign against the destruction of Ogoni fishing beds and Niger delta wetlands by international oil companies, in particular Shell, had won international attention, particularly among environmental and human rights groups, like Greenpeace and Amnesty International. Moreover, attacks against oil pipelines and demonstrations against oil workers had forced Shell to shut down its operations in the Ogoni areas, interfering with the stream of petroleum revenues that fed the dictatorship. "Some opposition groups were still able to get away with a lot of things, criticizing Abacha just about as harshly as they wanted," the United States ambassador to Nigeria, Walter Carrington, told me. "But MOSOP was hitting the Abacha people in the wallet, and that is the one place where they just don't fool around."

The biggest threat went well beyond the question of a few tens of thousands of barrels of oil, though. In his impassioned, literary way, Saro-Wiwa had begun to successfully articulate a challenge to the revenue-sharing formulas that kept the vast bulk of oil revenues in the hands of whoever was in charge of the central government. Under the traditional arrangements, the main oil-producing areas of the southeast—areas where powerless minorities like the Ogoni were legion—had remained as poor and despoiled as ever. Groups like MOSOP did not stop at questioning the military dictatorship's right to salt away billions of dollars worth of oil receipts in Citibank accounts, in Switzerland and elsewhere. They were attacking the very rationale behind the resource-poor north's determination to cling to power: wealth redistribution, at gunpoint if necessary.

In 1994, Lieutenant Colonel Paul Okuntimo, the local security task force commander in Port Harcourt, the capital of Rivers State, responded with a plan that called for "wasting operations," or what amounted to murderous raids on Ogoni villages. In May of that year, Saro-Wiwa himself was caught in the dragnet and arrested, but not formally charged, for ordering the murder of more conservative rivals among the Ogoni leadership.

The following March, I flew into the Ogoni area, at the invitation of Shell. By then, Okuntimo had completely sealed off the region and a corporate invitation was the only sure way in or out. It is difficult to say with precision what responsibility for the welfare of the local people a company like Shell should bear when it interlopes and extracts billions of dollars worth of oil, fully aware that virtually none of the money is being locally reinvested by the government. But if Western countries have slowly become sensitized to the need to help recover the wealth stolen by dictators like Mobutu and Abacha, in countries like Nigeria and Congo-Brazzaville and Angola, they must also acknowledge the fact that extraction without local development equally amounts to theft.

The Shell helicopter that ferried us around that day flew in low over the glistening Niger delta. It was such an extraordinary maze of wetlands and wending waterways that for a long time after their arrival in these parts, Europeans who came in search of gold and slaves had no idea that this vast area was the mouth of a single huge river.

The crew pointed out Oloibiri, the village where oil was first discovered in Nigeria in 1958. Back then, the villagers had demanded sacrifices from the Dutch oil explorers—chickens and the like—to bless the site. It is reported, too, that libations were poured, to celebrate. Now, search as one might, it was impossible to find anything amid the thick foliage and swamplands below that looked substantially different from how it must have looked thirty-seven years earlier, except, that is, for the huge flares that burn off the natural gas emanating from the wells all around the area. Millions of barrels and more than $300 billion in national oil revenue later, Oloibiri remained a little village in the mangrove swamp, lost in time.

Tracts of dead swampland surrounded many of the other sites we were allowed to approach. The heat from gas flares had burned off all of the aboveground vegetation, and the oozing of oil, slow and steady over many years, had killed most of the aquatic life.

At the little village of Aminigboko, where we landed, the Shell folks proudly pointed to a village school they had built for 1,250 students, one of forty or so they claimed to have built in the district. "These are some of the things we have done," said Lawson Jack, a Nigerian Shell spokesman, with a hint of weariness. "We tried agriculture first, but the people said that it was of no help to them. So we began building schools, and turning them over to the government. The government was neglecting them, though, so we took over their maintenance, too."

Small children observed us shyly but playfully from a safe distance, their torsos nude and their feet bare. The only adults around seemed to have been urged to turn out by Shell, perhaps for promises of drinks or small cash handouts. In any event, we had been told that a busy schedule lay ahead, and that we could spend only a few minutes on the ground, so there was no way to interact.

When the tour ended I returned to Port Harcourt and went to see Claude Ake, a respected Nigerian intellectual and an expert on the local political and environmental situation, to hear what he had to say about Shell's public relations effort. "When the soldiers were running rampage through Ogoni-land shooting people, and we were asking for aid for the wounded, where was Shell? They didn't contribute anything. Their callousness is breathtaking. The building of those classrooms is just a trivial matter. They have polluted the entire water table underground; they have left oil scum everywhere. There are flares burning, polluting the air everywhere you look, and they talk to you about classrooms. How much money do they spend on advertising by comparison? Let them keep their classrooms. They are rubbish."

In November 1994, a special Civil Disturbances Tribunal was created to try Ken Saro-Wiwa and fifteen others, and in January 1995, the dissidents were finally charged. The special tribunal's powers included the right to use the death penalty, and its judgment was beyond appeal. Okuntimo's permission was required for Saro-Wiwa to even meet with his lawyers.

Tensions rose inexorably throughout the year as international human rights groups beat their drums over the Saro-Wiwa case. The trial and prospect of executions even made leaders of neighboring countries, many of them dedicated authoritarians, jittery with apprehension, and delegation after delegation was sent from throughout the region to urge restraint and clemency.

Mindful of his unpopularity, particularly in the south, Abacha had long ago given up visiting Lagos, and remained cloistered instead at his heavily guarded presidential compound in Abuja. Many assumed that he was playing a strange new kind of poker, using the fate of the nation as the cards. Surely, many Nigerians thought, when the right time came, he would release the extraordinary pressure that had been building up, issue pardons and for once savor some favorable press. The alternative was just too terrible to contemplate.

As October 1, Independence Day in Nigeria, approached, the entire country anticipated a peaceful denouement. In a recent speech, Abacha had promised "important news" for the nation, and with Nigerian newspapers speculating feverishly over whether this would mean a series of pardons or the announcement of new elections, I managed to get a visa and flew to Lagos. Abacha was anything but easy to read, but the city had managed to convince itself that he was going to use the occasion to turn things around.

On the day of my arrival in Lagos, I headed to Chief Abiola's house on a whim, together with Robert Grossman, the photographer who accompanied me on many of my travels, and Purnell Murdock, the Voice of America correspondent, to see Abiola's senior wife, Kudirat, to ask if we could be with her to watch the Abacha speech at her house the next day, hoping to witness the celebrations that would take place if her husband's release were announced.

Although he was Yoruba, Abiola was a Muslim, and therefore allowed to marry more than one wife. Certainly, as a reputed billionaire, there were no financial obstacles. Kudirat, a handsome, dark-skinned woman who appeared to be in her forties, had a powerful voice and exuded the authority that comes with her matrimonial rank. Indeed, during the long months of fear and frustration over her husband's solitary confinement she had emerged as a force in opposition politics in her own right. "Abacha is moving the country at a very great speed," she told me, pausing for dramatic effect before bellowing, "backwards! There is grief in every home in Nigeria, and the most graceful thing for Abacha to do at this point is to have the military step aside."

Kudirat Abiola immediately accepted our request to visit her house for Abacha's early-morning speech, and even offered to prepare breakfast. "By all means, you must come," she said, exuberantly. "You are welcome."

One after another, Nigeria's dictators had deceived themselves into believing that they could muzzle Africa's most determinedly free-spoken population. Abacha was the fiercest, but as Kudirat's courage showed, not even he had come close. Like some child's toy rigged with springs, a crackdown in one spot led only to opponents popping up somewhere else. In Lagos, when feisty magazines were shut down by the police one week, they merely opened in another neighborhood or under another name the next.

When we left Kudirat, we set out to look for a different sort of opposition leader, Nigeria's most famous musician, Fela Anikulapo Kuti. The first thing I had noticed when I arrived in Lagos was how the city had been plastered with posters announcing that Fela would be performing that night at his own club, the famous Shrine. I had never seen Jimi Hendrix perform, nor had I seen Miles Davis—two other musical heroes of my youth—and having been a fan of Fela's since college, I was determined not to miss his show.

Fela came from Abeokuta, a remarkable city in the country's southwest that is located a couple of hours' drive from Lagos. The city was founded in the 1830s by refugees from the Yoruba civil wars, and since most of its 500,000 residents come from the same clan, the Egba, many claim that this makes Abeokuta the world's largest village. In a badly divided country, though, the city's main source of renown was the extraordinary gallery of national leaders it had produced. The famous sons and daughters included the once and future president Olusegun Obasanjo; the rightfully elected and now imprisoned president, Abiola; and Ernest Shonekan, an interim president installed as a puppet by the military in 1993, before Abacha seized power outright. Abeokuta had also produced Wole Soyinka, the Nobel Prize–winning author and political exile, and his aunt and Fela's mother, Funmilayo Ransome-Kuti, a matriarch of a clan as impressive as any in Africa and a political firebrand who successfully led a two-year demonstration to repeal a "women's tax" in 1948, twelve years before independence.

In Nigeria, easily the most famous person from Abeokuta, though, was her son Fela, the dissident musician-bard who had been arrested by the army and police as many as two hundred times because of his unrelenting criticism of military misrule. In one bid to silence him, Fela's mother was thrown off the balcony of his home in 1977, killing her.

Fela's music, Afro Beat, had its roots in Highlife, a creolized dance-band music that first blossomed in Ghana in the 1920s, catering to a semi-Westernized elite. Fela's songs usually eschewed the feel-good themes of Highlife, though, and swiftly evolved into a bitter and incisive oral history of Nigeria and, by extension, of the African continent. "I no be gentleman at all. I be Africa man. Original," Fela declared in one vintage song from the 1970s that bristled with African pride at a time when many Africans were soaking up Western influences as fast as they could. With time, his songs became even more trenchant and political, with titles like "Zombie," "Army Arrangement" (about the country's rigged politics), "ITT" ("International Thief, Thief," about Abiola), "Colonial Mentality" and "Coffin for Head of State" (about the murder of his mother) that denounced the soldiers and dictators laying Africa low.

Our driver, David, took us to Fela's famous home, which was known as the Kalakuta Republic. It was a sprawling urban commune with a large open courtyard where people smoked pot, washed clothes, cooked and dozed by day. Fela didn't have Abiola's excuse of being a Muslim, but he had married twenty-eight women simultaneously in the late 1970s nonetheless. Many of that original number had long since left him, but new women, for the most part the statuesque dancers who enlivened his shows, were constantly joining his lair.

We were scarcely noticed when we walked in, so utterly preoccupied were the people with either getting high or sleeping off the effects from previous highs. I spotted a gorgeous woman, nearly six feet tall, who was grilling fragrantly spiced chicken over charcoal by the building's concrete outer stairway, and approached her to ask if we could see Fela. With a low-key nod, she directed me upstairs, where I advanced feeling a touch of trepidation.

People were smoking dope everywhere on the second floor, either sitting or lying on the ground with vacant stares. I asked someone where Fela was, and was directed to the end of the hall, where we found the musician asleep in a room, sprawled on a bed with several women. The man who had directed us asked us to sit down in another room while someone announced us, and after a few minutes, he came back to tell us that Fela had invited us to be his guests at the concert that night. Fela did not feel like talking now, but if we liked, the man said, we could interview him after the show. Purnell, warming to the idea of doing a radio piece on the concert, asked if he could use a tape recorder at the Shrine, to which Fela's aide said, No problem. "If anyone gives you any trouble, just ask for Morgan, and I will straighten things out."

David had not wanted to drive us for a concert late at night, and hooked us up instead with Friday, another trusted driver I occasionally worked with. Friday had been an amateur boxer, and though not huge in size, exuded a tough, take-no-nonsense attitude.

We got to the Shrine at midnight, and it was still only sparsely filled. Fela's concerts were famously late and long lasting, so we made our way through the security check, taking care to clear Purnell's tape recorder, before finding some seats. The legendary club, it turned out, was a shoestring operation. It was a large performance space with a huge elevated stage, as well as platforms for Fela's female dancers along the sides. It was little more than a shoddy, rusting hangar, with cheap and uncomfortable metal chairs that were crowded closely together. I was far more impressed by the crowd. True to Fela's hell-raising populist image, at least 80 percent of the people who filled the seats were "area boys," Lagos slang for the city's hardened street youths. But there were plenty of other types, too, including radical-chic intellectuals and clusters of tourists from Europe and Japan.

Within minutes of striking up the first notes, Fela's band had the place rumbling. Soon, huge joints were making their way back and forth between total strangers; the crowd was working itself into the kind of hypnotized frenzy that the music was famous for. Some area boys who had been smoking and drinking heavily were sitting immediately behind us. The higher they got, the more preoccupied with us they became, fixating on Robert's cameras and pestering us with annoying questions. Friday kept a wary eye on them, though, and told us not to pay them any mind.

When Fela finally came out, the area boys behind us were content to flow with the music for a while, as were we. He seemed in particularly fine form, strutting and hopping bare-chested in his red tights, like a barnyard rooster. The music was angry and joyous by turns as Fela prowled the stage, shouting and preaching the ills of military rule and materialism. Every song was drenched in politics, but there was another constant theme as well—love; not love as in peace and love, but physical love as in bump and grind.

I had seen and enjoyed the best of Congolese soukous, arguably the most enthusiastic celebration of the female rear end anywhere in Africa, but the show Fela and his dancer-wives put on that night reached a whole new level. It was burlesque meets gymnastics, all set to a driving, unrelenting rhythm, and it was as raw and powerful a display of sensuality as I had ever seen.

Sweating profusely, Fela stripped down to his red underpants and began working his saxophone furiously, clearly influenced by both James Brown and Pharoah Sanders. He was fifty-seven, but appeared to have the stamina of a man in his twenties as he blew his way through the chord changes, riffing against the insistent beat. Many minutes later, when he finally paused, Fela introduced the dancers one by one, and as he did so, each of these tall, powerful women performed a solo of her own, writhing under the spotlight like dancing yogis.

In the midst of this exhibition, though, the area boys behind us interrupted our reverie. They had noticed Purnell's tape recorder and were making an issue of it. One of them insisted that he was a member of Fela's security force and demanded that we hand it over to them. We stood our ground, encouraged by Friday's calm, but the area boys were now passing word through the crowd that the Americans had snuck a tape recorder into the concert and were stealing Fela's music.

As the crowd drew tightly around us I pleaded our case to all those who would listen, invoking Morgan's name and recounting our visit to Fela's commune. The threats continued to multiply, though, and it was obvious there was no way we could fight our way out of there. Eventually, the crowd began jostling us, and things started to look desperate. I urged one of the people confronting us to summon Fela's security people. Agreeing, he threatened, "If you're not telling the truth, you will be sorry."

A few moments later, a huge security man walked up, parting the crowd by his mere presence. I had to crane my head to meet his gaze. I began to explain our story, but he showed no interest in hearing it, simply gesturing for the tape recorder and ordering us to follow him.

It was close to 4 a.m., and for most of the hall the concert continued undisturbed, as loud and frenzied as ever. But as we approached the exit, with the rowdiest elements of the crowd taunting us from behind, I saw one of Fela's dancers and immediately recognized her from the courtyard. It was the woman who had been grilling chicken over hot coals that afternoon. "Don't you remember me?" I asked desperately. Her face was as noncommittal as it was beautiful as she scrutinized me impassively. "You saw me this afternoon at Fela's house. I asked you where I could find him."

"Ah, yes, I remember you now," she said, and then turned to the giant security man. "These people are journalists. Fela invited them to the concert. He told them to bring their equipment." At that, there was an audible sigh from the crowd and the pressure quickly dissipated. The huge security man handed Purnell his tape recorder, and we walked to Friday's car and drove off, skipping our chance for a backstage interview with Fela. The sun would be coming up soon, and Abacha's speech was due in a few hours.

I was exhausted and dispirited from the confrontation, and asked Friday to drop me off at the Sheraton, where I decided to watch Abacha on television. Robert continued on to Kudirat Abiola's house as planned, to take her picture, and promised to bring me back some comments on the speech from her. As it happened, Abacha's big news was the commutation of the bogus death sentences against Obasanjo and Yar'Adua, which he reduced to twenty-five years. For the first time, he explicitly denied the legitimacy of Abiola's presidential mandate, though, and said a pardon for him "would be wrong and a poor precedent for the democratic system for which we are laying a foundation."

Kudirat Abiola was murdered the following year, on June 4, 1996, in what New York or Chicago police would call a gangland-style slaying, when her car came under heavy gunfire in Lagos traffic. The government denied any responsibility, but after the dictator's death, two years later, Sani Abacha's son, Mohammed, was charged with ordering the hit. Fela died of AIDS in 1997. He was only fifty-eight years old.

With the disappointment of Independence Day behind them, Nigerians sensed one more chance for Abacha to change direction. But the special tribunal organized to try Saro-Wiwa delivered its guilty verdict barely a month after Abacha's big speech. The dictator was the only person who could prevent the executions from taking place, and a parade of African leaders, including Nelson Mandela, had been urging lenience. On the morning of November 10, the very day that a Commonwealth heads-of-state summit was to open in Auckland, New

Zealand, however, Saro-Wiwa and eight other Ogoni defendants were marched to the gallows at the Port Harcourt jailhouse and hanged.

In eloquent defiance, Ken Saro-Wiwa's powerful last words recalled Mandela's statement from the dock before his life imprisonment in 1964, but in a final insult to justice—one that not even Mandela under apartheid had suffered—Saro-Wiwa was not allowed to speak before the court.

"I am a man of peace, of ideas," Saro-Wiwa wrote. "Appalled by the denigrating poverty of my people who live on a richly endowed land, distressed by their political marginalization and economic strangulation, angered by the devastation of their land, their ultimate heritage, anxious to preserve their right to life and to a decent living, and determined to usher to this country as a whole a fair and just democratic system which protects everyone and every ethnic group and gives us all a valid claim to human civilization, I have devoted my intellectual and material resources, my very life, to a cause in which I have total belief and from which I cannot be blackmailed or intimidated. I have no doubt at all about the ultimate success of my cause, no matter the trials and tribulations which I and those who believe with me may encounter on our journey. Neither imprisonment nor death can stop our ultimate victory.

"I repeat that we all stand before history. I and my colleagues are not the only ones on trial. Shell is here on trial and it is as well that it is represented by counsel said to be holding a watching brief [or friend-of-the-court status]. The company has, indeed, ducked this particular trial, but its day will surely come and the lessons learnt here may prove useful to it for there is no doubt in my mind that the ecological war that the company has waged in the Delta will be called to question sooner than later and the crimes of that war be duly punished. The crime of the company's dirty wars against the Ogoni people will also be punished."

CHAPTER THREE

Plague

B razzaville is one of those African capitals that manages to remain still and sleepy throughout the day, save for rush hours that are as brief as cloudbursts. The airports and borders are the only places where one can count on round-the-clock business and the vigilance that comes with it. When I arrived, the Congo Republic was not being infiltrated or facing attack, but for the men born into poverty who filled the ranks of the army, customs and immigration services, guarding the country's entrances and exits was the surest chance they would ever have to make a quick buck.

It was three in the morning when I landed, having taken a six-hour flight from Abidjan, on the west coast, to Brazzaville, in the continent's center, but it took only a few minutes for my photographer and me to run into trouble. The immigration agents spotted us from afar amid the crowds of yawning Congolese passengers who were carting home shiny new boom boxes and monstrous battered suitcases from their overseas voyages. Speaking with a deadly straight face, an immigration officer told us that the transit visas we had been issued at the Congolese consulate in Abidjan—at an "expedited" price of nearly $200 a person—were invalid. We would have to wait until morning, under police custody in an airport office, when we would be taken to the Ministry of the Interior to request new papers. Alternatively, we could pay something on the spot—perhaps another $200 would do, one of the green-uniformed soldiers suggested with a smile that mocked helpfulness.

Reaching difficult destinations and surviving with one's money and other possessions intact were life's daily challenge in Central Africa, and it was both a point of pride and principle with me never to surrender any of my belongings voluntarily. The customs agent seemed to have us over a barrel, but I had one trick left: a fancy-looking presidential press pass I had taken pains to procure after a previous hassle-filled stay in Brazzaville. I flashed it, and after a few minutes of consultation, to my mild surprise, the soldiers let us through.

Brazzaville had once been among the most orderly of Central African cities, making it and Kinshasa, a mere two miles away and the Dodge City of the region, an oddball pair of twins. This was always the place that one looked forward to visiting, with a small pinch of guilt, on the way into or out of the bedlam of Zaire. With its beautifully shaded streets, its solid, French-backed currency and a French-run café or bistro never far away, Brazzaville was capable of transporting me back in time, removing me from the region's misery and grime, and dropping me into my own little Casablanca, a charming and settled French provincial city peopled by colonial Africans.

The city had been changing a lot recently, though, and law and order were fast breaking down. The subtle north-south ethnic divide that had always driven this forgotten little African oil emirate's politics had devolved into a raw contest involving a proliferation of militias and fierce street battles. I would be lying if I said that I had already imagined then, back in 1995, that Brazzaville would be joining its fraternal twin across the Congo River in utter chaos just two years hence, which is how long it would take to go from gang warfare to spectacularly murderous artillery duels in the middle of the city. But if an accredited consul could no longer issue a visa for his own country, it was already clear to me that there was trouble in store.

On this night, though, my concerns lay elsewhere. I had been dispatched to Zaire, and planned to make my way by ferry across the oily expanse of the Congo River at dawn. My assignment was to report on the outbreak of the Ebola virus in that country, and making a bad situation worse, I was late. I had been on a special assignment when the epidemic struck, and the Ebola outbreak had been huge news around the world for days. Reporters had come from everywhere, many of them getting their first taste of Africa in what was possibly the most dilapidated and confusing country on the continent. In the process, more than a few of them were busying themselves overworking clichés drawn from *Heart of Darkness.*

Within moments of thanking the customs agents who had waved Robert and me on, we were driving through the sandy, pitch-dark streets of Brazzaville, on our way to the Sofitel, a French-run hotel kept so bracingly cold that the huge glass windows looking out over the river toward Zaire next door steadily threw off sheets of condensation. Our plan was to take the first ferry, at 6:30—barely two hours away. So we napped sprawled on the stuffed leather sofas in the Sofitel lobby and waited for the breakfast buffet. Getting into Zaire unscathed would be a lot harder than getting into the Congo, and not knowing when we might eat again, it seemed smart to fill our stomachs.

By now, living in Africa was not only required for my job but had also come to involve an intensely personal quest. The continent I had known in the early 1980s, poor and politically backward to be sure, had now settled into a spiral of bloody traumas and chronic disorder. I needed to understand why, and over and over again this question drew me back to Central Africa, a region that, together with a small cluster of West African states, with Liberia at its epicenter, rested atop the continental hit parade of mayhem and decay.

Because of the scale of the 1994 genocide, Rwanda was the site of the one African tragedy people in the farthest reaches of the world knew of. But in political terms, Rwanda's nearly bipolar society of Hutu and Tutsi made it more of an anomaly than a paradigm for the rest of the continent. More than any other place, Zaire—a country as vast as the United States east of the Mississippi, which shares land borders with eight other countries and is separated by a lake from a ninth, Tanzania—seemed like the country where I might find answers. By African standards, its contact with Europe had been extraordinary both for its duration, going back to the time of Columbus, and its destructiveness. From the earliest days of independence, in 1960, with the destabilization and overthrow of Patrice Lumumba, the country's first prime minister and only democratically elected leader, Western meddling had been persistent and profoundly destabilizing. And like most African countries, only even more spectacularly, Zaire had been misruled for decades ever since—in this case by Mobutu Sese Seko.

Our ferry ride would last only twenty minutes or so, and yet to me, the river crossing loomed like a passage into another world, making it impossible to sleep in the chill of the hotel lobby. Brazzaville, even with all of its recent problems, still seemed comfortably like Africa Lite. If worst came to worst, one always knew that the French were never too far behind the scenes, usually guaranteeing some kind of order or due process—at least for a Westerner. Zaire, by contrast, had never represented order of any kind, unless it was an order of the Cold War type, which dignified despots by dressing them up as indispensable allies. These were the waning days of the biggest despot of them all, Mobutu, and by now there was no longer any Cold War order, only disease and rot.

The presence of hundreds of foreign journalists chasing the Ebola story with their expensive equipment and wads of cash had made things only worse, sparking a feeding frenzy among Zaire's chronically unpaid soldiers. The Kinshasa airport was already renowned for body searches that left their victims dispossessed of whatever valuables they had brought with them. Too vigorous a protest could land one back on the next airplane stripped of everything but a pair of shorts and a tee shirt; the less fortunate wound up in jail.

Slipping into Zaire by the back door—steaming across the river from Brazzaville—seemed like a far better idea, and had worked wonderfully during an earlier trip, when I was watching what had seemed to be the first death throes of the Mobutu regime. That trip had gone beautifully until Robert and I were arrested at a ramshackle tuberculosis sanitarium on the edge of the city, where the patients had been abandoned by the government but where undercover police agents lurked nonetheless. It was a patient-run facility in the most abject sense of the term. People lay coughing and moaning in unlit rooms. There were no medicines, there was no food, and there were no doctors, either, unless a family could scrape together the means to keep paying one to come see their dying relatives.

Just as we were ending our time there, still reeling from the desperate pleas of patients wasting away on beds with no mattresses or sheets, we were encircled by a handful of heavily built men who began shouting, "What do you think you are doing in here? Do you think you have the right to come and take pictures in a place like this and ridicule our country?" Before we knew it, we and our timorous driver, Tony, had been bundled into our own battered little Toyota, where four of the policemen were brandishing pistols and threatening to kill us as they stripped away our watches, cameras, wallets and passports. The harvest of only a few hundred dollars had disappointed them, and their threats continued as we all rode stuffed together in the little blue sub-compact through the potholed streets of Kinshasa, until finally we stopped at the gates of the city jail. There we were told that if we could not come up with more cash, they would have us locked up.

It was the oldest racket in Zaire, and one I would face countless times in the future. Policemen, like soldiers, went unpaid, so they took their guns and badges as licenses to steal. Mobutu himself had openly sanctioned behavior like this, once telling his unpaid army to "live off the land," an instruction that set off the first of two stem-to-stern looting rampages in Kinshasa in the early 1990s. The two free-for-alls were known starkly as *les pillages*, and by now they were akin to the B.C. and A.D. of the modern calendar, scarring the psyches of Kinshasa's inhabitants so deeply that people spoke of their lives in terms of the before and after.

Theft had become the modus operandi for the entire country. Struggling to survive amid the country's organized chaos, many Zairians shrugged off their degeneration, saying that things had been pretty much this way since the time of the country's colonization by Belgium, and in fact, this little bit of folk wisdom wasn't far off the mark.

King Leopold II of Belgium had appropriated this huge colony at the 1884–85 Berlin Conference, the official kickoff for the European scramble for Africa, cynically claiming his motives were humanitarian. "Had Leopold been a different kind of man," writes Pagan Kennedy, "he might have been content to languish in his greenhouses and plea-sure gardens, and to cavort with his parade of prostitutes, some of them as young as ten years old. But he considered such treats to be only appetizers. He wanted to become one of the most powerful men in the world. In order to do that, he had to get his hands on a colony."

In his more candid moments, Leopold fondly described his newly acquired territory, which he ran brutally as his personal domain, as a "magnificent African cake," and for Leopold and subsequently for Bel-gium and others, the Congo, as it was known then, became synony-mous with a succession of cruel and shameless get-rich-quick schemes. For ivory, tropical hardwoods, rubber, and finally copper, cobalt and uranium, the country saw one European rush after another.

Leopold's African adventure is both stranger-than-fiction history and tragic fable, one whose legacy of theft and fraud has haunted the Congo ever since. Through stealth and extraordinary deceit, the king of Belgium, one of Europe's smallest and least consequential nations, persuaded his mighty neighbors to allow him to control more land than any other individual in the world, a territory as vast as all of Western Europe. In an era of rapacious global imperialism, Leopold somehow managed to convince his European peers that he intended to create a "confederation of free Negro republics."

"His political insignificance made him invisible, and so he could do whatever he wanted without attracting notice. If he flattered enough politicians, if he started enough rumors, if he spoke stirringly about the evils of the Arab slave trade, if he kept a stable of spies, then perhaps he could win his colony," writes Kennedy. Better yet, excelling at the Big Lie, the Belgian king told his fellow sovereigns that his work in the Congo would be driven strictly by Christian benevolence. "I do not wish to have one franc back of all the money I have expended," Leopold pledged.

What followed instead, under the self-ennobling banner of "the white man's burden"—an avowed mission to end slavery in Africa and bring civilization to a supposedly dark continent—was in truth one of history's greatest rapes. Farming was made a crime wherever African labor was needed for rubber cultivation, and men who did not produce enough had their hands chopped off. But instead of trailing shame and guilt through the ages, this rape has mostly bequeathed to us tales of Western heroism.

Explorers like Henry Morton Stanley are still celebrated with stories about their great exploits, while the details of how he made Leopold's conquest possible, by driving long columns of heavily chained Africans to their death as they bore his boats and guns and supplies through the great forests of the Congo River basin, are forgotten. Stanley was, in fact, something of a sadist, and was known for shooting Africans on a whim, simply because he didn't like the way they looked at him. Westerners have forgotten these truths, basking instead in the comforting myth of our civilizing mission, but unsentimental memories of Stanley live on with the Congolese, who even today remember him as Bula Matari, or the Stone Crusher, because of the murderous way he drove press gangs to forge roads where there had once been primordial rain forest and immense boulders.

Sheer greed and a shocking lack of what we might identify today as humanity drove the Belgian enterprise in Congo, like so much of the early European imperial exploitation of Africa, and the more carefully one examines the record of Leopold's behavior, the more it comes to resemble pure evil.

In little more than a generation, the Belgian king's yearning for empire and fortune may have killed ten million people in the territory—half of Congo's population, or more than the entire death toll in World War I. Even today Japan continues to face international ostracism for its brutal imperial conduct in China, Korea and other parts of Asia in the 1930s, which followed Leopold's Congo holocaust by a mere two decades. And yet there has never been any remorse in the West over the fallout from Europe's drive to dominate Africa. Indeed, few have heard these grim facts.

In view of the vastly larger scale of Leopold's atrocities, it is worth asking how he escaped remembrance alongside Hitler and Stalin as great criminals of the twentieth century. If Leopold's legacy had been millions of deaths alone, the impact of Belgium's takeover of the Congo would have been horrible enough. But the Belgians also created a tragic example of governance, essentially teaching Zairians that authority confers the power to steal.* And the practical corollary to this lesson was that the bigger the title, the bigger the theft.

For an entire generation of Congolese, Mobutu had been the undisputed heavyweight champion of this organized larceny, and although everyone knew what he was up to—a French minister once aptly described him as a "walking bank vault in a leopard skin cap"—he remained the West's favorite partner in Africa to the bitter end.

In the image of Leopold, Mobutu looted the copper and cobalt wealth of Shaba Province until industrial-scale mining all but ceased to function. His next El Dorado was the diamond fields of East Kasai. When the famously rebellious East Kasaians entered into a state of near revolt, refusing even to accept a newly issued "national" currency, Mobutu focused his greed on Kilo Moto, the fabulously rich mine in Zaire's remote northeastern corner that would temporarily slake what had become an unquenchable thirst. Kilo Moto became known as the

*Mobutu changed the name of the country from Congo to Zaire in 1971. After his overthrow in 1997, the name was changed again, to the Democratic Republic of the Congo.

president's very own gold mine, and though it does not excuse him to say so, Mobutu was clearly following in the footsteps of his illustrious predecessor, Leopold II, staking out a personal claim to the wealth of an entire region.

On the morning of our river crossing from Brazzaville to Kinshasa, the memories of troubles on our previous trip seemed almost quaint amid the air of hysteria produced by the rush of foreigners—journalists, doctors and relief officials—all seeking a piece of the action in the Ebola outbreak.

The word "Zaire" is a corruption of "Nzere," the name for the Congo River in a local language, which means "the river that swallows all other rivers," and the moniker could hardly be more appropriate. In the generalized absence of roads, the Congo has always been the country's lifeline. Three thousand miles from end to end, its watershed covers over a million square miles and includes over seven thousand miles of navigable tributaries. Between Brazzaville and Kinshasa, the world's closest capitals, the river is as broad as a lake, and though its appearance is leaden, even strangely solid in spots, its currents are notoriously strong. Our own docking maneuvers required heading upstream a good way, taking us well beyond our final berth, past a large fleet of huge freighters.

In this once-booming land, the ships were the equivalent of a rail stock and tractor-trailer fleet wrapped into one. But they were all badly rusted now, immobilized by an economy that with each passing day was growing more informal. Some had turned into floating apartment buildings, and here and there, men could be seen on their decks, squatting naked, taking their morning baths out of plastic buckets.

Even in this advanced state of ruin, though, Zaire, or more precisely Kinshasa and its skyscrapers, was an impressive sight from the low vantage point of our battered blue-and-white ferry. Mimicking Leopold once again, Mobutu had dreamed big. For a time, during the 1970s and early 1980s, when I had first visited, Mobutu's hold on the country, no less than that of his European predecessor, was built on a foundation of seductive, but ultimately outlandish, lies: rehabilitating African culture through a series of gimmicks, like banning neckties and Christian names, and through a demagoguery that promised a state whose power would reflect the country's immensity. At the height of his glory in those years, the tricked-out carapace of Mobutu's creation glittered with the illusion of promise. By now, though, every one of the country's forty-five million citizens bitterly understood that the Mobutu system had never been anything more than an empty shell.

At its core, Mobutu's program had consisted of little more than manipulation of symbols, fear and greed. But in the end, it was the president's outsized, Leopoldian appetites and ambitions that had laid his country low. These days, when Mobutu was not savoring champagne breakfasts in one of his European chateaus, he confined himself to his gaudily overbuilt village, Gbadolité, or to his gleaming white luxury riverboat, the *Kamanyola*, a ludicrous, James Bond–style prop, with a helicopter parked on its prow. All the while, a keen personality cult cranked out flattering names for him—the Guide, the Helmsman or, in a more atavistic mode, honorifics derived from the names of animals, like the Eagle, and his favorite, the Leopard, which hinted more candidly at his rapaciousness.

No one had declared Mobutu's Zaire dead yet, but something definitely smelled, and the country's decomposition had become an open secret. In the space of a mere year or two, by virtue of processes foreseen by none of the outside parties that had served for so long as Mobutu's allies and handmaidens—not by the Belgians or the French, not by the World Bank or the United Nations, and it seems not even by the CIA—this gigantic country would become a geopolitical fiction. There would still be a flag and an anthem, to be sure, along with a mortally sick and isolated ruler determined to cling on to the last. But like nature, politics tolerates no vacuums, and politically speaking, Zaire was already becoming an empty pit in the heart of the continent—a pit waiting for someone, by yet another unforeseen process, to fill it up and make the earth level again.

On this day, however, with sunshine streaking through the looming skyline of downtown apartment complexes and office buildings, it was still possible to sense the immense dreams this land had inspired, and not just the horrible ruin. Indeed, the best gauge was a glance back across the immense river at Brazzaville, ever modest, but now as shrunken and reduced as a postcard portrait. The only building that stood out on the distant shore, in fact, was the headquarters of the Central Bank of Central African States, a creation of France that circulated the CFA franc, a version of the French franc decked out in colorful African disguise, for use in Paris's former colonies. The tall copper-colored tower was a play on famous Central African statuary, and it shimmered from afar like a bronze scimitar, jealously warding off Belgium, or Zaire, or whoever else might be tempted to encroach on France's preserve. But one tower does not a city make, and it shimmered alone.

I had taken the precaution of alerting the American Embassy to my arrival, and as a courtesy, they had arranged for an embassy staffer, a Zairian "expediter" named Manzanza, to meet us at the quay. This was unusual procedure for both me and for the embassy, but the diplomat, a woman from the United States Information Service, extended me the courtesy with this comment: "Sure, that makes sense. If we don't greet you, we'll have to bail you out when they arrest you anyway."

As the scene at the docks came into focus, I rejoiced at my foresight. The Zairian quay, Ngobila Beach, was teeming with people: beggars in tatters, the handicapped smugglers in wheelchairs who spent their lives trafficking across this border, hefty market women wrapped in printed cloth and sweating over the quantity of goods they would have to surrender as "tax" to the vultures from the customs service, and every manner of security personnel, including soldiers, policemen and plainclothes intelligence agents.

We'd never met before, but Manzanza, who was dressed in the kind of neat two-piece outfit worn by the diplomatic corps' senior African personnel, spotted us immediately. "Don't give anything to anyone," he said, ushering us through the glutinous crowd toward the low-slung buildings with their dark rooms. There the customs and immigration officers waited as grimly as executioners, sure that each arriving passenger would surrender something, in cash or in kind.

In fact, not all the voyagers paid. Some never even approached the musty barracks, where stacks of used immigration forms, some of them easily a decade old, provided cozy nesting for rats. The big fish that passed this way relied on expediters of their own, known as "protocols" in the zestfully euphemistic lingo of Kinshasa. Some people are more equal than others in every society, but in Central Africa, Mobutu's Zaire had always provided the most colorful illustrations of this rule, and the protocols were slicksters in loud-colored shirts worn under European jackets, impossibly bold ties and showy gold-rimmed sunglasses.

While Manzanza haggled, some of the customs officers began

to take a worrisome interest in Robert's cameras, insisting on every imaginable kind of paperwork, from photo permits to sales receipts. It was an obvious prelude to a rip-off. While I watched, with mounting anxiety, one after another huge gilded Mercedes and shiny four-wheel-drive vehicles vroomed into the tightly enclosed space of the immigration retaining area to collect the diamond dealers and cosseted VIPs, who immediately disappeared behind heavily tinted windows. The protocols doled out cash and gifts from their small briefcases, thus ending the formalities. The cars then sped away again as quickly and as suddenly as they had arrived.

We were receiving a lesson in the way Zaire works, and as much as it offended the broad egalitarian streak in me, I took careful note. Robert and I would never enter or leave Zaire again without some form of reception or escort, be it the major we eventually cultivated at Ndjili airport or, later, the right-hand man of Mobutu's own son.

The last time Africa had received the kind of attention that the Ebola outbreak was drawing had been during the Rwandan genocide, and even then, after 800,000 people were slaughtered, the interest abated quickly. More than a million Africans die every year from malaria without raising a peep in the wealthy countries of the world. Struggling for a way to depict the scale of this disaster, the Tanzanian researcher Wen Kilama said, Imagine seven Boeing 747s filled mostly with children crashing into Mount Kilimanjaro each day, and you begin to get an idea of malaria's horrifying toll. In some African countries, 30 percent or more of the population is infected with AIDS, and yet the common bonds of humanity that are said to exist between us have never drawn the rich and the wretched of the world together in an emergency.

If "the claim of the stranger—the victim on the TV screen—is the furthest planet in the solar system of our obligations," as writes the essayist on global conflict and nationalism Michael Ignatieff, crises like these placed Africa somewhere beyond planetary space, consigned alone to a moral Oort Cloud.*

But the massive hemorrhaging and projectile vomiting associated with Ebola were such cinematically compelling new grist for the world

---

*The Oort Cloud is an immense spherical cloud surrounding the planetary system at the edge of the sun's orb of gravitational influence.

media's insatiable market in images of horror that African disease was guaranteed a spot on the nightly news for as long as the epidemic lasted. Besides sheer prurience, though, the outside world's interest was being driven by old-fashioned fright and narrow self-interest. Ebola aroused the fear in America and Europe that in today's shrunken and interconnected world, a deadly threat like this was only a plane flight away (like the SARS virus) from lives that truly mattered—those of Westerners.

"Where Africa is concerned, there is a constant search for tragedy with a new face; it's like what else is new in genocide," Ali Mazrui, a prominent Kenyan scholar, told me on the telephone a few days into the Ebola panic. "There is a hardened insensitivity to things which happen in Africa which are regarded as on the margin of human importance, even if hundreds of thousands die, which can only be called malignant neglect."

All too often, Africa coverage has come to resemble the cowboys and Indians games of my boyhood. We are quick to find heroes in the Westerners who are always seen as rushing to the rescue, while unconsciously concluding that the Africans served better in the role of, at best, passive spectators. We have too often gotten our explanations from the outside experts and the Western diplomats who professionally wander these parts, rushing right past the very subjects of Africa's dramas, the Africans themselves. I was determined to be different, and yet here I was, just like everyone else, rushing toward another lurid African mess that, thanks to the magic of television, had become the global story of the week.

Our first day in Kinshasa was spent in a blur of formalities, trying to obtain the necessary letters. Along the way, we successfully navigated the Ministry of Health, which wanted proof that we had received all of the normal vaccinations (no protection, of course, against Ebola), and, above all, the Ministry of Mines, whose authorization (for a $500 fee) signified that we were allowed to visit the zone of epidemic—the western Zairian city of Kikwit—for any purpose, except for mining, that is.

Dr. Kissi, a Zairian officer at the World Health Organization's offices in Kinshasa, was hardly reassuring. His advice to us was clear and concise. If you must eat in Kikwit, only eat hot food, or fruits and vegetables that have been carefully washed. And above all, avoid all contact with vomit, feces and urine. "It is important that we keep our neighbors in Kikwit contained where they are while we try to put out this fire," he said. "If not, the flames will arrive in our own home." He paused for a second, before adding gravely, "Which is to say, Kinshasa. We are lucky in the sense that the more powerful a virus is, and this one is as strong as they get, the more fragile it becomes. And this virus doesn't seem to be able to survive outside of the human body for very long, thank God. Because if there is one country that is ill prepared to face a large-scale epidemic, it is Zaire."

Dr. Kissi sent us off with those hopeful words, and with the last of our precious letters, and thankfully this time there was no fee. All of the other letters had been painstakingly typed and stamped by mid-ranking officials with a care bordering on reverence. The bureaucrats were so caught up in this farce that they had come to take it seriously themselves, and explained with great solemnity how our growing collection of expensive laissez-passer would assure our freedom of movement and safety even in the farthest hinterlands. Experience, though, had already shown us that in a pinch they were next to worthless. At bottom it was all nothing more than a racket that allowed poorly paid officials to supplement their monthly salaries.

I had been snared in this Catch-22 so many times already that by now I regarded it as one of those weary, immutable facts of life. You reach your destination with all of your paperwork just right, only to have some red-eyed official blow smoke in your face and invent yet one more piece of paper that you are supposed to be carrying. Often, there was no way forward except to pay a bribe.

Outsiders might call it corruption, or perhaps even anarchy, but for Zairians the games officials played with "formalities" was an unremarkable part of what was called "Système D," for *débrouiller*, the French verb meaning "to make do." Stealing was not just all right in Zaire; it had become an absolute imperative—a matter of survival, especially for unpaid officials assigned to distant provinces.

Early the next morning we drove to Kinshasa's general aviation airport, which was run-down even by the standards of this run-down country. First and foremost, it was a boneyard, the final resting place for the rusty DC-3s and other workhorses that had flown incredible numbers of hours with minimal maintenance ferrying Mobutu's troops and his private merchandise—diamonds, gold, pineapples, cassava— around this huge country. Mobutu had largely given up on territorial control by this stage of his rule, having concluded that it was as tedious as it was costly. The one thing that counted, he had concluded belatedly, was control over markets, and from this point of view, the president's fleet of planes, though barely airworthy, was his most vital asset.

Every few months one of these loose-riveted aircraft would crash somewhere, typically in a remote forest. It was the kind of thing that people around here shrugged off as happenstance. This casual fatalism changed forever a few months after our trip, though, when the inner-city airport itself was the scene of a dramatic crash: A Russian Antonov running guns and diamonds back and forth to Angola did a belly dive, plowing through the adjacent, zinc-roofed shantytown and killing scores of residents in its huge fireball.

On this particular day we were looking for a much smaller plane; anything, really, that could ferry us to Kikwit, 370 miles to the southeast. In our rather desperate circumstances, Robert and I, together with David Guttenfelder, a photographer from the Associated Press who had been working the Ebola story for nearly a week, were willing to spend a couple of thousand dollars. With speculation rife about a coming quarantine, just about everyone else was trying his or her best to flee Kikwit, so we had to find a pilot who would wait for us on the ground there until late in the afternoon, rather than taking someone else's money for the return run. Otherwise we would never make it back to Kinshasa in time to file our stories and pictures—or, for that matter, to eat a meal free from worries of contamination.

David, who had flown in and out this way a couple of times since the start of the epidemic, had a lead on a small, two-engine plane, and within forty-five minutes of arriving at the airfield, we were taxiing for takeoff. We had a surprise guest, however, in the form of a potbellied Zairian colonel in full khaki uniform. Presumably, he had finagled a seat for far less than we had paid.

All over the continent, I had made a practice of turning down soldiers attempting to hitch rides in my car—including many with guns. It was a matter of safety, yes, but of principle, too. Almost everywhere ordinary people associated soldiers with thievery, repression or worse, and I didn't want any part of those associations. As we watched the colonel load several duffel bags full of Zairian currency into the small plane's hold, though, I began to think that this time luck might be on our side. The pilot had whispered to us that the money was meant to pay the troops in Kikwit, which seemed like an inspired decision by Mobutu, aimed at avoiding mass desertions amid the general panic brought on by the virus.

From the air, with all its greenery Zaire looked like a set for *Jurassic Park*. As Kinshasa's huge sprawl slowly receded and then finally disappeared, the landscape molted suddenly and repeatedly. We went from forests as thick as heads of broccoli bundled tightly together, to golden savannahs resembling the American Great Plains, and finally, as the earth began to rise and fold upon itself, to extraordinary mesas. Green and flat, rising sharply from the surrounding plains and neatly covered with grass, they looked as if Norse giants had conceived them for putting practice. A trancelike state of relaxation settled over me with the unexpected nature show. It was a precious instant to be savored, like a final cigarette before an execution, and then, just as suddenly as it had begun, the sound of the small plane's deceleration and initial descent snapped me out of my reverie.

As the plane taxied, the simple cinder-block building that served as a terminal came into clear view. It sat near the edge of one of those steep escarpments we had been admiring from the air. In my lap I clutched a small plastic bag containing what I realized at that instant was a thoroughly silly emergency medical kit: rubber gloves, disinfectant and bandages. Suddenly, the reality of our destination and the plague that we had decided to visit was upon me.

Our little airplane had the effect of chum on sharks, and the soldiers who were guarding the landing strip began making their way toward us even before the engines were cut. As we deplaned, though, I realized just how correct my intuition about the colonel had been. The soldiers smiled at the sight of him and jostled one another to help with his bags. Normally, this would be the moment of our arrest, but we made off with scarcely a show of our papers after agreeing with the pilot to meet at the latest possible hour, which he said was 5 p.m.

A battered old taxi bore us creakily into town, toward the hospital that had been ground zero of the epidemic, in search of the kinds of stories we had been reading and hearing—stories almost too terrible to believe, scenes of patients whose very innards were dissolving into blood and mucus, expelled in agonizing bouts of diarrhea that ended in death. Italian missionaries from an order known as Little Sisters of the Poor had run the small hospital, with its pastel blue walls, but the Catholic sisters, who had always imposed a strict order on this place, preserving it from the powerful tug of equatorial decay, were themselves among the first to die in the epidemic.

Our first glimpse of the outbreak was of the parties of mourners who gathered under the eucalyptus trees that surrounded the small complex, aged women shrouded under lengths of colorful printed cloth who sat on the ground or on straw mats rocking back and forth. It was impossible to tell if they were mouthing words or simply moaning, but their powerful and eerily rhythmic wailing was painful to hear, and clearly bespoke the recent or imminent death of loved ones.

The moment we got out of our car, our noses were assailed with the stinging odor of chlorine. Healthcare workers in uniform, volunteers recruited for the task, were constantly spraying the area with a powerful solution of the disinfectant; where traffic was heaviest, nearest to the wards, the chlorinated ground had even turned muddy in patches.

Officially, there had been three hundred or so deaths so far, and most of the sick had ended up in this hospital, working their way from one makeshift ward to the next as their horrible symptoms grew relentlessly worse. First came the sore throat and headache, and then came the violently bloodshot eyes and runaway fever. Finally, the commencement of vomiting and constant diarrhea irrevocably confirmed the diagnosis.

Katuiki Kasongo, a forty-two-year-old army doctor, received us in as friendly a manner as one could hope for under the circumstances. Herds of Western reporters had galloped and brayed through the very scene that stood before us, jamming their cameras into the faces of terrorized, dying patients and their relatives, and now they were gone, although the tragedy had still not completely run its course.

Dr. Kasongo did a quick calculation and said there were fourteen remaining patients. But after a glance into Pavilion 3, the last stop for patients, those practically beyond hope, he corrected the tally. A couple of men draped in sheets lay inside, moaning faintly but showing few other signs of life. "The dangers are different, of course, but for us, the medical staff, the treatment is the same as for our AIDS patients," Dr. Kasongo said. "We don't treat them. We only try to comfort them. With all of our training, we feel totally helpless and discouraged, especially given the risks we are facing here. We are doing our best, but being incapable of offering people anything more than a couple of Tylenols eats at you. It is a terrible situation."

There was no sign of pining for recognition when he said matter-of-factly that Kikwit's small medical community had been sounding alarms for weeks about the strange and sudden apparition of people struck down by violent bouts of bloody diarrhea. He spoke with a depressingly familiar African weariness that comes from fighting against long odds, waging an extraordinary struggle with few means at your disposal—least of all the attention of outsiders. It would be easy to mistake his tone for fatalism. It was the sound of being completely alone in the world, a supposedly interconnected world, and it is a feeling that many Africans, particularly well-educated people like Dr. Kasongo, experience every day.

In matters of knowledge, science and medicine in particular, the outside world has never grown accustomed to listening to Africans, or respecting their knowledge of "serious" matters. Listening to Dr. Kasongo, I recalled a story I had often heard when I was in Haiti. During a debate about that country in the United States Senate early last century, Secretary of State William Jennings Bryan had expressed surprise to learn that black people could speak the language of Molière. "Imagine that," he said. "Niggers speaking French!"

Kikwit emerged from obscurity when the number of deaths had simply become too great to ignore, and perhaps most important, when foreign missionaries began to die along with the villagers they had attempted to treat. So many of the gripping stories I had read or heard, outside of the vignettes of blood and death themselves, were of the intrepid Afrikaner "bush scientist" or the brilliant French doctor or the American experts who had landed from the Centers for Disease Control as if beamed down from a spacecraft with their impressive anti-infection suits. The Africans were simply the victims, like props in a play, and the surfeit of suffering and the preternatural modesty even of the frontline workers like Dr. Kasongo combined to make them ideal for the role. Few of us had stopped to notice, but these were the real heroes.

The head nurse, Césarine Mboumba, a sturdy thirty-six-year-old woman dressed in a faded blue uniform, had worked at the small Kikwit Hospital for the last six years. She was present at the terrifying start of the epidemic, and had watched her closest colleagues die one by one for reasons no one understood. All she could think of was that God, for his own obscure reasons, had decided to spare her, because they had all been doing the same work.

"At the beginning we had no idea that this was an epidemic, never mind an Ebola epidemic," she said as she walked me through the wards. "I was the nurse who operated on the very first case. My anesthesiologist died, the second nurse died, then two of my assistants died."

That initial patient had himself been a laboratory worker named Kimfumu, she said. He was transferred to Kikwit Hospital complaining of severe abdominal pain. With new patients trickling in, complaining of similar symptoms, and invariably progressing toward the same bloody diarrhea and vomiting that announced their pending death, worry mounted, and the alarms started sounding for outside help. Two weeks later, two of the Catholic sisters succumbed. And two days after that, another pair of sisters followed them.

"When this began, the only thing we could consult was an old book on tropical medicine," Mboumba said. "It says nothing about the kind of bleeding that we have been witnessing, but when people ask me if I want to leave Kikwit, I say absolutely not. My work is here. I am no longer afraid."

Near Pavilion 3 sat a faded lime-colored building that now served as the morgue. Just outside, a dozen or so bodies that had been wrapped in heavy plastic sheeting lay in the shade of a high row of flaming red flowers, awaiting burial. Every now and then, I could see workers in masks and gloves leaving the morgue pushing wheeled carts atop which perched flimsy wooden coffins. When I left the hospital, I discovered their destination.

Just down one of the narrow dirt roads that led to Kikwit Hospital, fresh trenches had been dug by heavy machines. There, the virus's poor African victims were being given hasty burials. I arrived on the scene to find a delicate young woman dressed in a simple cloth wrapper, striking even in her grief as she used a narrow little shovel to fill in the dirt over her mother's grave. "Today it is my mother I've come to bury," said the woman, who gave her name as Julienne Kinkasa. As she spoke, another younger female relative looked on. "The other day it was my sister. She was a trainee at the hospital."

When I asked her if she thought she, too, was now at risk of dying, she said, "At this point I am not afraid of the disease. What I am afraid of is starving to death. We have been abandoned by society. People are so worried about the epidemic that they flee from us. What will we do now to survive?"

I decided to drop in on the headquarters of the foreign scientists who were said to be tracking the virus like bounty hunters, competing to discover its source both for the resulting good and perhaps also for the personal recognition and gain it would bring them. I found them in a dimly lit building not far from the hospital, a handful of men poring over computer printouts, composing messages for transmission by satellite fax back to their headquarters. Occasionally they looked up to exchange tightly clipped remarks among themselves.

It was clear from the moment they noticed me that they had already seen more than enough of my kind, and one of them announced, sharply, that they were all very busy. No longer expecting an interview, I pressed for a few leads. Could they tell me which neighborhoods of Kikwit had been particularly hard hit? Were there still new cases being reported? Where might we find someone who was newly sick?

At this, one of the foreign experts, a Frenchman named Rodier, snapped, telling me that the hordes of poorly behaved foreign reporters had made it nearly impossible for them to work. "We have had enough of your types looking for people with blood coming out of their ears," he said. "The epidemic is over. You are too late. Go back home!"

With what time we had left, I told our driver that I wanted him to take us through Kikwit's poorest neighborhoods, where we could inquire if there had been any reports of unusual deaths. The mention of poor neighborhoods in this city of half a million—a place without lights, telephones or even running water for most people—appeared to create some confusion. Poverty was everywhere, and in such circumstances its very definition begins to change. But within fifteen minutes, after winding and crossing back through a dusty quarter called Mkwati, where mud-walled houses were separated by bramble hedges, we had found what we were looking for.

There, a man who sat in the shade repairing a bicycle near a bend in the road told us what the all-knowing WHO experts had been unable or unwilling to say. "Six people died in that house right there," said Mpouto Kalunga, a peanut farmer who wore a worried look and said he lived nearby. "There are others dying, too. They are not my friends, just my neighbors."

Kalunga was clearly wary of us. A carload of foreigners was a rare sight in this neighborhood, and in these times of plague it was unlikely to mean good news. We told him that we were journalists, but he seemed scarcely mollified. All over town there had been wild rumors of suspected carriers of the virus being rounded up and disappearing.

"After the first deaths, the foreigners came and sprayed all of the houses," he said, as if he hoped we would disappear. "Are you going to spray again?"

We insisted that we merely wanted to see the sick, and finally he pointed up the slope toward a house on the right. There, three young women, girls really, their heads shaven in a sign of mourning, sat morosely in a dusty courtyard. I asked them if a relative had died from the virus, and immediately regretted having been so direct. "Our father died of the hiccups that he got from eating bad fruit," said the eldest of the sisters.

She was the only one of the three who could manage a bit of French, which made it easier for me. She continued in her defensive vein, "The disease you are looking for is not around here. It is in the hospital. You must go back there." As she spoke, a man arrived on a bicycle and interjected himself casually into the conversation of total strangers, as had happened so often to me in Africa. As Westerners, the privacy we are accustomed to is one of large homes and separate living quarters, of a life with telephones and automobiles. This, I was reminded, was the world of villages, where secrets were much harder to keep.

"Their father died of Ebola," he shouted, once he had confirmed our interest in the outbreak. "Don't believe what they are telling you."

With that, a small fight broke out, and though I did not understand the specifics, it was clear that an exchange of insults was under way. We continued onward by foot up the red dirt road's incline. One block away we found Mula Kinvita, a slender twenty-nine-year-old man wearing pink rubber gloves, washing himself painstakingly with a bucket filled with soapy water. "My mother died this morning at ten a.m.," he said, confirming my suspicion that there had been a death in his house. "She got sick with a fever last week, and it just kept getting worse and worse. Yesterday she began vomiting and having diarrhea. This morning, she just lay there trembling, and then she was dead."

I asked why he was washing himself this way, and he told me that he had just finished washing his mother's body in preparation for her burial. When I asked where she was, he pointed meekly to their one-room, mud-walled home.

Sure enough, inside his house, lit at this hour only by the fading rays of late-afternoon sunshine that streaked in through a small square window, lay his emaciated mother. She was stretched out on a straw mat, partially covered with a sheet of faded cloth.

The washing of cadavers is a solemn family duty in the Central African hinterland, and in a world of short lives and infrequent joys, sending one's loved ones off properly into the hereafter becomes all the more important. By tragic coincidence, this ceremonial preparation of the dead had become one of the prime means of transmission, and yet even after it was known that the virus was spread this way, it was difficult to persuade people to forgo their last rites.

Kinvita insisted that nobody had warned him of the danger. "A couple of days ago, when the Red Cross people came through here, I told them about my mother and they gave me some Tylenol to give her. When they returned in their truck this morning, I asked them to help me bury her, but they told me they are not allowed to carry the dead, and drove away in a hurry."

With the hour of our charter's return flight to Kinshasa fast approaching, numbed by our neighborhood tour, I asked our driver to take us back to the airfield. We boarded the plane with a minimum of fuss from the soldiers there. Once again, the colonel sat in the front seat of the plane. Back in the capital, only he would know how much of the soldiers' pay had actually reached the troops. Indeed, back in Kinshasa, only he would care.

Once airborne, we spoke little among ourselves. Perhaps as a release, David took pictures as we flew. My thoughts turned to Kinvita. I had urged him to go to the hospital and tell the people there about his mother's death. I had no idea if he would heed my advice, but I was skeptical. What good had the hospital ever been to him before?

Perhaps he would be coming down with the headaches soon, I thought. Perhaps the virus would kill him next. Perhaps there would be others in the neighborhood. It seemed clear that I would never know, and perhaps neither would the experts who sat in their makeshift office compiling their reports.

Discouraged by these thoughts, I began watching the landscape down below, and once again was hypnotized by the awesome tables and folds of earth. There was the natural, and there was the man-made.

CHAPTER FOUR

The Golden Bough

The easiest way back to Abidjan was a return flight from Brazzaville. So we decided to go home just the way we had come, taking
the westbound ferry back across the Congo River and stopping off for
a few days. I wanted to reacquaint myself with a country I had known
well a decade earlier, when I had visited often as a translator at World
Health Organization conferences, and later as a journalist.

As the ferry made its return passage, I recognized the same languid
Zairian rumbas playing on the tinny speakers on the open deck above
that I had heard from my seat in the cabin on my way to Kinshasa. As
the boat rocked gently and its engines chugged against the river's
strong currents, cutting silently through huge clusters of floating
hyacinths, instead of the deep anxiety I had felt a couple of weeks
before, I found myself fighting off sleep.

Somnolence seemed like an altogether appropriate state for my
return to Congo-Brazzaville. Other than an intense but brief burst of
killing during the country's transition from its Central African variant
of "Marxism" to an equally tropical form of "democracy" back in 1992,
nothing much ever seemed to happen here. Indeed, bored foreigners
often joked about the place, calling it Rip Van Winkle's village, because
of its reputation for immutable sleepiness.

The broad boulevards cut decades ago by the French during colonial times were filled as ever with sand. The polio-afflicted beggars with their loopy limbs and wooden crutches gathered in clusters at the stoplights, just as I had remembered them. And you could still set your watch by the abrupt halt to business activity at the start of the noon-time siesta.

I had been rereading one of my favorite novelists, the Congolese author Sony Labou Tansi, and having heard that he was secluded in a village somewhere, together with his wife, Pierrette, both of them dying of AIDS, I was thinking of trying to find him.

If an African god had set out to make a country, a land resembling the Congo would not be an unlikely result. Zaire next door had always been spoken of as Africa's "geological scandal," because of its disproportionate share of the continent's mineral wealth, but the real scandal was here, and it merely began with minerals. This little country seemed rich in just about every way that nature allowed—large oil deposits, huge expanses of virgin tropical forests, untouched minerals of just about every kind, great rivers, the sea. Congo-Brazzaville was as big as Montana and almost as empty, with barely two million souls to share all of this wealth. But in the end, the folly of the country's leaders, propelled by the boundless greed of outsiders, proved too much to overcome in spite of the innate wealth.

Governance in Congo had been as deranged as any other in Africa, but the place was too small ever to command much attention. The dividends it paid to its benefactors in France, the former colonial master, were too generous for them to complain about the political mess. Indeed, the French had long profited from the chaos by deftly pulling the strings. Most of all, Congo had remained obscure because it never had a dictator like Mobutu, who dominated the much larger country next door, commanding attention on the world stage with his solicitude toward the West during the Cold War and through his outrageously colorful style. When Congo-Brazzaville did rouse itself from long bouts of quiet, the place became very complicated.

At the height of the Cold War, the Soviet Union was squeezed out of Zaire—then also confusingly known as the Congo—in the CIA-backed coup that overthrew Patrice Emery Lumumba in 1960. It is hard to imagine world powers competing fiercely for influence anywhere in today's Africa, but in the 1960s intense rivalry was the name of the game all over the continent. So when a group of young officers in Brazzaville took power in a 1968 coup, creating the purest version Africa had yet seen of a Marxist-Leninist state, Moscow rushed in with aid and advisors, seeking the much smaller, former French Congo as its consolation prize.

The heavy industrial and agricultural machinery sent to Congo was intended to turn the country into the Soviet Union's showcase in the region. Moscow was about to learn that among the political forces at work in Central Africa, entropy has few rivals, least of all an imported ideology from the cold lands of the north called Marxism. For the Russians, even with all of the latent and unexploited wealth of Congo-Brazzaville at hand, trying to create a New Man there would prove as futile as it had back home.

The French at least had the advantage of their lengthy colonial experience, which allowed them to better understand the Congolese. When commercially viable quantities of oil began to be discovered in Congo in the early 1970s, Paris easily outmaneuvered Moscow, restoring what it called *relations privilégiés* with the country that had been the base of the Free French forces during World War II.

For all of the Soviet Union's advisors, for all the MiGs that took off and landed at the airports in Brazzaville and Pointe Noire, lending the leadership a macho blush of power, for all of the model farms created and for all of the monuments to Marx and the streets named for Lenin, the French had an answer. It was a softer, more seductive form of power, something called joie de vivre—bespoke suits, *les meilleurs crus*, haute cuisine, *hôtels particuliers* on Paris's most prestigious boulevards for the richest—and the Congolese elites, like their peers just about everywhere else in Central Africa, lapped it up.

Once the oil began flowing in earnest, nothing but fat years seemed to lie ahead for this obscure little land, but in fact, all the pieces were in place for a big fall. The country's predicament was part of a recurring drama in Africa, where the outside world's lust for some raw material, be it rubber, timber, cocoa, cotton, uranium or oil, knocks a society off balance and sends it careering into disintegration. The basket cases of tomorrow can be fairly easily predicted today. One need only glimpse quickly at the oil rushes under way in Equatorial Guinea, Chad and Angola or, on a smaller scale, at the scramble in eastern Congo for exotic minerals, like coltan (there was also a fad among Japanese for African ivory for use in carved personal seals in the 1980s), to sense the approaching disaster. And yet the consequences of this commercial predation are no more debated today than in the time of Leopold; perhaps less.

In Congo, the beginning of the end was ushered in by Denis Sassou-Nguesso, a strikingly handsome army officer with a keen taste for the good life. It has long been said that even tinier, oil-rich Gabon next door was the world's leader in per capita champagne consumption. But surely under Sassou, Congo's Pierre Cardin Marxists were not far behind.

After a brief interim, Sassou had succeeded Marien Ngouabi, a more earnest communist who was mysteriously assassinated in 1977, just as the petroleum boom was starting, and under the new leader it wasn't long before an arrangement was reached that seemed to leave all the big players happy. Congo's communist elite went through the motions of Marxism-Leninism, holding as many plenums and Central Committee purges as it wished. For many, ideology became a hairsplitting, almost religious obsession, allowing leaders and party cadres to live up to the Congolese reputation, built up by generations of brilliant sculptors, musicians, priests and writers, for creative imagination. The Russians contented themselves with the country's Marxist label, and with its supportive votes at the United Nations. Paris's main demand—and it was one that the Congolese elite, never too keen on dirtying its hands in the battle for national construction in the first place, was only too eager to grant—was to stay out of the way while Frenchmen ran the oil industry.

In its own absurd and tragic way, Congo functioned reasonably well like this for nearly two decades, on the surface, at least. The Marxist leaders ran a tightly policed dictatorship, providing meager but steady returns to the population while they and their foreign partners salted away billions of dollars worth of oil revenues in Western banks and luxury real estate in Paris, Switzerland and the French Riviera.

"Your situation is rich with rewards. But you'll have to be resourceful," a minister of national education instructed a newly appointed minister of health in a telling passage in Sony Labou Tansi's novel of the wretched excesses of sudden wealth and absolute power, *La Vie et Demie*. "A minister is made from his 20 percent share in the expenditures of his ministry. If you are clever, you can even tease that figure up to 30 percent, even 40 percent. . . . You must build things. We build all the time, because building pays the minister. In short, be daring and you will see how little streams turn into big rivers."

A hallucinatory tale that remains purposely ambiguous about the identity of the country where its action takes place, the novel speaks equally well to the situation of both its author's native Congo and of Zaire. The only thing is that in both countries, as ruin set in like a bad case of gangrene, the greed grew so intense that ministers were soon too busy stealing to build anything at all.

In a brief foreword to *La Vie et Demie*, which was published in 1979, Tansi calls his work an attempt to see "tomorrow with the eyes of today." In a reference to the repression on both sides of the Congo River that prevented artists like himself from describing their countries' situations more openly, he writes, "when the occasion comes to speak of the present day, I won't take such a roundabout path; nothing, in any event, so torturous as a fable."

From the time of brutal tribal kingdoms that competed with one another to sell slaves to the Europeans, to European colonization itself, with its forced labor and Draconian punishments for failure to meet production quotas for things like rubber or cotton, the Congolese people had never known a good deal. Strong-arm tactics were used to keep intellectuals quiet during the Marxist era, too, and few others were inclined to complain during this period, when amazingly, the majority of the population was kept on the public payroll. In effect, the latest triumph of the Congolese imagination was building a workers' state without workers. But despite having absorbed the worst lessons from Moscow (including dictatorship of the proletariat and hopelessly inefficient heavy industry) and from Paris (limitless bureaucracy and Latin-style corruption), as long as ever more oil kept flowing, the semblance of a functioning state could be maintained.

"This was the capital of l'Afrique Centrale Française, so what did the French do when they set up here? They put all the elite grandes écoles for Central Africa here and began training bureaucrats and officials," said an American diplomat whose cynicism was the fruit of several tours in the region. "Then the Soviets came, and the Congolese who already had a centralized state began adopting the idea that the government does everything for the people.

"I served here through some of the period of Marxism-Leninism and Scientific Socialism, and even then it struck me as a bunch of baloney. I don't think that Sassou and his friends believed any of it, not for even a minute. It was simply a wonderful tool for maintaining control, and it coincided perfectly with the tribal model that everyone here already knew inherently: The leader is chosen through some form of consensus, but rules with a pretty heavy hand. Under the old system, whenever you had an enemy, you accused him of sorcery. Under communism you call it deviation from the ideological line, and you purge him. The results are the same: liquidation, banishment or reeducation."

One such victim was Bernard Kolelas, the mayor of Brazzaville and a leader of the Bakongo ethnic group. Kolelas was a voluble and headstrong politician whose messianic crusade against one-party dictatorship was fueled in equal parts by Christian zeal and by his outsized ego. "Nine times I was arrested for speaking out against totalitarianism," Kolelas told me in his spacious Brazzaville home, which was heavily guarded by unsmiling youths with machine guns. "They would keep me tied up from morning till night, and torture me with an electric cable."

This treatment may not have kept Kolelas quiet for long, but most other Congolese got the message, and sought refuge in beer and palm wine, in the loose and easy sensuality of this land near the equator, or if they couldn't bear it at all, in exile. But as well as it seemed to work for a while, the Congolese system was just as surely never built to last. Oil prices fell throughout the late 1980s, creating huge problems for a state that had grown addicted to the manna. Simply put, no one had made provisions for declining oil prices or for declining reserves.

By the time the bottom finally fell out at the start of the 1990s, the little Congo that hardly anybody had ever heard of accounted for one quarter of the French state-owned oil giant Elf Aquitaine's proven reserves, and according to many estimates, an even higher percentage of the firm's profits. "They didn't know a thing about the oil business and let the foreign companies define all of the terms," an American diplomat said. "Throughout this period, Elf was the leader, and all they had to do was deal with Sassou and a few other people, buying them off at a fairly modest price. We are talking about a few tens of millions of dollars skimmed off of the top."

So what do you do when you can no longer pay salaries in a country full of civil servants? In February 1991, after Congo had been refused new credits by France and by the International Monetary Fund, Sassou convened an extraordinary meeting that he called the Sovereign National Conference to discuss the jam he had gotten himself into. An unprecedented debate about the state of the nation took place there, one that was intended to lance the boil of public discontent, while reinforcing Sassou's rule. But instead the conference turned into a raucous, three-month-long trial of the communist leadership.

"The national conference basically boiled down to one central question," said Kolelas. "The people said that we have been laboring all of these years and you've been pocketing our money. We refuse to go along with a system like that any longer. There's no point in working anymore."

Sensing that he could not hold on much longer, Sassou boldly sought to get out in front of history by volunteering to become a figurehead transitional president, and hence reinventing himself, however improbably, as the father of Congolese democracy.

Next door, giant Zaire was becoming the spectacle of Africa, steadily disintegrating while Mobutu, a recluse in his village palace in Gbadolité, clung to power. Meanwhile, unnoticed amid the attention lavished on an Eastern Europe that was suddenly casting off its communist dictatorships, Congo-Brazzaville was joining a small club of African nations—initially including Mali and Benin—that, without foreign help or fanfare, were "going democratic," as largely peaceful civic movements brought down longstanding dictatorships.

Congo's brief democratic experiment and its collapse turned out to be deeply influential, not least in once-mighty Zaire. Looking back now, the obvious lesson to be learned from this—whether or not it has been grasped—is that in Africa, both big advances and huge disasters often begin in small countries. Congo's democratic honeymoon ended almost as suddenly as it had begun. As would prove the case in country after country in Africa in the 1990s, the experience was derailed by regional, and then, even more narrowly, by ethnic and then, finally, by tribal efforts to monopolize power, accompanied by bloodshed and warlordism. Without sturdy institutions, and with little experience in the rule of law—problems whose roots go back to colonial rule—politics was reduced to a game of ethnic brokerage.

Here and there, fledgling democracies quickly assumed a sectarian hue, as, for example, when predominantly Christian southerners united against northern Muslims in Ivory Coast, or when Muslim majorities in northern Nigeria interpreted majority rule to mean that they were justified in imposing strict Sharia Islamic law in the states they controlled. In Congo-Brazzaville, officers from the sparsely populated north had dominated during the oil boom years, and when the Sovereign National Conference chased Sassou from power, southerners rejoiced, uniting briefly around a simple but potent theme commonly heard all over an ethnically splintered continent: It's our turn.

"After the disaster of one-party rule we had the tragedy of democracy, and it has lasted so far for three years," said Emmanuel Dongala, a Congolese novelist I went to see to talk about Sony Labou Tansi and about the state of his country. "We went straight from dictatorship to multiparty politics without any transition. The attitude was, Aghh, the old regime has fallen and the northerners are gone. Now it is our turn to hoard all of the money, to have the most beautiful women and to drive the fanciest cars. The rude awakening that we had here was to learn that in Africa political parties are still composed on the basis of the lowest common denominator, and for the Congolese, that still means the ethnic group."

With Congo producing an alphabet soup of political parties, each pretty much organized along ethnic lines—and sometimes consisting of nothing more than a clan leader and his extended family—the handwriting of this country's demise was written on the wall for all to see. Pascal Lissouba, a southerner, a thick-spectacled Marxist with a background in plant genetics, won election as president. Sassou complained that his supporters had not been given enough jobs and refused to participate in any multiparty "unity government." The former president then made common cause with Kolelas, making Lissouba's party the minority in government and setting the stage for the first battle for Brazzaville in 1993.

Almost no one outside of Central Africa, except perhaps France, paid any heed to the urban warfare in Brazzaville, which pitted the president's militiamen against Kolelas's private army, but the fighting showed as much resourcefulness in its disregard for human life as any war in recent memory. For weeks, rival gangs composed of soldiers and neighborhood toughs pounded one another and residents of the city with anti-aircraft guns and heavy artillery aimed at one another's neighborhoods.

"It all began when the Aubervillois led a charge into the Bakongo neighborhood, bashing and banging for a day and a half with heavy-caliber field guns that didn't have any business being used in a city," a foreign diplomat told me, in a reference to Lissouba's militia. "Kolelas's people, the Lari, responded by cutting off the railroad lines that came in from the coast, and then going after Lissouba's people with equal viciousness in the streets of Brazzaville. The fighting didn't end until pretty much everybody in Brazzaville had lost an uncle or a brother or a nephew. This had always been a country where people from different groups intermarried, and it was an amazing thing to watch the hatreds boil over. You have to wonder now if it can ever be put back in the bottle."

Kolelas had a different explanation for why the fighting stopped. And in his reasoning, in retrospect at least, one could also see the seeds for the coming conflagration, which would pit the two southern leaders against Sassou. "By the end of three months of this kind of killing we had cases where people would capture their enemies' babies and beat them to a pulp with a wooden mortar for revenge," he said. "Finally, I believed there had been some sort of divine intervention when I started hearing people say, 'We are all blood brothers, descendants of the same Kongo kingdom. Why should we massacre each other if all we are doing is giving the northerners a chance to take over again?' "

No one was predicting it at the time of my visit, but a new and far more destructive war, fought precisely along these battle lines, was to arrive on the heels of Mobutu's downfall in 1997. It was much more intense than the cakewalk campaign that would topple Mobutu and bring Laurent Kabila to power, and it may have killed more innocent people, but this was the near-invisible little Congo, and its suffering, like its progress, would go unnoticed.

For reasons I could still not fathom, Tansi had inserted himself in the middle of this venomous equation, first running for parliament in the 1993 elections, and then boycotting the institution altogether, along with the rest of Kolelas's supporters. The stories of his final, declining months were as dispiriting as anything I had heard about this country. Congo's greatest writer, a man whose brave satirical fiction had subverted dictatorships throughout the region, had taken up the tribalist Bakongo cause of Kolelas's most hate-filled supporters with a virulence that he married to his gift for the verb. John Updike, writing about Tansi in *The New Yorker,* said that his late works were haunted by a "personal dying." Updike quoted a passage from Tansi's last novel, the surrealistic *The Seven Solitudes of Lorsa Lopez:* "In this country, night has the appearance of divinity. It smells like infinity. Day here will never be more than a pathetic hole of blue, sickly light." The words capture beautifully Tansi's almost fanatical disgust with the Central African condition, but give little hint of his own growing political folly.

Tansi's concerns were never with the cookie-cutter countries bequeathed by Europe's arbitrary partition and colonial subjugation of the continent. Subtly underpinning all of his art, but always at the forefront of his increasingly rabid politics, was a deeply felt nationalism. It harkened back to what was for many African intellectuals a myth-infused antediluvian past, before the time, that is, when Europe's imperial mapmakers and colonizing armies destroyed Africa's nascent states.

There was tragic irony in Tansi's rage for redemption. Europe had undoubtedly wreaked untold destruction by shoehorning Africans of different languages and cultures together inside arbitrarily drawn boundaries at the end of the nineteenth century, by halfheartedly imposing its models of governance and economics on the continent for a few short decades in the twentieth century. Then, by washing its hands of Africa and walking away long before the mold had set, it vastly compromised matters even further.

Though born of the indignities of domination by Westerners, Tansi's passions were nonetheless based on a narrow, ethnically driven sense of identity. Everywhere one looked in Africa, runaway ethnicity in politics had the same impact: blinding carnage and chaos. Surely this was not the germ of African renaissance. An ideology like Tansi's struck me rather more like a stick of dynamite thrown into a crowded marketplace—a recipe for death and destruction.

While dying of AIDS, a disease he refused to so much as acknowledge, Tansi was experiencing a delirious streak of energy, which he unleashed on foes both old and new. Among them were the other ethnic groups, whose history he felt was nothing but backwardness compared to that of the descendants of the grand old Kongo kingdom. There was France, which had thrown Congo's disparate peoples together in the same doomed formula for state creation seen all over Africa, and had been despoiling his country ever since. And finally, there was the vanity, nihilism and greed of Africa's modern leaders, whom he condemned mercilessly, harkening back all the time to a putatively purer Africa, the Africa of his ancestors, who enjoyed order and light before the golden bough of their culture had been defiled by wave after wave of European slavers, explorers, missionaries and colonists.

From the stories I was hearing secondhand, Tansi had worn out his welcome in Paris, where until recently he had been undergoing treatment for AIDS at the expense of both French and African friends. He had been sighted briefly in Brazzaville, together with his wife, and then they had disappeared again. Although Robert and I had heard all kinds of tales about him—that he was already dead, that he was in Zaire—most of the accounts seemed to converge around the idea that he had gone deep into the bush to undergo what French-speaking Africans call *traitement à l'indigénat,* or traditional cures. The village that was named most often in this context, the one that was cited with the most conviction, was a tiny place named Kibossi, located on the banks of a medium-sized tributary of the Congo River.

Because of the infrequent air connections out of Brazzaville, we knew when we set out that Sunday morning that we had only one day to find Tansi. Everyone had told us we would require a four-wheel-drive vehicle, and although I wondered if I was setting myself up for a rip-off, I submitted to the idea and negotiated the least ruinous fee I could with the only rental-car agency that was open for business on that sleepy Brazzaville Sunday.

The driver, André, collected us at our hotel, and we hit the road immediately, leaving Brazzaville's sandy streets behind us. Within a few minutes, following the banks of the river, we passed the looted and destroyed compound of the World Health Organization, where I had done my stints as a translator, and finally hit the winding, pitted two-lane road that after twenty years of booming oil exports was still the closest thing Congo had to a national highway.

I had been talked into the necessity of a true off-road vehicle, a huge and heavy Toyota Land Cruiser, and not one of the recreational vehicles that serve as oversized cars for suburban adventurers back home. But droopy-eyed André, skinny, almost dainty in his fancy shirt, designer sunglasses and gold chains, looked like anything but the type of guide one would want to have deep in the bush. What is worse, he had brought his sportily dressed girlfriend along for the ride, seating her far in the back. There was a strong hint of pique from both of them over the fact that André's French boss had made him work on a Sunday because of a couple of Americans with a peculiar request.

The trip started out badly between us. During the first hour I repeatedly had to ask André to turn down the music. And though he grudgingly did so each time, he gradually turned it back up, until the bass pounded so heavily that it masked even the noise that the brutal banging from the steadily deteriorating road was delivering to the car, and to us. The songs were heavily rocking Congolese rumbas, with fantastic, bouncing guitar runs, and lilting vocals by a roly-poly singer whose name I soon learned was Madilu System. In the popular manner of many Congolese singers, Madilu seemed to weave the names of every person he knew into his lyrics, laughing deeply as he pronounced words like "enigma" and "paradox" in his booming tenor.

Like an endless loop the same tape would play over and over throughout the day, producing the same scratchy attempts by André and his girlfriend to match the singer's trills. But however much it had grated on me at first, I was gradually won over. Indeed, in time, I was playing the guitar parts in my head, tapping my feet and occasionally even puzzling over what the enigma was.

The ride was giving me my second lesson in the geography of this region in as many weeks. Although we never strayed far from the banks of the Congo or one of its many tributaries, climbing the grassy hills and then plunging into incredibly lush bamboo-filled valleys, I realized that I was seeing more of what I had been admiring from the air on the flight to Kikwit. Africa is extraordinarily empty. The Sahara and Kalahari Deserts, each huge, have climates far too dry to support more than a few wandering nomads. The forbidding Sahara alone, which is scarcely smaller than the United States, is a little less than one third of the continent's total area. At the opposite extreme of the continent's ecological spectrum, the Central African rain forest, a biosphere of over 500,000 square miles, is a world of water and vegetation so dense that one could fly overhead for hours and never see the ground.

However lush it may appear, though, for humans life in the forest is almost as rude as it is in the desert, which is why only small numbers of pygmies eke out a life there. We drove atop one of those grassy plateaus that had so hypnotized me from the air, and dipped into the well-watered valley that led to Kibossi. Everywhere, I was stunned to remark that apart from the road we had turned off onto—a loamy track that seemed at times as if it would swallow the car like quicksand—there was no sign of man's hand anywhere.

The Congo River had excavated the soil from the bowels of the continent all along its immense arc through southern, then eastern and finally Central Africa, and then deposited it here like molehills of compost. This was earth of an almost impossible richness, and yet for miles at a time there was not a soul in sight. Tropical pestilences had plagued Africa from the beginning of time, and this primordial curse had meant that much of its best land remained underpopulated, almost uninhabitable. Western science has never given these problems its best shot, far from it, and technology has been failing miserably in the face of menaces as commonplace as the mosquito and the tsetse fly.

Water was everywhere in abundance, but the dampness bred an amazing proliferation of parasites, from larvae that bore their way into the skin of those who wade in streams, causing blindness years later, to fly-borne parasites that attack cattle, making it impossible to raise a herd. Malaria and common diarrhea alone kill millions of African children each year. And though hard to measure, the toll of disease on the survivors is easy to grasp: generalized lethargy and shortened lifespans. More recently, AIDS had descended on the continent like a coup de grâce delivered against those who had survived against already long odds. In countries like Congo-Brazzaville, perhaps a third of the population had already become infected.

We pulled into Kibossi toward the end of lunch hour to find a Sunday afternoon scene pretty much typical of any village between Senegal and Zimbabwe. As scrawny chickens pecked for specks of grain by their feet, the village men, their clouded eyes bloodshot with a hint of yellow mixed in with the red, sat on benches alongside low-slung concrete buildings talking loudly and drinking beer from brown bottles as long as their forearms. The women were still at work, bending low to sweep their courtyards with their long African brooms of splayed straw bunched and tied loosely at one end; feeding naked, runny-nosed babies; or deep-frying batter-dipped delicacies for their young daughters to sell by the roadside as the afternoon stretched into evening.

Foreigners don't pull into little villages like this very often, and as we got out of the Land Cruiser everyone stopped what they were doing to watch us. André approached the most sober of the men nearby and asked him in the local language if Tansi was to be found anywhere nearby.

The hubbub increased, drawing people out of their homes and attracting lots of bystanders. Through experience, I already had the distinct feeling that we were about to be led on a goose chase. Some people claimed to have heard of the recent arrival of the man we were looking for. They said he wasn't staying in this village, but rather across the nearby river, and a good walk upstream.

Having come all this way at such expense, we couldn't turn back without having a look, so we haggled over the boat ride we would need to take, recruited a guide and were soon on our way. Robert and I sat, along with our guide, in a pirogue, a dugout made from the long but shallow trunk of a local hardwood tree, along with two young men who steered us across the river, sometimes paddling with a crude oar and sometimes standing and pushing against the bottom with a long wooden pole. With the boat wobbling jerkily, bringing the warm and muddy water to the very lip of the low-slung hull, I was convinced that we would end up swimming for our lives. And yet somehow, we made it across.

To my chagrin, it took only a few minutes on the far bank to confirm that Tansi was not living in, nor had he ever lived in, this village. He had never even been heard of there. Going with the flow, however, even when it is hard to discern much of any direction, is a necessity in Africa. It is not my style, but I had learned to enjoy it, making a virtue of momentarily surrendering control. I had seen too many foreign correspondents tearing their hair out in frustration over Africa's chaos or cursing the venality or supposed incompetence they claimed to see everywhere, even as they offered to bribe their way through situations unbidden.

An improvised trip, and the experiences like these it provided, sometimes overshadowed the destination itself, becoming a source of understanding, or at least of feeling for a continent so many others were content to damn. So, having had an opportunity to admire the boatmen's uncanny balance—and little more—we returned to Kibossi, paid our various helpers and companions, and set off for the return trip to Brazzaville.

The advantage of a good travel companion goes beyond plain company; his real value is in the kind of moral encouragement he provides in situations like these. Robert had maintained his usual cheer in Timbuktu, even as I succumbed to dysentery. We had kept each other going on huge overland trips—navigating by the moonlight in the near-desert wastelands between Ouagadougou and Niamey, rushing to cover the overthrow of one of the region's rare elected governments, or surviving the horrible road between Burkina Faso and Ghana that we had taken on with a battered taxi with broken seats.

As weary as I was this time, Robert, who sat in the bumpy back seat of the car with the loud music and with André's still-complaining girl-friend in her showy but faintly ridiculous faux-Chanel blouse, had to be even more exhausted. But just as I was about to give up the search for Tansi, he asked what we should try next. So once back in Brazzaville we did what we should probably have done from the very start: We went to Tansi's city home in search of information.

The afternoon had turned so hot it even seemed to slow the bulbous green equatorial flies that swarm around restaurants and refuse heaps in Brazzaville. We found the house with little difficulty. It was an unassuming place in the Bakongo quarter, a little larger than most, perhaps, but nothing special in this dusty grid of streets. A couple of teenagers sat on the veranda with machine guns, posting guard, which we took as a good sign. But once under the awnings, a glimpse at the near-total darkness inside made me think Tansi was not there.

After a moment's wait, Tansi's son, Regis, appeared, sporting a look much like our driver's, complete with gold neck chain. The style, popular all over Africa, was innocuous enough, but as an African-American, and thereby, by definition, as a descendant of slaves, I always found it ironic. Africa had been taken over and Balkanized by Europeans eager to find gold. And from there, one commodity led seamlessly to another, resulting in the trade in human beings, with black people in chains shipped off to their death or bondage by the millions from places all up and down this coast.

Regis said he knew where his dad was and seemed eager to see him, so I invited him to come along as we set off once more in the Land Cruiser. The new destination was a place called Foufoundou, a tiny village not found on Michelin's maps of the region, which I always carried. Regis seemed confident, though, so we forged on, traveling well past the turnoff to Kibossi.

As the afternoon wore on, though, despair gradually displaced my earlier serenity. We were driving on sandy secondary roads now, and the tracks in the soft earth brought here by the Congo basin's rivers were so deep that the car could often steer itself for minutes at a stretch. The massive growth of grasses and bamboo had overwhelmed what had been roadway. The heavy stalks of bushes and vines that constantly scratched and banged away at the car had turned our pathway into a tunnel of thick greenery. I distracted myself from my growing fears of our breaking down and of the approaching darkness by imagining this terrain in prehistoric times. I was back to my visions of *Jurassic Park,* and found myself imagining encounters with some hitherto uncatalogued beast.

There was that music, too—the record by Madilu, playing over and over. I didn't know any Lingala, the language of most Congolese pop, outside of the most common expressions of romantic affection that are repeated in almost every song, but somehow I was beginning to intuit the meaning of his fulsome valentines. When the tail-wagging intensity of the music slowed, it was just possible to imagine that the repeated references to enigmas and paradoxes evoked by the singer were about the dilapidated state of this "rich" country and its nonexistent roads, rather than some melancholic expression of the singer's romantic obsessions.

According to the guidebooks, this former French colony boasted a total of 770 miles of paved roads, but from the evidence of our travels, even that modest figure seemed impossible to believe. André was characteristically laconic in explaining the shortfall. "Why don't we have roads in this country after so many years of oil exports? Because the money came in, and the politicians spent it. The worst part is that we told them: Take your time, eat well. The Congolese people have contented themselves dancing while their leaders ate sumptuous meals."

Whether or not we would ever find Tansi, André's words had just brought us closer to him, I thought. He knew almost nothing of the writer, but taking different routes, the two shared conclusions.

We eventually came to a clearing, an old railway town on an abandoned line. Children were playing soccer half naked in the muddy streets. The local language had changed since Kibossi, as it does every few miles in many parts of this continent, but with a bit of struggle André was able to understand enough to know that we were drawing close to our destination. Just when I thought the road could not get worse, it did. To exit this forgotten settlement, we had to move the rotting trunk of a tree from the path, and as the overgrowth became ever heavier, the car groaned and brayed through the sand and bush, threatening to stall or seize up every few minutes.

When we finally reached another clearing, this one a patch no bigger than a two-car garage, André spotted a toothless old woman loading up a sack of kindling to carry home to prepare her evening meal. He called out to her and then approached. With only a couple of hours left to go before the sun's demise, I was not encouraged to see her pointing off into the distance.

When he returned, he said we would have to leave the car there and walk. "She said it isn't too far," André told us. "We just have to cross a river and climb the next foothill over there."

Robert and I got out, detecting a recurrent theme, and together with Regis, the four of us began our hike. I was in city clothes, clearly made for concrete sidewalks and tiled floors, but with a minimum of slipping and sliding, down I went, until we reached the river, which was really more like a creek. There we had to clamber across a fallen tree, all mossy and slick, to reach the other side. Then, as we huffed and puffed up the hill, Regis began to speak up a bit for the first time. I asked him why his father would come to a place like this. Was it his village? Regis said no, and tried his best to explain. "He had no peace in Brazzaville," he said. "He must have come here to find peace."

At the crest of the hill I could indeed make out a small village. A few puffs of smoke were wafting up from a cluster of huts, indicating that it was inhabited, and my spirits followed them skyward.

All the huts were constructed with bamboo and mud walls and thatched roofs, and were arranged in a semicircle around a broad, open space. As I approached, I noticed a skinny unshaven man of indeterminate age. He was barefoot, and rocked backward on a wooden chair. He was holding a pipe and turned as he heard our footsteps. "Mysteries still exist," the man exclaimed. And as he turned toward us in greeting, his mouth opening into a huge toothy grin, I recognized him as Sony Labou Tansi. "They told me you would come, and now you are here."

I had no chance to ask Tansi what he meant. His hair was wildly overgrown and bore a distinctive patch of white on the crown of his head, and as I drew close to him, he began to speak agitatedly. He began explaining how he had come to this place, and his words tumbled forth, lucid enough, but still somewhat scattershot. "The treatments they were giving me in Paris were not having any effect," he said, scratching himself constantly against the wooden chair's backrest. "When I returned to Brazzaville I met a prophet who told me to come here."

As he spoke, growing more and more excited, I could hear soft murmurs coming from a bamboo and straw cabana at the edge of the carefully swept clearing. Tansi said it was his wife, Pierrette. She was very weak, he said, too weak even for the African miracles that seemed to have revived him.

"There is sacred writing in this place. You will soon see for yourself. The Mother has been reading the Scriptures, and the Scriptures said that foreigners were on their way." In a few minutes, I would understand to whom and to what he was referring.

Tansi had shown a flash of tenderness, an affectionate smile, toward his son, who was trying to be brave but looked devastated. Tansi now had an audience and was holding forth, all the more vigorously since it had all been prophesied. Regis wandered off to find his mother, who, as we later saw for ourselves as we fed her peeled grapes while she lay on a cheap mat, was very near death.

"I've been writing a lot. Some of my best work," Tansi said. "But the French people don't want to publish it. They said I am too hard on France, but in their egotism, they've missed the point. Asia has come into its own. Latin America has come into its own. Africa alone has failed, and I will not mince my words about the reasons why: We are still sick from a sort of contamination that began under colonization.

"Our leaders follow the examples they were taught by the Europeans, stealing money and never doing anything for the people. I'm calling my newest work 'La Cosa Nostra,' because it is about Africa's dictators and their protectors in Europe, but I am asking the world to reconsider Africa, too. I am asking for a Marshall Plan to rescue us. The cultural richness here is incredible, and it is being destroyed. It cannot be allowed to go to waste."

Briefly, Tansi discussed his latest passion, Solzhenitsyn, and said he had read *Cancer Ward* over and over in his Paris hospital room. "We are all doomed, fated to die," he said, emitting an enthusiastic deep-voiced cackle that triggered a rattling cough. "But in the meantime there is nothing to stop us from living."

At this instant, we began to hear the sound of chanting in the distance. Then, emerging suddenly from the bush, came a procession of villagers led by a robust woman draped in white. At the sight of us, they began cheering ecstatically.

Tansi identified the woman who led this troupe as Emilie Kiminou, the "Mother who receives the messages," and suddenly the swept earth of the clearing had become a stage. Tansi produced a sheaf of loose papers filled with bold, loopy scribblings that looked like the work of a deranged child. Instructing me to watch carefully, he handed them to Mother Emilie, who, half singing, half chanting, proceeded to "read" these messages, speaking in tongues at a breakneck speed.

When the clamor reached an end, Tansi looked at me as if I should by then have had all the proof I needed of his African miracles.

"Kongo has existed as a nation since Beatrice," Tansi said, growing drunk with excitement on a mixture of his own Kongo nationalism and Mother Emilie's syncretic evangelism. But ironically, he had mangled the kingdom's significantly longer history in the process.

Dona Beatrice had indeed been a legendary female prophet in the Kongo kingdom in the late 1700s. Her real name was said to have been Kimpa Vita. The kingdom had controlled much of present-day Congo, Zaire and Angola, until its final defeat by the Portuguese, the first to cull slaves from the area for shipment to the Americas. Beatrice had become powerful, convincing people that she was possessed of the spirit of Saint Anthony of Padua, a popular Catholic saint of the time and reputed miracle worker. Her followers believed that Jesus, Mary and the saints were all Kongolese. Ultimately, like Joan of Arc, she was burned at the stake for heresy at the instigation of European missionaries.

I was now implicitly being asked to believe that Mother Emilie was an incarnation of this forgotten Kongolese saint. Tansi had been longing for the resurrection of *his* Kongo his entire adult life, and now, only two weeks away from death, he had found it.

"You must understand why I am feeling better now," Tansi said to me in an embrace as we parted. "I am home at last. Finally I am in my own land. I should have come here a long time ago. It has revived me, and if I had not taken so long to come, Pierrette might have been saved, too."

CHAPTER FIVE

Greater Liberia

Our small Russian prop plane finally dropped down beneath the murky mass of clouds that hung low like a gray lid over Liberia, after a two-hour flight west-by-northwest from Abidjan. If I hadn't known better, I would have thought that we were about to make an emergency landing, for all I could see below were brackish swamplands and the lush green of the West African bush. It wasn't until the very final moments before landing that the first reassuring glimpse of solid land, and then, at last, the pitted landing strip of James Spriggs Payne airfield came into view. There was always a nagging thought at times like these that if anything went wrong, death was a certainty. I often wondered if there would even be a rescue operation, as I pictured instead the salvage effort by villagers living nearby who would undoubtedly come scurrying to the crash site to recover whatever they could haul away from the wreckage.

Displaying an extraordinary and totally unfeigned cool that seemed native to this corner of Africa, people on bicycles and on foot hurried their pace just enough to get across the runway in time as we landed, disappearing down orange clay footpaths that led away into the bush. As the noisy little aircraft taxied and came to a final halt, I thought there could be few better introductions to this country than Spriggs Payne. Outside, a crush of excited relatives of the two dozen or so passengers aboard our flight was already forming on the tarmac nearby. And alongside them, the ground was already thick with a demi-monde of porters, greeters, "facilitators," beggars and outright thieves.

If you had come to Liberia just once before, you would have earned celebrity status among this crowd, for whom memory was part of the hustle, and since I had come often, as I descended from the plane cries of "Hey Mr. Howard," "Hello Boss Man," "My friend, come this way," rang out from every direction.

Beyond the distractions of this unofficial welcoming committee there were the police and immigration officers, health inspectors and the other dubious officials waiting to accost you, demanding to see travel documents before you could even make it inside the decrepit little terminal. These were people who stole by official sanction, and inside that dark and sinister place, hassling travelers had long ago become stylized ritual.

As I headed for the immigration building, a tall, broad-shouldered Nigerian soldier dressed in that country's distinctive green fatigues and matching cap swung a swagger stick at the jostling touts, bellowing in his deep voice for "Order!" It had all the impact of someone swatting away flies from rotting fish. They feigned scattering for just an instant, then came back just as quickly as they had dispersed.

The confusion that attends the landing of every airplane in Liberia should be patented, I thought, so thoroughly was it Liberian. In microcosm it reflected the chaos of a country that had been bled heavily during a long civil war, and kept on knife's edge by a myriad of rival militias ever since. Tiny Liberia, just 2.6 million people at its peak, had lost 200,000 people in a conflict that had been cruelly indiscriminate.

We usually think of wars as having identifiable adversaries. In Liberia, search as one might, it had become impossible to discern any clear lines. The sheer number of deaths seemed to warrant a label like "genocide," which might have drawn more attention from CNN and perhaps roused the diplomats of the world. But the Liberian civil war's victims came from every class and description, and perversely, because there was no longer any sharp ethnic focus to the killings, the country's atrocities eluded easy categorization, and thereby escaped attention in a world already eager to ignore Africa's nightmares.

Still, it was hard for me to observe the airport's choreographed confusion without concluding that this tragic little country's chaos also had its comical side. Almost everything in Liberia did. But it was vital never to forget that the easy joking and breezy nonchalance masked a raw struggle for survival, and that after five years of brutal civil war, nearly everything here, including airport begging and bribe-taking, had become deadly serious. It took a mere instant to lose your wallet, your passport or your laptop here at Spriggs Payne, and anywhere else in Liberia you might just as quickly lose your life.

In August 1995, the country's factions had negotiated a ground-breaking agreement to come together in a national unity government. Most important, the pact allowed for the war's instigator—and all along its most stubborn protagonist—Charles Taylor, to return to the capital, Monrovia, for the first time in many years.

Like a Roman outpost under permanent threat from Germanic warriors, during Taylor's time in the bush Monrovia had remained a city under siege. Because of the constant skirmishing in the country-side, half of the population now lived in Monrovia, a city without electricity or running water. Another third of the nation had simply fled Liberia, and were living in UN refugee camps scattered about the region. By now, save for the fighters and their peasant captives, the hinterland was largely empty. Residents of the capital were kept alive only by the grain shipments of international charities like CARE and Catholic Relief Services, and Taylor's rebels were kept at bay only by the presence of a huge garrison of troops from the Economic Community of West African States (ECOWAS), which was overwhelmingly dominated by Nigerians. ECOWAS had originally deployed for the same purpose five years earlier, amid a major refugee emergency: to prevent Taylor from storming the capital.

Lacking refugee camps or any other appropriate shelter, Monrovia's huge internally displaced population took up residence in the gutted and bombed-out shells of what had been a once-proud city's most prestigious addresses. Somehow, the entire front facade of the massive, boxy structure of the Libyan-built Foreign Ministry, for example, had been neatly sheared off in the artillery duels between the Nigerians and Taylor's fighters during one of the rebel leader's attempts to capture Monrovia. And squatters now used the ministry's offices as overcrowded apartments, seeming to pay no mind to the fact that their whole lives were on display to the passersby on one of Monrovia's busiest avenues.

This same gritty resourcefulness was at work at the Intercontinental Hotel, once a majestic skyscraper that stood on the city's high ground like an exclamation point, announcing the cosmopolitan pretensions of the old Americo-Liberian elite—the class of freed American slaves that had founded this country in 1847. As they settled the land, the Americo-Liberians fondly strove to reproduce the only model they knew, the plantation society of the American South. Affecting top hats and morning coats, the freedmen ruled Africa's first republic in a clannish and conservative manner, established their own curiously paternalistic brand of apartheid, systematically excluding so-called aborigines from positions of privilege and power until 1980, when a coup by an unschooled soldier and "man of the soil" from the Krahn ethnic group, Master Sergeant Samuel Kanyon Doe, brought this anachronistic little universe to a bloody end.

Like nearly every other monument to the Americo-Liberians, the Intercontinental Hotel had been shattered and left to rot in the moldy damp of Liberia's persistent tropical rains. Nowadays, in exchange for their lofty sea views, and the generous breezes that served in lieu of air-conditioning on the upper floors, the hotel's squatters had to cart their water, and anything else they consumed, up the many flights of dark stairs to wash, drink and cook.

In fits and starts, between repeated disastrous setbacks, Monrovia had been struggling ever since Doe's coup to resuscitate itself and rejoin the late twentieth century. But the mood of desperation had never been greater than during these last few grim years of the war, which the city's residents had spent living under a dusk-to-dawn curfew, and every time I visited I thought there could be no more cruelly Draconian punishment for one of Africa's liveliest people than to keep them locked up in their stifling and unlit homes from sunset to sunrise every day.

Now, the curfew was being drastically scaled back, and I decided to test the truce and take advantage of the brightening outlook by trying to drive to Charles Taylor's would-be rebel capital. For years, Taylor had been holed up in a small city called Gbarnga, well to the northeast of Monrovia, across a broad no-man's-land and then deep into what everyone in the capital considered certifiably hostile territory.

Once I'd finished the airport formalities, the *Times*'s stringer in Liberia, Jackson Kanneh, and my regular Monrovia driver, Old Man Bah, greeted me at the airport exit. In all the countries I visited frequently, I had made a priority of finding an exceptional driver to work with. Old Man Bah, a native of Guinea, the land next door, was reliable, which was essential, but he also had a good knowledge of the terrain and the local factions, a nose for news and a keen sense of danger, of which Liberia offered plenty. And invaluable in a country accustomed to mayhem, this pious Muslim man in his sixties, who unfailingly dressed in a knitted prayer cap and Liberian-style safari suit, also boasted some of the best nerves I had ever seen.

When people were scattering through the streets in panic at the outbreak of gunfire, a fairly common occurrence in Monrovia, Old Man Bah would calmly roust me from a meal or an interview and say, "Mista Howard, I think we haffa go now." While others raced wildly through the streets looking for shelter, he would drive us at his own stately pace in his gently decaying blue Peugeot to Mamba Point, the rocky promontory on the Atlantic Ocean where my hotel was located, in the shadow of the UN headquarters.

As we drove to the hotel, Jackson, whom we often jokingly called the mayor for his countless social connections and for his famous ease with women, announced with a wicked grin that the downtown bars had decided to celebrate ladies' night that evening in honor of the curfew's suspension. On Carey Street, the heart of the nightclub district, raunchy, unself-conscious Monrovia was in full blossom, and for all the smuttiness of the place, there was something utterly bracing about its lack of pretension.

Husbands and wives, sons and daughters had been bottled up in their dark and airless little homes for months, and suddenly, like sailors on a rare shore leave, they were enjoying the outdoors again. Cheek to jowl at El Meson, Monrovia's most famous bar, sat the threadbare and the well-to-do, knife-scarred prostitutes and pretty girls next door, the shiny-faced daughters of what remained of the country's middle class, who had managed to slip out of the house. People of every description were mixing, talking, pouring down Club beers, cursing the ennui of their recent lives under curfew and, above all, hitting on one another with an almost total lack of inhibition.

The house band that night was singing what had become local standards during the war, songs with titles like "Iron Titty," about the virtues of young flesh, and "Gorbachev," a ditty about people who trade sex for money, and men and women of all stripes were lustily joining in.

Jackson told me that he and another friend of ours from Abidjan, Purnell Murdock, the regional Voice of America correspondent, had spoken to Charles Taylor in Gbarnga by satellite phone and received permission for us to drive there and interview him. We were to leave in the morning, stay overnight in Gbarnga and return to Monrovia the next day, just before Taylor himself was to make his grand entry into the city he had destroyed but never managed to capture.

I was excited about the prospect of seeing Taylor, hitherto a disembodied voice we heard almost every day, orating more than speaking, in that cocksure manner of his, via satellite telephone to interviewers from the BBC World Service's African radio programs, where he claimed victory in battle or denied defeat with equal aplomb. Taylor's bombastic performances had made his interviews the longest-running theatrical act in the region, and since there was little other news or entertainment available, work literally stopped in Monrovia at 5:05 p.m., when his favorite forum, *Focus on Africa*, began to the sound of echoing clarions.

From Monrovia, throughout most of the war it had been impossible to visit Taylor country, a rump state that the rebel leader fancied as Greater Liberia. The alternative route in, overland via Ivory Coast, was possible only by invitation, and as a frequent critic of Taylor, who avidly followed what was written about him, I knew I would never enjoy such a courtesy.

"Big Man" is a term that has been heavily overworked by Western journalists. It is tossed about to describe African leaders in the same cavalier and disdainful fashion that the press displays with the coded language it sometimes uses for black American politicians, like "flamboyant" or "street smart." Quite recently, Latin America had been full of Big Men, as had Eastern Europe, and much of Asia for that matter, but only in Africa did the term—actually borrowed from anthropologists' descriptions of Pacific island societies—become a fixed moniker employed by writers too bored or lazy to get beyond such labels.

For Taylor, though, Big Man seemed, if anything, like a painfully inadequate description of someone with such a monstrous ego and raging paranoia. I had chuckled earlier in the day when Old Man Bah told me that the Ministry of Finance's old Cadillac had needed to be pushed to a garage after a brief trial run in preparation for the new government's swearing-in ceremonies. Then at the bar I overheard details of the grand entrance Taylor was planning to mark his return to the capital. Liberia was a country where most people felt lucky if they had two or three changes of clothing and enough to eat any given week, and yet Taylor's convoy was to consist of thirty-two shiny new Nissan Patrols and fifteen Mercedes-Benzes. The only suspense was over what sort of vehicle he would arrive in, and it was taken for granted that the choice would be designed to make as grand a statement as possible.

Robert, who had come with me from Abidjan, Jackson, Purnell and I set out the next morning with an unknown driver suggested by Bah. Taylor had become an outsized myth in the minds of Monrovia's long-suffering residents, and even someone as cool and sure-handed as Bah imagined that the road to Gbarnga was littered with skulls and bones, so he had declined to drive us. Taylor had assured Purnell that the fighters who were guarding the route would be notified in advance of our arrival. All we had to do, he said, was show up. But as we drove through the suffocating heat, soldiers at roadblocks manned by the Nigerian-led West African peacekeeping force, ECOMOG,* expressed ever graver doubts about our prospects.

All morning long we had to submit to the tedious formality of walking through the checkpoints, carrying our belongings for inspection into bamboo huts manned by droopy-eyed soldiers, while the car was searched. Some of the peacekeepers openly questioned our sanity for wishing to drive into rebel territory, but there was nothing they could do to stop us. We had all of the necessary paperwork from both ECOMOG headquarters and the Liberian government.

Early that afternoon we reached the first checkpoint controlled by Taylor's National Patriotic Front of Liberia (NPFL). We were now leaving the tightly circumscribed little world of Monrovia and its surroundings and entering so-called Greater Liberia. It was a "country" recognized by no other state, but the frontier had all the makings of a typical African border crossing. And by way of confirmation, there was even a rusting metal sign proclaiming: "Welcome to Greater Liberia. Land of Peace, Progress, Prosperity and Pleasure." I was braced for trouble as I mounted the hill to the barracks that housed the immigration offices, which peered down menacingly over the crumbling two-lane highway. But the NPFL officials were crisply efficient, if unsmiling, once I announced when they asked me my business, "The president has invited us for an interview."

African borders are, above all, marketplaces, and a quick glance can speak volumes about the state of the nation you are entering: how fla-

---

*ECOMOG, or the ECOWAS Monitoring Group, was the peculiar name given to the regional peacekeeping group in Liberia.

grant the corruption is, how well fed and clothed the people are, how smoothly things function. Here, women naked from the waist up sold little cakes on the side of the road, while skinny children dressed in the faded hand-me-down clothes imported in bulk from America scurried about. Apart from a few old-timers, there were no men in sight. They had all been killed or pressed into service as killers themselves.

We were officially in Taylor-land now, but most of the drive beyond this first checkpoint was spent passing through a much older country within a country, the immense Firestone rubber plantation. Firestone, as Liberians called it, was a poignant example of Africa's abiding generosity to the outside world, from the earliest days of the slave trade to the present, or perhaps better put, of the continent's wholesale plunder.

Liberia was formed from a Tennessee-sized sliver of coastal West African rain forest, wedged between French- and British-claimed territories—today's Ivory Coast, Guinea and Sierra Leone. Some five thousand of the original settlers were former slaves whose return to Africa was arranged by the American Colonization Society, a group whose most famous founding member was the sitting American president of the time, James Monroe. The Colonization Society had proclaimed the lofty goal of establishing a West African beachhead for Protestantism, but its sponsors, including many of the leading American lights of the early nineteenth century—on both sides of the Mason-Dixon line—also felt that it was better to be rid of freed slaves than to have them hanging around. The specter of a slave revolt like the one successfully led by Toussaint Louverture in Haiti at the turn of the century provided strong motivation for the idea of shipping freed blacks back to Africa.

The territory they were being sent back to sat next door to Sierra Leone, a land the British had long called the White Man's Grave, because of the deadly epidemics of malaria and yellow fever that plagued the area. When the first settlers arrived aboard a brig named *Elizabeth* in 1822, a quarter of the eighty-six freedmen aboard quickly perished, forcing the survivors to flee to British-controlled territory. The same fate quickly befell a second shipload of settlers who set out from New York harbor. When a third group of freedmen arrived in the place that would come to be known as Liberia, the Colonization Society negotiated the purchase of a sixty-mile strip of coastland from the Bassa, a local people, marking the first permanent settlement of a place whose chosen name, Monrovia, for James Monroe, already bespoke sweet but misplaced gratitude.

The new promised land was one of the meanest environments in a continent full of difficult climes. Heavy rains fell for months at a time—forty inches in an average June alone—and tropical diseases took devastating tolls. To further complicate matters, the Bassa people, who had no understanding of the contract they had signed, surrendering rights to their land, soon began mounting deadly raids against the settlers.

Beset with myriad difficulties, the new state began to founder, and American interest, tepid at best even at the outset, waned. In the 1920s, Washington refused to lend the Liberian government $5 million to tide it over a severe financial crisis, and the American millionaire tiremaker Harvey Firestone of Akron, Ohio, suddenly stepped into the picture, changing everything. Firestone was seeking new sources of rubber to meet the booming demand from the era's big new industry, automobiles, and in 1926 he was given a ninety-nine-year lease on a one-million-acre tract.

Firestone's Liberian holdings instantly became the world's largest rubber plantation, and it had cost the company only six cents an acre, barely a third of what the British had paid for their competing plantations in Malaysia. Despite the huge cost advantage over his British competitors, Firestone imposed an aggressive drive to cut corners, and for years afterward the plantation was dogged with charges of employing slave labor and coercive recruitment of laborers, eventually provoking a suspension of relations with Liberia by the Hoover administration and an investigation of the plantation by the League of Nations.

For mile after mile as we drove through the oxygen-saturated air of the plantation, all we could see were row after lush green row of rubber trees slowly oozing their thick white sap into small cups spiked into their sides. Besides the occasional bent old man carrying a broken branch home for firewood, or small groups of stunted, dwarflike girls carrying heavy loads on their heads and bundles on their backs, the place was totally deserted. Sporadic roadblocks were the only thing to remind us that we were not in the Republic of Chlorophyll. But even when we were stopped, the mood was usually loose. Taylor's boy soldiers and their officers were already partying over the apparent end of the war. Whenever we pulled up just short of the crude iron-spiked barriers that were laid across the road, a few words about an interview with the president usually sufficed to get one of them to drag it lazily out of the way, letting us through.

"Wha [white] man say he gone interview da Pappy," I overheard one of the boy soldiers say, using their customary paternal moniker to refer to Taylor in their heavy Liberian pidgin.

Well into the afternoon, though, as the forest finally began to thin and we sensed we were drawing closer to Gbarnga, a couple of Taylor's fighters emerged from the trees looking all business with their guns raised, and a tense interrogation ensued. One of the young men wanted to inspect the trunk, and I opened it for him. "Anything for me?" he asked, with no hint of humor. I held my ground and said sorry, but no. The other fighter stepped forward and said the two of them were hungry and wanted some food. Since we were carrying nothing more than some loose peanuts, baguettes and a few oranges, I declined once again, politely but firmly.

As I had often felt in this region, my accent, this time in English— passably Liberian—had thrown him. Living in West Africa now for the second time, I could usually tell where someone was from after hearing only a word or two. I also found that without too much effort I could reproduce a local patois in West Africa in pretty short order, whether it was English- or French-based, without embarrassing myself.

When a hungry man wielding an assault rifle is inspecting your car at an isolated roadblock, the value of accents might seem questionable, but more than once in my experience merely getting the tone or inflection right had proved enough to stop a menacing person in his tracks, forcing him to pause and wonder how someone who is so obviously an outsider had become so intimate with his world. The hope was that the next thought would be one of prudence; this outsider might have other unexpected powers as well.

Seeing that I had left lots of reading material lying on the front seat, the first fighter demanded some newspapers from Monrovia. This surprised me, since I had assumed they were illiterate, but I sensed an opportunity to defuse the situation by ceding something, while avoiding any sign of submission, which I knew could be fatal. Since we didn't have any Monrovia newspapers, I handed him a copy of *The New York Review of Books* that I had just finished reading and climbed back into the car, hoping that he would give the order for us to proceed before he realized the nature of my gift. It worked perfectly, and with his signal to the boy holding a rope attached to the two-by-four studded with nails that served as their roadblock, we sped off, emitting a collective sigh.

We reached Gbarnga shortly before 5 p.m., and after passing a couple of final checkpoints at the edge of town, we were escorted by Taylor's presidential security agents to the grounds of a compound of brilliantly whitewashed buildings surrounded by neatly manicured lawns. From the sight of things, we quickly gathered that this was where Greater Liberia's Boss Man, as many here called him, the "Pappy" to a horde of orphaned boy soldiers, lived and worked.

We were told to wait, and while we sat outdoors our handlers warily sized us up. I described our arrangements and insisted that an interview had been promised. They answered: By all means, of course we would see the president. Taylor went to great lengths to avoid submitting himself to unflattering questioning, and our handlers had obviously been assigned the task of making sure that we would cause him no embarrassment.

More than an hour passed, and I relieved my boredom with the tiny Sony shortwave that I took with me wherever I went. Shortwave radio has gone the way of the vacuum tube in much of the world, but the BBC remains the state of the art in globalization in these parts, requiring only two batteries to stay connected.

Darkness came upon us swiftly, and in the last light I began to ply Moses, the gaunt secret policeman assigned to watch us, for information. After much prodding, he slipped away to make inquiries on our behalf, and while he was gone, a lower-ranked flunky who had also been watching us drew near to me and said, "Man, we want this war to end so badly. We have no food. We're not paid. There is no school for our children. I can't even find clothes to put on my back."

When Moses returned, he apologized sheepishly for an abrupt change in plans. "I have been asked to escort the honorable journalists to the presidential guest lodge," he said, echoing his master's grandiloquence. "There is no problem, though. Don't worry. The president will see you tomorrow, by all means." By that point, the news was neither a surprise nor total disappointment. We were all dead tired, and famished, too, after a long day without food. Knowing Taylor's penchant for ostentation, I had visions of a sumptuous meal awaiting us at the presidential guest lodge.

As we drove away the sky opened up, unleashing the kind of diluvial rainstorm that is typical in Liberia. The raindrops fell like shot, each issuing its own little explosion, and we could barely make out the road as we plodded through the torrent with the high beams on. Moses told us that we had better get something to eat before we reached the lodge, puncturing my banquet fantasy, so with the driver sticking his head out the window every few seconds to verify his course, we crept through the unlit streets of "downtown" Gbarnga as good as blind-folded by the rain.

After a few minutes we arrived at the town's only sit-down restau-rant, a dingy little one-room shack with wobbly tables and steel chairs that grated noisily against the cement floor. Next to it, like a scene out of a western, stood Gbarnga's only nightclub, the Dream House Bar, and with the music already pounding away despite the early hour, we guessed the people inside had been caught in the downpour and decided to have a little party. Our spirits took another hit when we learned that the restaurant was serving only sweet tea and bread. As some of Taylor's officers sat there in the dimly lit room partaking of this miserable fare, a shifty-looking man approached to ask me in a whisper if I wanted to buy some gold. "No," I said, "but I would really love something to eat."

Keeping despair at bay in situations like these required resource-fulness. Leaning over the railing separating the restaurant from the disco, I called out to a couple of the bar girls inside and explained our problem. They wore skimpy dresses and hot pants, and giggled incred-ulously as they asked if I wouldn't join them. I insisted gently on food alone, and within a few minutes they cheerfully rounded up some canned sardines, bottles of beer and a few other odds and ends. We thanked them for "saving us," paid them for what they had brought, adding a little extra for their kindness, and headed off for the lodge.

The rain had let up just enough for us to backtrack down the high-way a few miles in the direction of Monrovia. We headed down a narrow muddy road and were guided the final few yards by a man on foot to the dark, windowless building that we were told was the presidential guest-house. Containing our dismay as best we could, we used flashlights and candles to unload our things and have a look inside. There were beds and a few chairs, but no sheets or tables. It was going to be a long night. The effect of the beer lightened the mood, though, and as we ate the bread and scooped sardines and Spam from the cans, Purnell kept us laughing with hilarious stories of his troubled early sex life, when, hard as it seemed to believe, he said he had been painfully shy with women.

We rose with the sun the next morning and were surprised to find a few other presidential guests sitting in the living room where we had eaten. They had arrived overnight, after we passed out, and to my surprise, I had not heard a thing.

Someone from Taylor's protocol eventually came to collect us, and we set out immediately for the presidential compound. In Monrovia we had been warned that the highway back to the city would be closed that afternoon to ensure security for Taylor's arrival by road, meaning that if we didn't head back soon, we would not arrive in time to cover events there. Morning edged toward noon, and our stomachs growled as we sat on a veranda waiting for some word about our promised interview, just as we had the night before.

Losing patience, I summoned Moses to tell him that we couldn't wait any longer, and this produced a lot of nervous exchanges between our handlers. One of them, a security man, said in a menacing tone, "Nobody leaves Gbarnga without seeing the Pappy." Out of prudence we waited another fifteen minutes. But with no sign that we were going to be ushered in for our audience, we piled into our car and drove off. We quickly collected our things from the lodge and sped out of town, wondering what would happen if the Pappy sent some of his boys to arrest us after having stood him up.

On our way out of town we followed the same route we had taken in the rain the night before, and we could now see downtown Gbarnga, the capital of Greater Liberia, in all its glory. It was nothing more than a desolate strip of bombed-out buildings and filthy little chop-bars, or greasy spoons. In lieu of a proper market, the cornerstone of urban life in West Africa, there was a large slab of broken concrete under open skies, the foundation of a demolished building. There, on the ground, the local women traded in produce and cheap goods. Then and there I understood the future that awaited Liberia should Charles Taylor ever succeed in his obsession to become president: unlimited comfort and glory for the chief and unmitigated misery for his people.

We had been on the road for just a few minutes, speeding as fast as our rickety taxi could carry us, when one of our tires exploded with a boom. We were all so jittery that we thought we had come under fire. Clambering out of the car, we began to help our hapless driver with the repair, only to discover that there was no jack. Together we lifted the car while the driver jammed a new tire into place, and at that very moment, a large jeep came speeding toward us piled high with fighters, including some hanging from its sides, waving their guns. Barreling ahead as fast as it could go, the vehicle began swaying wildly from side to side, making us all dive for the bushes as it closed in on us. From the glimpse I got, I could tell immediately that these were not boys on a joy ride, but fighters on their way to battle, and we immediately understood that something big had just happened in Gbarnga.

As we sped warily toward Monrovia, even the most carefree checkpoints of the day before had turned into nightmares manned by jumpy boy soldiers who pointed their rifles at us with fingers playing on their triggers. Word had already reached them that there was trouble in Gbarnga, and they grilled us with suspicion about what we had seen and heard.

At one roadblock a group of children with battered assault rifles forced us off the highway at gunpoint and began shouting at us furiously. The boy in charge could not have been more than fifteen years old. His eyes were deeply bloodshot, and the smell of the marijuana that Taylor's commanders supplied to the child combatants, along with harder drugs, hung thick in the air. I remained seated when he ordered us out of the car, and attempted to gently reason with him, trying to strike the right balance of self-confidence with respect for the authority conferred by his gun, but he would have none of it, and resumed shouting and waving his rifle.

After a few minutes of electric tension, an officer arrived and began to calm the boy down, and when the child's anger had slackened a notch or two, the officer waved us through. A few miles later, still well within Taylor territory, our car blew a second tire, and we discovered that there were no more spares. Desperate now to get out of Greater Liberia, we drove for ten miles on the rim alone, finally reaching a town called Kakata. There I paid the driver for his services and gave him a little extra money to get his tires fixed, and we hired another car to carry us back to Monrovia.

Not until we reached Monrovia did we learn what had happened in Gbarnga that morning. Just moments after we had left the presidential guesthouse it had come under fierce attack with machine guns and rocket-propelled grenades. We were told that the other men who had arrived there while we slept were senior commanders who had been summoned by Taylor, and then were killed after an assassination plot was uncovered. Others dismissed this explanation, though, saying that the incident was a cold-blooded political execution of a kind common in Taylor's senior ranks.

"I started with a shotgun and three rifles and a few dozen men behind me," Charles Taylor said in an interview with *Harper's*. "The first garrison we came to put up no resistance, they ran without a fight. My dear, they thought we had a multitude. It was dark, it was night, and they just assumed. Their guilt and their corruption magnified their enemies in their sight. Now we had arms to take the next garrison. General Varney and Prince Johnson, seasoned military men, lifelong soldiers, joined our cause, of course, with many of the troops under them. Suddenly we'd become formidable!"

Taylor's initial drive for power began on Christmas Eve, 1989, and had very nearly succeeded, but when his rebel army reached the edge of Monrovia, its leadership split. Nigeria had rushed into the void at Washington's urging to block the armed takeover of the capital, and Taylor, showing rare prudence, pulled his men back, sensing that a face-off against Africa's largest army was a fool's gamble. At the head of his splinter faction, Prince Johnson, Taylor's volatile and wild-eyed former chief of staff, pressed ahead, and managed to capture President Doe in the process.

Johnson's murder of Doe on September 10, 1990, gruesome, drawn out and filmed in a herky-jerky cinema verité style, would become one of the signal events of West Africa's post-independence history. As men sliced off Doe's ears, kicked him and stabbed him, Johnson repeatedly demanded that Doe provide the numbers of the Swiss bank accounts to which Doe, in the long tradition of African dictators, had been sending off the money he stole from the treasury. Doe would reveal no secrets, and took his time dying; at Johnson's insistence, the president's captors kept the camera running throughout his agony. It was more than a gruesomely innovative twist on hunters' stuffed and mounted cadavers. It was irrefutable proof of the victim's demise in a land where superstitions about magic and invincibility still have a lock on the popular imagination.

A barely literate master sergeant, Doe had disemboweled his predecessor, William Tolbert, in a 1980 coup and summarily executed twelve senior government officials on a Monrovia beach. Thus, as enthusiastic street kids cheered the firing squad, 111 years of Americo-Liberian rule came to an ignominious end. The slayings took place just one year after the Ghanaian military leader, Jerry Rawlings, a young junior air force officer who had recently seized power, publicly executed three of his predecessors. An awful, matching bookend for the end of the decade, the videotaped dismemberment of Doe confirmed for shocked West Africans that their politics were undergoing a hideous transformation, from the gentle venality they were long accustomed to into a horror show of almost biblical cruelty. Few could have imagined, though, that far worse was still to come.

In his *Harper's* interview, Taylor insisted that he had held his men back in order to mollify Washington during the 1990 offensive against Monrovia, showing restraint even while Prince Johnson pursued his Genghis Khan–style campaign against the city, skewering children, slaughtering people in churches, targeting anyone who might be from Doe's ethnic group, the Krahn, and even killing people for sport. "Your American ambassador came to the Ivory Coast to see me in the middle of the night with a bunch from the CIA," Taylor said. "Oh yes. They just appeared at our perimeter suddenly from the darkness, out of thin air. What your ambassador told me was that if I waited, if I didn't plunge the capital into a bloody battle, the U.S. would back me one hundred percent. They and the West African peacekeepers would quickly take care of Prince Johnson, and I would be installed as president of Liberia. . . . They lied to me. Why did they do that?"

The belief in mysterious powers operating in the fast of darkness, in the stealth and omniscience of the CIA, and in his own victimhood and constant betrayal by others, was classic Taylor, whose melodramatic airs and paranoia were emphasized by his practiced use of the tremolo tenor voicings of a Mississippi preacher. Taylor apparently believed that the CIA had tried to help him before, too.

Taylor, Liberia's most powerful warlord, had been an official in Doe's disastrous government but fled the country after reportedly embezzling a large sum of money. In Massachusetts, where he briefly studied at Bentley College, Taylor was arrested and sent to prison, to await extradition to Liberia. Somehow he managed to escape, but the story of how he was able to flee has never been convincingly explained. "I wouldn't even be in this country today if not for the CIA," Taylor told *Harper's*. "My escape from the American jail in Boston—I think they must have arranged that. One night I was told that the gate to my cell wouldn't be locked, that I could walk anywhere. I walked out of jail, down the steps, out into America. Nobody stopped me."

However tempting, it would be wrong to dismiss Taylor's CIA stories out of hand. Washington and Paris, each in its own way, exercised immense sway in this part of the world throughout the 1980s, and they conducted most of their important business covertly. The biggest distinction was that while France wore on its sleeve its eagerness for influence, even control, over its former colonial domain, the United States insisted on leaving as small a footprint as possible in West Africa. Although 12 percent of its population traces its roots to Africa, America's steadfast position was to insist it had no vital interests on the continent, even as its dependence on African oil and other minerals grew steadily. It was easier to run African affairs on the cheap that way, by using spies and special envoys instead of high-profile diplomacy and costly programs. In the end, it was a world not so far removed from Taylor's own obsessive paranoia.

There were countless other stories about this smallish man of gargantuan vanity and seemingly unquenchable ambition, but the most compelling ones were told by men who had fought by his side. Over the years I had gotten to know several of Taylor's former officers, from his top generals to simple platoon commanders, and their stories were steeped in the kind of fear and respect I imagine wild animals must have for whichever beast sits at the pinnacle of their particular food chain.

A former commander who had broken with Taylor and fled the country related the details of Taylor's life after returning to Africa, following his escape from the American prison. "Taylor received training in Libya to overthrow Doe, and was sent later to Burkina Faso to continue his training and make preparations, recruiting fighters from around the region," he said. "I was with him there, so I know what I am speaking of. Thomas Sankara [the late president of Burkina Faso] was supporting him, but when he [Taylor] began pressing Burkina for the green light to invade Liberia, Sankara grew impatient with him. Taylor left for Sierra Leone to seek permission to invade Liberia from there, but he was kicked out after he seduced the defense minister's wife. Then he went to Guinea, and he was kicked out there, too, and to Ghana, where I heard he was arrested twice.

"We have a proverb that you may have heard," Taylor's onetime commander told me. " 'Snakes don't make pets.' That fits Taylor to a T."

Sankara, a charismatic young leftist officer, had seized power in Burkina Faso in 1983 and was killed four years later. With his death, Taylor finally found an opening. Blaise Compaoré, Sankara's former number two, his successor and the man who is widely believed to have arranged his assassination, quickly jettisoned the progressive politics that had made Sankara a hero throughout the region and drew his country close to France once again, and even closer still to Paris's most important ally in the region, Ivory Coast.

The story of Taylor's rebel beginnings in Burkina Faso is a convoluted one, but its twisting contours reveal much about the way Africa has worked in the four decades since independence, with personal rivalries and grudges between leaders, and sordid under-the-table maneuvers by outside powers and their commercial interests, often driving change.

Doe, who had proclaimed himself a general and had accumulated fictitious degrees from Liberian universities to compensate for his near illiteracy, was well on his way to becoming a West African Idi Amin. Sankara detested him as an offense to the dignity of Africans. Ivory Coast's archconservative president, Félix Houphouët-Boigny, was also offended by Doe, but for very different reasons. Doe had executed William Tolbert, the Ivorian leader's neighbor, close friend and deeply conservative ally, along with Tolbert's son, who was Houphouët-Boigny's son-in-law. Taken together with the executions in Ghana, Ivory Coast's neighbor to the east, the killings represented a terrifying precedent for Ivory Coast's president-for-life: succession by murder.

For all of Liberia's connections to the United States, Washington had done virtually nothing to help rein in Doe, even as his rule became wildly murderous and flagrantly corrupt. In 1985, I had witnessed firsthand the reluctance to say or do anything that might offend Doe, when the once skinny and timid sergeant—now turned bloated and arrogant president—stole the presidential elections in a manner so blatant that the scenes at polling stations resembled slapstick. Ronald Reagan's secretary of state, George P. Shultz, breezed through Monrovia shortly afterward to endorse the "election," badly undermining American claims of support for democracy in Africa. Had democracy been Washington's concern, it might have called for an international observer team to monitor the vote, or it might have condemned the massacre of university students by Doe's army a year earlier, or at least raised questions about the fact that the two leading opposition candidates were banned from the race.

To be sure, Shultz's endorsement did not stem from any great enthusiasm for Doe, whose presidential priorities after several years of misrule had finally boiled down to one essential—clinging to power. In fact, the secretary of state expressed his distaste for the man after meeting him, telling the American ambassador acidly, "Perhaps I made a wrong career choice, if it was people like that I was going to meet. Doe was unintelligible." With the Cold War on, though, America's objectives in a region that forever seemed to dangle from the margins of the world stage were as rudimentary as Doe's: clinging to strategic assets, sewing up UN votes and containing enemies, from Moscow to Tripoli.

America's political involvement with most African countries has been both recent and sporadic. Liberia, though, is a screaming exception to the pattern. The Firestone plantation served as America's strategic reserve of rubber supplies in World War II. Robertsfield was Africa's largest airport, a huge, air-conditioned, brushed aluminum structure that sat strangely out of place in the middle of a fetid swamp, before it was destroyed in the country's civil war. The airport was built with Department of Defense funds, but the project had nothing to do with Liberian passenger traffic. The "gift" of an outsized airport, which Liberian society was not even remotely prepared to maintain, was meant to accommodate the largest of cargo planes, and Washington used the facility for years as a refueling point for large arms shipments to the anti-communist Angolan rebel movement, UNITA, sent by the CIA and the Pentagon.

Liberia was home, too, to Omega, a forest of soaring antennas maintained by secretive American technicians on the edge of Monrovia. Officially, this vast farm of steel towers that crackled with more electricity than all of downtown Monrovia was part of a maritime emergency navigational system. It also served as the regional rebroadcast center for the Voice of America. Liberians in the know, however, whispered that it had a less innocent function as well: transmitting coded American diplomatic and intelligence communications traffic around a large slice of the planet.

For American policymakers of the time, interests like these easily trumped notions of democracy in a land where diplomats had always taken a patronizingly long view of Africa's potential for political and economic development. Thus, instead of denouncing Doe's election and exerting strong pressure on the former master sergeant for human rights improvements, Shultz's visit was rewarding him with an extraordinary pat on the back.

For a man like Doe the satisfaction must have been great upon hearing word of the December 1985 Senate testimony of the assistant secretary of state for African affairs, Chester A. Crocker. Straight-faced, Crocker called Doe's fraudulent elections "the beginning, however imperfect, of a democratic experience that Liberia and its friends can use as a benchmark for future elections." Over the next few years, Washington routinely opened its checkbook to the tune of $50 to $60 million in annual aid for the Doe regime, making Liberia sub-Saharan Africa's biggest recipient of American largesse.

Democracy movements had just begun to sprout here and there throughout much of the continent, with Liberia at the forefront. Within five years, Africa's political landscape would begin its most dramatic shift since the independence era in the early 1960s, with the advent in many countries of free presses, competitive elections and presidential term limits. Yet, schooled as they were in low expectations for Africa, American officials were blind to the coming changes. What is worse, in places like Liberia, the closest thing America has ever had to an African colony, Washington had placed itself on the wrong side of history, and however unwittingly, helped grease the path of Africa's first republic toward another, far more ignominious, record: the world's first failed state.

It is foolish to think that Washington should carry the burden of blame for most of Africa's problems, or even of tiny Liberia's. But a thread of ignorance and contempt ran through American covert sponsorship of Africa's first coup d'état, the overthrow in 1960 of Patrice Lumumba, the elected prime minister of the Congo, to our steadfast support for dictators like Mobutu Sese Seko and Samuel Doe. It would be dishonest to pretend there is no link between what has perhaps been the least accountable and least democratically run compartment of America's foreign policy—African affairs—and the undemocratic fortunes of the continent.

With Liberians left to groan under Doe's rule, Taylor was able to amass the support of a large, if incidental, coalition of local and regional powers: France and Libya were both eager to knock the United States down a rung in what each considered its own backyard; Ivory Coast wanted to show that regicide would not go unpunished;

and Blaise Compaoré wanted to turn Burkina Faso, his dusty, impoverished backwater, into a force to be reckoned with in the region, and was obsessed with blotting out the lingering popular memories of Thomas Sankara.

All Monrovia was abuzz with anticipation of Charles Taylor's arrival. Volunteers had been enthusiastically scouring the city for days, and for a city that had the utterly charred look in some neighborhoods of Dresden after the bombings, it fairly shone. Late in the afternoon of our return, Taylor's huge motorcade made its grand entrance into the capital. Massive crowds gathered along the route, starting in Sinkor, a once comfortable residential area built around a broad main avenue leading to the center of town. Sure enough, there were all of the Mercedes and four-wheel-drive escorts filled with gun-toting NPFL thugs that we had been told to expect, and for his own transportation Taylor had chosen an armored, gold-trimmed Land Rover, an all-terrain vehicle the likes of which Liberia had never seen before.

I tried to suspend judgment, but watched in dismay as the people of the city waved and cheered the man most responsible for the country's miserable fortunes. Then I rushed with my colleagues through the packed streets to get downtown for Taylor's arrival news conference, the first he had ever held in the city.

The scene inside the large villa that Taylor had chosen as his temporary residence was almost surreal. The thirty or so reporters allowed in after a huge crush at the heavily armed entrance were ushered into a large room where Taylor's top aides scurried back and forth, brandishing victory grins and looking busy as they prepared to receive us and to hold a banquet for Taylor immediately afterward.

Victoria Refell, a tall, domineering Americo-Liberian woman who favored long shaggy Cruella De Vil wigs, spectacularly painted fingernails and heavy makeup, gave the press a lecture about how we should address "the honorable" Mr. Taylor, who, she promised, would be with us in a minute. Most of the reporters were from Liberia's heavily bled press corps, and they looked frightened and incredulous at finding themselves inside the Boss Man's home. When Taylor finally walked in, I had a second premonition about how this man would wield power if he ever became president.

As a child, Taylor had been given the nickname "Bossy" by his schoolmates, because of an already pronounced obsession with author-

The Grand Mosque of Djenné (Mali)

General Sani Abacha, president of Nigeria, addresses the nation.

An unclaimed body lies on the roadway in Lagos, Nigeria.

Fela Anikulapo Kuti performs at the Shrine, in Lagos.

Shell Oil flares unwanted gas near a village in Nigeria's Delta region.

An open-pit diamond mine in Mbuji-Mayi, (Congo)

National Highway No. 1, just outside of Kinshasa, Zaire

Sony Labou Tansi, the late Congolese novelist, in Foufoundou

A victim of the Ebola virus being wheeled to a grave in Kikwit, Zaire

The Liberian president Charles Taylor at James Spriggs Payne airfield, Monrovia, Liberia

Lawrence Moore, a Liberian boy soldier, Broad Street, Monrovia

Children wandering across the runway at Spriggs Payne

Squatters in Monrovia

President Mobutu Sese Seko: The Leopard,
The Helmsman, The Guide

Hutu refugees on the run, Tingi-Tingi, Zaire

A Serbian mercenary training a Zairian soldier in Kisangani, Zaire

A pro-democracy march in Kinshasa led by Etienne Tshisekedi (center), dismissed as prime minister by Mobutu

Borrowing a page from Mobutu, President Laurent Kabila built a personality cult in Congo before his death in 2001.

The former Foreign Ministry headquarters,
Monrovia, now a home for squatters

ity. By now, no one who had watched him as a warlord could believe in his transformation into a democratic leader. Indeed, his every symbol and gesture—from the gaudy motorcade, followed by praise-singing supporters who ran for miles behind his vehicle, to the Mobutu Sese Seko outfit—presented him as a throwback to the dinosaurs of an earlier era in Africa, the worst of the first-generation leaders of the continent who had built powerful personality cults and clung to power for decades. Liberians were still in rags, but here was a man impeccably coiffed, manicured and groomed, and dressed in a finely tailored two-piece African-style suit with the same kind of Mao-cut jacket popularized by the illustrious Zairian despot.

Exuding haughty self-contentment, Taylor seated himself in a high-backed rattan chair reminiscent of the one in the famous picture of Black Panther leader Huey Newton. In his hand he held an elaborately carved wooden scepter. When he began to speak it was, as usual, pure bombast. "We must take a moment to thank God," he said, "for this popular, people's uprising was, in reality, God's war."

This was the man who had revolutionized warfare in Africa by making generalized use of child soldiers, binding them to him through terror and drug addiction. This was the man who had pursued a war in his own little country that had killed as many people as all the wars in Yugoslavia.

He carried on for a while in the same vein, and when he finally finished speaking Refell stepped forward to ask for questions from the press. Many of the Liberian reporters were literally trembling. Virtually every Liberian had lost relatives in Taylor's war. Almost every Liberian had lost his livelihood. And I could not know if their reaction was due to fear or to barely stifled outrage. To say that lives had been shattered would be a trite understatement. For all of the inequality under its Americo-Liberian apartheid, a half generation ago Liberia had been one of Africa's most advanced countries. Now people were living in abject poverty and degradation, without a formal economy or even a government. For all of this, the only thing Taylor saw fit to say about the destruction he had wrought was that it had been God's plan.

An eerie and absolute silence lasted for two or three minutes. Finally, Refell stepped forward and tried to get someone to ask a question, and when no one did, I raised my hand and spoke. I have seldom had trouble staying within the emotional confines that American newspaper journalism calls for when conducting an interview or writing a story. By convention, our work is about studied neutrality, or at least a semblance of it. But when I opened my mouth to speak, I began to feel the tremor I had seen in my Liberian colleagues, and I found that I was unable to contain the anger I sensed boiling in the room among my cowed peers.

"Isn't it outrageous for someone who has drugged small boys, given them guns and trained them to kill to call this God's war?" I asked. Unaccustomed to being in the company of anyone but syco-phants or people terrified of him, Taylor averted his gaze. Meanwhile, Refell and the other aides glowered at me. "How dare you call the destruction of your country in this manner and the killing of two hun-dred thousand people God's war?"

In truth it wasn't really a question, but Taylor knew that he couldn't allow this to be the last word. "I just believe in the destiny of man being controlled by God, and wars, whether man-made or what, are directed by a force," he sputtered, momentarily confused. "And so when I say it is God's war, God has his own way of restoring the land, and he will restore it after this war."

The press conference was over, and Charles Taylor, despite a rare moment's embarrassment, had achieved his objective. The snake was finally inside the capital.

CHAPTER SIX

Falling Apart

Wild rumors had been circulating in Kinshasa for weeks. Mobutu had suffered a heart attack. Mobutu was dying of AIDS. Mobutu had succumbed to a mysterious curse. Mobutu lay in a coma in the south of France. Then, one hot day late in August 1996, a street kid ran through one of the city's largest markets screaming, "Mobutu is dead, Mobutu is dead." Within a few panicked seconds, the huge market had emptied, demonstrating just how raw nerves can be in a city that had experienced repeated bouts of looting. Indeed, a scarce few minutes later, most of the shops in the surrounding neighborhood were shuttered.

Within the fraternity of Africa's longest-serving dictators, it had become a point of pride, a competition almost, to see who could spend the most time outside his country without inviting a serious threat to his power. Since the death of the founding father of Ivory Coast, Félix Houphouët-Boigny, in 1993, Mobutu, who liked to while away his summers on the Riviera, had been the continental champion, hands down.

Kinshasa is a singularly incestuous city of five million people. From the cool heights of Binza, where the rich live on the same baronial plots that the country's Belgian masters once inhabited, to the cratered streets of La Cité, where the heavy rainy seasons leave puddles so deep they are dubbed Lake Mobutu, big news traveled as if by superconductor. What was so unsettling this time was that nobody seemed to know what was going on, and yet everyone could sense that something was badly wrong.

In early September the guessing game was brought to an end by a laconic statement issued by Lausanne University Hospital in Switzerland: Mobutu Sese Seko suffered from prostate cancer and had just been operated on. Later that day, hoping to calm the public, the ailing president granted a brief interview to a local radio station, which was immediately rebroadcast in Zaire. The palpable fatigue in Mobutu's voice, like the noncommittal answers about when he would return home, had the opposite effect, though, and word immediately circulated that the man who had single-handedly run this country since 1965 was in the final stages of a deadly disease.

Barely a month had passed since fifty thousand people had marched through downtown Kinshasa demanding that Mobutu organize elections by May at the latest, as he had only recently pledged, or resign. Now, suddenly, the nation was suffering a case of the chills. Mortality was just not something one associated with Mobutu—most Zairians had grown up with him as their leader and fully expected to die with him as their leader as well.

Feisty and rambunctious in normal times, Kinshasa settled into an awed and wary quiet. Too jaded or simply too poor, most Kinois had long ago given up buying the scores of thin, poorly set newspapers that proliferated in the capital. Instead, they gathered around newsstands where vendors laid out the most popular titles in sprawling displays, allowing people to read at their leisure, often aloud, and with Mobutu dying, the crowds had never been bigger.

The hush even included the city's politicians. As a class, these men had made careers attacking the president during the last, relatively freewheeling decade of his rule. But the capital's politics still ultimately remained Mobutu's game, and he knew well that for most of his critics, the dissenter's soapbox was viewed merely as a stepping-stone to some kind of lucrative appointment. If you could shout loud enough and draw big enough crowds, there was hope that Mobutu might name you prime minister. The lucky few stole as much as they could, first for themselves, then for their villages and finally for their clans, before the president's revolving door would spin once more. The result was a political class that was thoroughly co-opted. The only standout was Etienne Tshisekedi, whose short-lived stints as prime minister had made him a popular hero because, though powerless, he clung stubbornly to democratic principles.

Mobutu ridiculed his critics with his Louis XV–type warnings that after him would come the deluge, and if the prostate scare proved anything, it was that no one had ever seriously contemplated a future without the Marshal at the helm. Like orphaned children, a galaxy of people who had made their careers as professional opponents now trembled at the prospect of Mobutu's disappearance.

Mungul Diaka, a short-lived Mobutu prime minister and governor of Kinshasa, was a fairly typical specimen. A man full of ideas for his country, and like every prominent politician in Zaire, equally full of himself, he spoke to me about the need for federalism and decentralization for hours one evening on the huge, pillared balcony of his princely Kinshasa house. Finally, as I made my way to leave, he turned to me and confided his fears.

"The way Mobutu ran this country, I pray God that he'll have a bit more time; enough anyway for him to organize elections, so that he can be beaten and replaced," he said. "If he were to die now, we have no structures in place to govern this country. The army would try to take over, and it would be a catastrophe for us all."

Kinshasa's politicians might have been sweating, but remarkably, for the man who was supposedly dying, life's routines continued much as before. Mobutu owned a twenty-eight-room mansion in Lausanne, but for his cancer treatment he opted for some spiffy new digs nearby, renting a whole floor at the Beau-Rivage Palace Hotel, on the shore of Lake Geneva, for a cool $16,000 a night. Throughout his treatment, Swiss investigators sought to question Mobutu over the tens of thousands of dollars worth of telephone bills and other accounts left unpaid by the huge presidential entourage in Lausanne. But the Leopard would not be disturbed. During the final nights before his surgery, he was often spotted by reporters in a Beau-Rivage bar, fondling the high-priced prostitutes who paraded before him in casting-call fashion while he downed $350 bottles of Dom Pérignon with hangers-on.

Here again were unmistakable echoes of Leopold II, who was named in a British courtroom in 1885 as a client of a "high-class" house of prostitution, to which he allegedly paid £800 a month for a steady supply of young women.

The farther away one got from Kinshasa, the less fazed people seemed by the looming uncertainties of an era already being dubbed "l'après-Mobutu." The countryside was so neglected that for years people must already have been feeling that they lived in l'après-Mobutu. So I began making the rounds of the various ministries for the travel authorizations Robert and I would need to go see for ourselves.

After our brief abduction at the tuberculosis asylum, Tony, the timorous, roly-poly man who had been my first driver in Kinshasa, begged out of working with me any longer. He had decided that getting roughed up by agents of SNIP, the National Service for Intelligence and Protection, was above the call of duty, no matter how good the money I paid. In his place, Tony recommended another driver named Pierre, who one morning showed up at the Memling Hotel, where I was eating breakfast in the crowded and dreary buffet-style restaurant.

Old Man Bah, in Liberia, was serenity personified. Pierre, on the other hand, with his permanent look of slight dishevelment, a battered blue Fiat that was forever in need of urgent repairs, and creditors and relatives who constantly pursued him for funds, was the picture of ill ease. For all of his complaints of ulcers and bouts with malaria, though, Pierre, who was crowding fifty and dressed constantly in a uniform of grease-stained jeans and hand-me-down tee shirts, knew his country better than almost anyone I had met. He spoke Zaire's two most commonly used languages, Lingala and Swahili, with equal ease, and after years of working with journalists, he often seemed to know our jobs better than most of us did, with the critical difference that he was unfailingly humble.

I learned more about operating in sticky situations from watching Pierre worm his way through dangerous neighborhoods or into buildings that were officially off limits or into meetings where he had no business being than from anyone else. It was almost impossible to turn him away whether you had a big gun or a big title, and on those rare occasions when he was refused, he always figured out a new angle of attack. When I asked Pierre once how he managed his magical access, he looked genuinely surprised by my question, the answer so obvious, so natural. "Monsieur French, you can go anywhere you want to go as long as you look like you are sure of where you are heading and that you belong there once you arrive," he said, smiling sheepishly.

Our last stop in pursuit of travel authorizations was the Ministry of Information, a huge skyscraper in the center of the city built in Mobutu's heyday, when his regime was still busily creating monuments. The Americans had "given" him the biggest, the Inga Dam, near Kinshasa. This pharaonic project had required the erection of high-tension power lines across 1,100 miles of jungle, all the way to Shaba Province, home to the copper and cobalt mining industries in the far south of the country, and home to secessionist movements ever since the Belgians schemed to break the province—then known as Katanga—off from the rest of the country shortly after independence.

Abundant hydroelectric potential already existed in the south of Zaire, but the rationale for projects like these was never economic—at least it had little to do with Zaire's very real economic needs. What the dam offered, instead, was huge contracts for GE, and for Morrison Knudson, and for Citibank, which would make a handsome profit from the financing—all guaranteed with American tax dollars through the Export-Import Bank. Mobutu and his minions would undoubtedly get giant kickbacks, too. For the Leopard, the biggest selling point of all, however, may have been the idea of using an extravagant power project to lash Shaba to the capital. Secessionists would have to think twice about making a break with Kinshasa knowing that Mobutu had his hand on the power switch. What good, after all, would the world's richest copper deposits and 65 percent of the earth's cobalt be if there was no electricity to drive the heavy machinery needed to extract and refine it?

The skyscraper that housed the Ministry of Information was part of another grandiose scheme, this one largely promoted by France under Valéry Giscard d'Estaing. A vast array of state-of-the-art microwave transmitters was intended to give Zaire the continent's most advanced communications infrastructure. The truth was much sadder. It was nearly impossible to make an ordinary telephone call anywhere in Zaire. "The Domain, with its shoddy grandeur, was a hoax," V. S. Naipaul writes of a ruler very much in the mold of Mobutu in his African masterpiece, *A Bend in the River.* "Neither the president who had called it into being nor the foreigners who had made a fortune building it had faith in what they were creating. But had there been greater faith before?"

When we pulled up to the ministry's outer gates, a sleepy-looking soldier approached swinging his old, rusted rifle and told us to halt. It was sheer redundancy, given that a chain stretched across the entrance. Pierre reached in front of me to hand his driver's license to the soldier through the passenger's side window and, instead of asking any questions, shouted, "Ba journaliste," identifying us as reporters. His sudden assertiveness took the soldier aback and the chain dropped immediately, allowing us into the sprawling complex.

The rest of the way would be more difficult, judging from the darkness inside the skyscraper. We had to reach the sixteenth floor of the building, but not even a distant hum could be heard from the elevator shaft. Even on the best of days, only one of the building's elevators worked, and since there were no functioning buttons to push, the only way to summon an elevator was by tapping on the metal doors, as Pierre began doing with his keys—to no avail. So we walked up the sixteen flights, passing breathless stragglers on our way up the pitch-black staircase, and receiving news from people on their way down, happily confirming that the people we needed to see were in their offices.

The sixteenth floor had two saving graces: It was never hot, because of the steady breeze that blew through the open windows at this elevation, and it offered majestic views of the city. We paid our fee for the travel papers and waited for them in a large conference room, watched over by a wall-length black-and-white photograph of a much younger Mobutu resplendent in his leopard-skin cap. The portrait was as faded as the regime, and yet like Mobutu himself, it still bore traces of a former grandeur.

After a long wait, Robert and I received our visas and were finally set. In the morning we were planning to head for Mbuji-Mayi, the capital of East Kasai Province and the diamond-mining capital of the entire country. We had chosen Zaire Airlines, one of the country's many makeshift carriers, all of which gamely attempted to make up in hustle for whatever they lacked in safety precautions. Never having been to Mbuji-Mayi before, and having heard many stories about the immediate arrest of "uninvited" foreigners, we decided to travel with one of the *Times*'s Kinshasa fixers, Kamanga Mutond. Pierre had also given us the name of an army colonel who, he said, might help us in case we ran into trouble there.

I had selected Mbuji-Mayi not so much for its diamonds, but

because of its own creeping, de facto secession. When the zaire was introduced as the national currency in 1977, it was worth $2. On the day we left for Mbuji-Mayi, $1 was worth 59,000 zaires, and the currency's value was falling at such a clip that at least two new rates were introduced each day on "Wall Street," the congested warren of streets in central Kinshasa where foreign exchange was traded by plump, busty matrons who sat on stools.

Inflation was strangling anyone in Zaire who still lived in the money economy, and the insult was especially acute in East Kasai, whose diamond production made it the equivalent of the country's Fort Knox. When, in 1993, Mobutu's government tried to introduce a new currency whose bills came with a plethora of additional zeros, the exasperation sparked a quiet rebellion in Mbuji-Mayi that all but ended the president's authority in East Kasai. The people of the province were already famously intractable, and simply said no to the new denominations, and since that date they had been using the country's musty old zaire notes—long invalid anywhere else in the country—as the legal tender.

Mbuji-Mayi's monetary solution was an example of Africa's genius for improvisation. If it could only be invested in institution-building, I thought, the country would be transformed. In the meantime, though, unable to print their own money, the people of Mbuji-Mayi were trading with carefully tied up stacks and bundles of the frayed, rust-colored banknotes, handling them gingerly to slow their disintegration.

The airplane had replaced the riverboat as the main means of commercial transport for these people. This was not because it was cheaper or safer—although it was clearly much faster—but because the country's big riverboat fleets had been decimated by years of corruption and poor management. Our six-hundred-mile flight was filled with hefty market women who wore their hair in fantastic braids that stood up like steel spikes pointing in every direction, and who swathed themselves in bright, printed cotton pagnes, the cloth wrap outfits that constitute the national dress. And while we flew, they drank from the fat half-gallon bottles of beer served by the flight attendants, preparing themselves for a few days of heavy haggling in some loud and sweaty market.

After a couple of hours in the air, we landed at Mbuji-Mayi's modest airport, where an abandoned old Boeing sat rusting on the apron and a handful of the smaller executive jets favored by the country's diamond elite glittered under a brilliant sun. Following the other passengers, we began walking toward the low-slung terminal to find a spot in the shade from which to observe the unloading of our bags, but the instant we paused a young man beckoned, saying that the police were waiting to speak to us. I waved the man off and tried to look as unconcerned as possible, while keeping my eye on the luggage, which was being towed to the airport building on a wagon attached to a small tractor. This seemed to make the man who was summoning us only more agitated, though, and after a few moments' standoff, I understood why. The SNIP officer in charge was watching the scene from the window of his office, glowering all the while.

Getting arrested had become so familiar that I associated physical sensations with the experience, almost like the onset of symptoms in a recurrent disease. There was always a feeling of heaviness, like carrying a dead weight, a shallowness of breath and a slight elevation of temperature, which in this climate quickly led to sweating. All the while, as you tried to maintain as cool an expression as possible, your mind raced with ideas about how to outfox your captor, how to convince him that keeping you would be more trouble than it could possibly be worth. At the same time, operating on another channel altogether—one totally bereft of self-confidence or optimism—the brain pours over a skein of what-ifs for those situations where nothing works in your favor.

The airport commissar was a bit young for his job, scarcely over thirty. He had a healthy, well-fed look and a face whose rounded contours suggested tractability. My assumptions were all wrong, though. The first thing he did was to separate us from Kamanga, from whom he had immediately demanded an "order of mission," a legacy of colonial times when Africans often required official documents stating their business to move from one part of the country to another. And because of its diamonds, Mbuji-Mayi had always been even more exigent. Before independence, Congolese residents of the town required special papers to move from one part of their city to another.

Naively, I had believed that Kamanga, who was born in Kananga, the capital of nearby West Kasai Province, would be able to circulate here with ease. But Mobutu had split the Kasai in two after the region had attempted to secede in the 1960s in sympathy with its native son, Patrice Lumumba. Ensuring they remained apart, the road between the two cities was allowed to crumble and dissolve under the assault of torrential seasonal rains. Old-timers told us stories about the three-hour bus rides they used to take to Kananga to attend soccer matches there, returning home in time for dinner. To reach Kananga nowadays requires at least three days with a robust four-wheel-drive vehicle, and even then the trip by road is possible only in the dry season. It was a perverse measure of Mobutu's success that few of today's young in Mbuji-Mayi had ever even been there. By the 1990s, Mobutu's divide-and-conquer approach had so atomized the country that only true locals trusted one another. And we were quickly confronted with the fact that here in Mbuji-Mayi, Kamanga was nearly as much of an outsider as we were.

The SNIP agent railed at Kamanga for a few minutes before finally telling him to move on. "Your employer must know where you are and what you are doing at all times, and approve of it." We had just landed in a province where the national currency no longer held sway, and where army deserters outnumbered men in uniform, but he seemed unaware of the irony of his words. Next he demanded our passports, and inspected them carefully, rubbing the pages noisily between his fingers, which he licked every few moments for effect. My passport was thick with dozens of supplementary pages, and he let them cascade out, accordion style, and read them one by one, taking his time, and demonstrating his cool by wearing a tracksuit jacket over his clothes while we dripped sweat in his airless little office.

"This is a very delicate time for our country, with the president ill and absent from Zaire," he lectured. "You call yourselves journalists, but people like you should know better than to come to Mbuji-Mayi at a moment like this. This is not just the center of our diamond industry; for Zaire it is a strategic zone."

We were asked to confess that we were spies, or that we were looking for gemstones. We were asked if we had come to fan the flames of separatism that flickered in East Kasai. Then, finally, we were asked what the airport commissar must have been wondering from the start: How much were we willing to pay to recover our passports and be allowed to circulate freely?

In situations like this, from the moment the conversation shifts to money, I usually feel that I have secured the advantage. This is for the simple reason that, as I said earlier, I have almost never agreed to part with any funds, and because the request for a bribe usually exposes the flimsiness of the arrest in the first place. This officer was more tenacious than usual, though, and when we had used up most of the afternoon, wasting a big chunk of our first day of what was meant to be a seventy-two-hour stay, I agreed to pay him $20, telling him that this was all I could afford. The tiny size of my offer shocked him, and forcing a smile, he said that we were free to leave the airport, but that we would have to collect our passports the next morning at the regional police commissioner's office.

The name Mbuji-Mayi means "big rock," appropriately enough for a diamond town that churns out huge stones like popcorn, but despite the stencil drawings of diamonds on many of the small storefronts that lined the road through town, the heavy battering that our car took from the rock-embedded road gave us a different appreciation of the name's meaning. For all of the wealth this city had produced for Mobutu, it had received nothing so much in return as one well-paved street. In fact, the rape had been going on for at least a century, since Leopold's agents combed the Congo region for elephant tusks, and later for rubber, killing millions of unremembered Africans in the process. Today, the West's latest obsession is columbite-tantalite, or coltan, the $400-a-kilogram ore that drives a civil war in the post-Mobutu Congo (Zaire) that is still festering after two and a half million deaths. But that is getting ahead of the story. Then, as now, what had mattered most in this part of the world was not human lives—particularly not the lives of Africans—but the extraction of something deemed valuable in distant but almighty markets.

In Leopold's day, frequent military campaigns were mounted to force Kasai villagers to venture deep into the forest to collect sap from rubber trees. Recalcitrant men and those who failed to come up with their quota were lashed with the chicote, a whip usually made of hippopotamus hide. Alternatively, they had their right hands chopped off, frequently resulting in death. But when it was not a matter of survival for the laborers themselves, the collection of rubber to feed Belgian industry was literally a life-or-death issue for their families. Heavily armed Belgian agents, often traveling by river, would surprise a village, capturing as many women and children as they could before everyone could flee, and hold them hostage until the husbands and fathers returned to the scene with enough rubber to satisfy Leopold's envoys. Just for good measure, chickens, goats and other domestic animals were slaughtered, while the captives were left unfed.

Mbuji-Mayi's routines have been brought up to date somewhat

since then. But as we found out when we were stopped by a policeman on motorcycle, even before we could reach our hotel, social control remains just as important now as it was in colonial days. Life has become a tad less brutal, but with almost no alternatives, survival nowadays still impels young men to subject themselves to extraordinarily harsh jobs in the industry that has replaced the rubber collection of an earlier time: the digging or panning for diamonds. For most that means descending into narrow pits, scarcely the width of their shoulders, and scraping out by hand soil to be sifted by others. Sheer heat kills some of the workers. But the biggest worry is the ever-present risk of a pit collapse, which almost always suffocates the digger before he can be pulled out.

East Kasai's plains roll and tumble endlessly under a big Montana sky, so the ubiquitous pits are invisible, except when you stumble upon one. Every now and then, a kid will get out a diamond big enough to put away some money, or to return to his village like the prodigal son. Sometimes it is even enough to make him feel rich. When I met Boaz Muamba-Nzambi, he was one of those diggers. Luck had brought him a fortune in diamonds, and all over town the fortune had won him fame. His success story had begun a few years ago, when he sold his goats for $300 and hired a digging crew. On their very first outing they found a stone worth $17,000. Strikes like these are rare, but by all accounts the thirty-year-old entrepreneur continued to have uncanny luck, and rather than squandering his earnings, he has used them to buy up several plots of land, as well as a shiny new Toyota Land Cruiser. By the time I met him, Muamba-Nzambi was into diversification, opening a drugstore and running his own traders back and forth to Nigeria to buy cheap manufactured goods for sale in Mbuji-Mayi.

"I have friends who have found twelve-thousand-dollar diamonds, and in three weeks they have nothing left," he said. "They simply went crazy, treating hundred-dollar bills as if they were tens, and running around with three or four women at a time."

The lore built up around rags-to-riches stories like these worked as an irresistible lure, bringing moths to the flame. It was free publicity for an industry that in these parts demands only dispensable young lives to keep it going.

Others prefer to prospect in the Mbuji-Mayi River, a deceptively lazy-looking waterway dotted with small islands where crocodiles lurk menacingly in the stagnant pools, regularly claiming human victims.

But the best prospecting, and probably the most dangerous, too, consists of poaching on the sixty-five square miles of the Belgian mining company MIBA's concessions, a huge quantity of land that the company has never managed to exploit fully. Imagine an army of James Bonds in the film *Dr. No* sneaking onto a forbidden island, only to be pursued and fired upon by relentless security patrols. That only begins to give an idea of MIBA's problem with the local diamond poachers who wait for the fall of night to creep onto the concessions to fill their rucksacks full of the mounds of earth freshly turned by the company's huge digging machines.

Mbuji-Mayi was built around MIBA's concessions, after an Englishman discovered diamonds in this region in 1918. And from the beginning, MIBA has operated like a state within a state, providing the city with its only electricity, its only drinking water, its only hospital and its best schools. But most of this bounty is restricted to the five thousand or so people who work for the company, and live at the factory's edge, clinging like a baby to its mother's breast. These small luxuries come from shipping off the company's precious product under tight controls, and sending the proceeds of the sale of the gems to faraway masters.

Mobutu may have Africanized the company in the early 1970s, but seeing black faces in the front office did little to change MIBA's economic model. Half of Zaire's diamond production comes from here, but almost nothing comes back to Mbuji-Mayi in the form of revenue. As with ivory and rubber—and, indeed, most of the commodities that Africa has continued to produce for the world since the colonial era—the real profits, the big fortunes, are being made elsewhere: in Antwerp for diamonds, London and Paris for cocoa and coffee, and France, Japan and Singapore for Africa's best timber. In any one of these markets, the money that put the swagger in Boaz Muamba-Nzambi would be considered nothing more than chump change.

But just as East Kasai tired of Mobutu's currency manipulation, Mbuji-Mayi was growing sick of being a company town built around MIBA. Indeed, the city's educated elite, men and women who had been engineers, doctors and teachers in Lubumbashi, the far southern city that is the capital of Shaba Province, seemed sick of diamonds altogether. Most of them returned here in 1992 when Mobutu orchestrated a murderous pogrom in the copper belt against migrants from this region. Overnight, well over 100,000 people from neighboring

Kasai Province were chased out of Zaire's copper belt, and untold thousands were killed in a bout of officially sanctioned ethnic cleansing that presaged the purge of the Banyamulenge, people of Tutsi origin from North Kivu Province, in 1996.

Mobutu had thrived by the very same divide-and-rule strategy that Belgium had used to dominate the country, his tactics growing steadily more violent over time. But the events at Kivu would prove to be one ethnic cleansing too many, because they persuaded post-genocide Rwanda, which was Tutsi-led, to invade Zaire in order to save its Tutsi kinsmen, and ultimately to bring Mobutu down.

Still, for the strivers of East Kasai, known throughout the country as the Jews of Africa, the massacres at Lubumbashi were a perverse blessing. After returning home by the tens of thousands, by foot or on the backs of badly overloaded trucks, they began to pick up the pieces of their shattered lives, little noticed by the outside world. Even if doomed to repeated setbacks, theirs is a vision of an Africa under design and construction by Africans themselves, and ultimately it is efforts like these that hold the key to the continent's resurrection.

Men like Kalala Budimbwa, fifty-one, a former copper mine manager who survived the ethnic cleansing in Lubumbashi, are now taking the measure of their native region's possibilities and plotting ways to develop East Kasai with its own means. "We have kept inflation down and steady here for three years in a country where it is rising through the triple digits," Budimbwa said in the courtyard of the prim residential hotel he built on the edge of town. "We have already built new roads with money raised locally. Our dream now is to build a highway to Luanda [Angola], nine hundred miles from here, and to build a hydroelectric dam to provide us cheap electricity."

The people of Kasai had never asked to belong to a country called Zaire. Indeed, like so many Africans locked into the fanciful creations of faraway mapmakers, this invention of the Europeans a century before had become a source of perpetual alienation and a huge cross to bear. Zaire was falling apart, and it seemed ever more likely that other parts of Africa would follow. But for Budimbwa and other Kasaians of his generation in a hurry to leave something concrete here for the next generation to carry forward, the beginning of the continent's necessary reconfiguration was now.

"Our dreams are the dreams of people everywhere, aren't they?" he said. "We want to be able to turn on the lights and read to our children at night. We want affordable cement so that we can build houses for our families. We want roads so that we can truck our produce for sale in other markets, instead of seeing it spoil. We want to be able to put money in the bank and know that it won't be stolen or have its value melt away. If we had our own state we could take charge of ourselves. But who can wait for that? Zaire has already lost the means to stop us from moving forward."

As we prepared to leave Mbuji-Mayi, lining up at the airport early in the morning, the air was still but refreshingly cool. I scanned the dingy little hangar for the SNIP agent who had demanded a bribe, fully expecting more trouble on the way out of town, but he was nowhere in sight.

After we had boarded the Air Zaire plane and were heading toward our seats, he suddenly appeared, dressed in another fancy tracksuit. He was showily accompanying a pretty young woman to her seat.

"I hope your visit went well," he said to me, with practiced oiliness.

"No thanks to you," I replied, without a smile.

"I hope you don't bear any hard feelings," he said, extending his hand.

Ignoring his gesture, I took my seat.

CHAPTER SEVEN

Where Peacocks Roam

For as long as one could remember, Zaire had been the oversized bully: the schoolkid who meddles willfully in the disputes of others, or steals their candy or lunch money on the least whim. Then came the attack, a brutal jolt awakening the country from its prolonged and self-indulgent dream. And in the sudden wakefulness, a nightmare was unfolding.

It all began with an implausible fiction. One of Zaire's most marginal ethnic groups, the Banyamulenge, had mounted a rebellion, and for Zairians in the west of their country, as for the international press stampeding into the region attracted by the scent of flowing blood and cordite, the question of the hour was, who are the Banyamulenge?

Suddenly, out of nowhere, all along a hundred-mile corridor of Zaire's Great Lakes region, an eastern hinterland a thousand miles removed from the capital, city after city—Uvira, Bukavu and then, finally, the provincial capital, Goma—was falling under a rain of mortar fire marshaled with uncanny precision. When the dust and smoke settled, a newly minted, and yet strangely disciplined, rebel army had materialized. Somehow, in a region of desperately poor countries, they showed up freshly tricked out with shiny new Kalashnikovs and Wellington boots.

In a matter of days the mysterious new rebels had achieved their first objective. While UN workers were being evacuated in neat convoys across the border to Rwanda, and relief officials from a hodgepodge of international nongovernmental organizations were still pinned down in their homes, unable to go outside safely, the rebels had emptied some of the world's largest refugee camps of their populations.

To be sure, the routed victims ranked high on any list of international pariahs. They were ethnic Hutu who had fled Rwanda after carrying out that country's 1994 genocide against the Tutsi minority. Nearly a million of them had been given temporary shelter in UN camps just across the border, on the unyielding lava flows in Zaire's North Kivu Province, where farming was next to impossible and even wells or proper latrines could not be dug.

Within two years of the genocide, the world had largely forgotten Rwanda's Hutu exiles, but the exiles had forgotten nothing, least of all the zero-sum game of hatred that once again had cast them as the losers to the much less numerous Tutsi. And with the connivance of the Mobutu government in Kinshasa, they had spent their time in exile sharpening their knives for another death match with their blood rivals.

The revenge-minded Hutu were discreet enough to eschew uniforms and military forms of address in the camps, but under the complacent eye of the UN refugee agency, which ran their huge camps, elements of the defeated Hutu army, and members of the machete-wielding Interahamwe militia, the main foot soldiers of Rwanda's terrible genocide, rebuilt their units and prepared for a new war.

The Rwandan genocide was not halted by any international intervention. Rather, after some 800,000 people had been slaughtered in a slow motion, low-tech, hundred-day bloodbath, an exiled Tutsi army that invaded from its bases in Uganda managed to take over. Since the end of the civil war, Rwanda's new Tutsi leaders had been demanding the arrest of the Hutu authors of the genocide, but the world had shown no stomach for a task that would have required a major international security operation to seal the region's porous borders and disarm the Hutu living in the camps. This was Central Africa, after all, a region where life had always been regarded as cheap, not Bosnia or Kosovo, places where European lives and interests were at stake.

The Clinton administration had already proved how feckless it could be in Central Africa. During the murderous summer months of 1994 in Rwanda, officials in Washington pointedly avoided use of the term "genocide" even as press accounts and intelligence reports detailing the extent of the slaughter—on average, eight thousand murders a day—flooded over the transom. For three months, throughout one of the greatest slaughters of the twentieth century, the Clinton administration never once held a meeting of its top foreign policy advisors to discuss Rwanda.

The aversion to the word "genocide" had nothing to do with honest disagreements in the American capital about the extent of the killing. Rather, it was all about ducking international calls for intervention. At one interagency meeting in Washington that April, Susan Rice, a rising young black star on Clinton's National Security Council, argued another justification for the semantic evasion—politics. "If we use the word 'genocide' and are seen as doing nothing, what will be the effect on the November [congressional] election?" said Rice, who would later be named assistant secretary of state for African affairs.

In a perverse repeat of that performance, scarcely three years later, Washington was doing its utmost to soften the condemnations of Rwanda for its cross-border attacks on the refugee camps in Zaire. Clinton's policy aides attempted to justify their hands-off approach as a reflection of their wish to promote "African solutions to African problems." But even a catchphrase this cynical doesn't begin to hint at the sludge of putrid crimes and misdemeanors that the United States was, in effect, sanctioning by turning a blind eye to the Rwandan blitzkrieg on refugee camps in Zaire.

Since independence, instability and bad governance had been Africa's twin Achilles' heels. They were the two internal weaknesses most immediately responsible for the continent's persistent misery, and the fighting that had just begun under Washington's generous political cover would spew both of these plagues across Central Africa, sowing political unrest, armed conflict and humanitarian disasters for at least the next decade.

With the camps in Zaire now under attack, hundreds of thousands of refugees were suddenly on the move. As they gathered their meager belongings and pressed forward together, footfall after terrified footfall back into Rwanda, the televised images of the pitiful fleeing hordes strangely mimicked the seasonal migrations of wildlife on the East African plains. Many other Rwandans, including thousands of ex-militiamen with guns, disappeared into the Zairian forest. Mass slaughter was anything but a new feature in Rwandan history, and it had cut both ways. Now, in the Congo, it was the Tutsis' turn to attempt a sort of final solution. But all was not as it seemed.

During those awful early days of the crisis, we in the Western press understood precious little. The usual sources of information in times of conflict in Africa were generally nowhere to be found. The United Nations had itself evacuated its workers from the main centers of the fighting, and where they had not been evacuated, they were in hiding. Scrambling for someone to unravel the mystery of the Banyamulenge, many of us fell back on the ever handy, ever available "Western diplomats" to explain what was going on. In principle, this has almost always meant American diplomats. But the problem with our heavy reliance on them this time was not just their usual ignorance about what was really happening in the thick of an African crisis. Rather, as would only slowly become clear over the coming weeks and months, it was that they were playing sides in the conflict and doing all they could to avoid owning up to it.

In time, we began piecing together the complicated picture of the mysterious Banyamulenge. They were pastoral migrants from present-day Rwanda who began settling in the Ruzizi plains, an area of Zaire's mountainous South Kivu Province, in the early nineteenth century. Their name meant, simply, "people of Mulenge," and was adopted from the name of a local mountain. Complicating things greatly, however, was that in time much more recent Tutsi immigrants into eastern Zaire, specifically relative newcomers to North Kivu, borrowed the Banyamulenge identity to bolster their citizenship claims.

The scramble to do some rudimentary ethnic detective work brought to mind just how normal it was for reporters to operate in nearly perfect ignorance of their surroundings on this continent. Africa remained terra incognita for most within my profession, whose job it was to inform the world, and for many of us an assignment here involved little more preparation than thumbing through a Lonely Planet guide. Anywhere else in the world we would have been judged incompetent, but in Africa being able to get somewhere quickly and write colorful stories was qualification enough. It was a repeat performance of the same contemptuous glossing over that characterized so much of Europe's colonial involvement with the continent, and though I had more experience here than most of my peers, I was in no way exempt. Only midway through Kabila's campaign against Mobutu did

I finally get around to reading *The Rise and Decline of the Zairian State*, Crawford Young and Thomas Turner's seminal 1985 study of Zairian politics and history, which should have been a prerequisite for any reporter. Scales fell from my eyes in the face of such detailed knowledge, and I felt a deep, physical sense of embarrassment at my own ignorance.

Before most of us could even begin applying our newfound wisdom about the Banyamulenge to the story at hand, the plotline had shifted dramatically. With the Hutu refugee camps suddenly emptied, the original pretense of a "tribal war" between the Banyamulenge and hostile local ethnic groups who had been persecuting them gave way to a newer, somewhat more plausible explanation: This was a Rwandan-led campaign to empty the refugee camps and thereby prevent a repeat of the 1994 genocide.

With eastern Zaire's biggest cities falling, however, it seemed obvious that we were witnessing something even bigger than a mere pre-emptive strike. The other shoe did not take long to fall, though, and the dramatis personae was rounded out by the sudden stage entrance of Laurent Désiré Kabila, a shadowy, retro-chic rebel who had been living on the murkiest fringes of East African life for two decades and was proclaiming the start of a Zairian revolution.

It was hard to take the first few audacious statements by this orotund figure seriously, and the initial reflex of the press was indeed to write off with a chuckle this would-be revolutionary challenger to Mobutu. But from the moment the international news networks began broadcasting images of the man, whose braggadocio strut seemed straight out of the South Bronx, his true aim—the overthrow of the government in Kinshasa—was announced for all to hear.

"We must remove Mobutu and throw him into the dustbin of history," Kabila exclaimed in Swahili, the language of the east, gesticulating confidently as he reviewed a battalion of his bug-eyed followers in Uvira, on the northern banks of Lake Tanganyika. "The alliance appeals to the rest of the Zairian population to rise up against the repressive system that has plunged the people of this country into misery. This is your movement. It is a movement against tyranny and corruption. It is a movement for freedom and human life."

From the very start it was a ludicrous boast from a man whose known past included illegally trafficking in gold, diamonds and elephant tusks for years, hiding out in the mountains, dabbling in Maoism, and even kidnapping Western tourists and holding them for ransom. But at least now Kinshasa had some fix on its foe, an army of boys supplied by Rwanda—and kitted out in Wellington boots and shiny AK-47s—which Kabila called his Alliance of Democratic Forces for the Liberation of Congo.

The mood in Kinshasa was one of shock, an emotion that is usually, indeed almost by definition, transitory. For the government, though, it would be both prolonged and paralyzing. Mobutu was absent and stricken with cancer, and although he had rarely kept a firm hand on the tiller these last years, with the Helmsman gone, his country had become totally rudderless.

For the time being, the task of trying to hold Zaire's pieces together was left to the prime minister, Kengo wa Dondo, himself half Tutsi, raised under the name Léon Lubitsch. Under the circumstances, this glaring ethnic liability only spurred the already frenetic jockeying for position of Mobutu's elite, a motley collection of bemedaled generals and sticky-fingered grabbers dominated by relatives and fellow northerners who had been rendered fat and plodding by years of unbridled greed.

With Kinshasa approaching the boiling point, Kengo had little choice but to take a hard line toward Rwanda and its Tutsi-governed ally, Burundi, which he accused of attacking his country. He would even lend his voice to the anti-Tutsi frenzy that was sweeping the capital. "We will not negotiate with anyone while a part of our national territory is being occupied by foreign forces," the prime minister shouted to an angry mob of students who surrounded his office. Armed with bamboo sticks and branches, which they wielded like guns, groups like these had been hunting down people in the capital for days, singling out anyone who had the long slender build and distinctly angular features of the Tutsi.

Kengo had every right to point an accusing finger at Rwanda, but that did not excuse the ugly reprisals against Tutsis in Kinshasa's streets. Moreover, Mobutu had provided the perfect excuse for the invasion by allowing the governor of South Kivu to order the expulsion of 300,000 Banyamulenge from the province in early October, just days before the fighting erupted in the east. Even at this early stage of the game, Washington and its key East African allies, Uganda and Rwanda, were alone in pretending that Kabila, a frontier bandit and small-time terrorist whose efforts to overthrow Mobutu had flopped disastrously years ago, was the real moving force behind the rebellion.

Everyone else in the region, indeed in Europe and within the relevant agencies of the United Nations, spoke openly of Kabila as the cat's paw for a Rwandan military operation. What no one could imagine yet, perhaps least of all the two principals most directly concerned, Mobutu and Kabila, was how quickly this African puppet would grow legs and take off on his own. Life was breathed into him by the jubilation his rebels met in Mobutu's long-neglected countryside, and by Kabila's own treachery in eliminating potential rivals in what was originally conceived as a collective leadership. The most important of them was André Kissasse Ngandu, a man from eastern Zaire's Nandi ethnic group, who, like Kabila, had spent years struggling, with little effect, against Mobutu. Kissasse became the alliance's first military commander and nominal vice president, but was assassinated under mysterious circumstances on January 6, 1997, in what was widely believed to be a hit arranged by Kabila.

The scene was now set for Mobutu's return, and the tension and dramatic potential were such that, even bedridden from chemotherapy, the old dictator, a performer at heart, could not resist. Decades of wretched excess involving money and power had ultimately bored him, but Mobutu still craved the kind of reaffirmation that only attention from others can bring. Indeed, his longing to be needed and the lure of the bright lights he had so often enjoyed on the international stage were what kept him going.

Filthy Kinshasa was being painted and scrubbed. Soldiers dressed in snappy green uniforms were suddenly putting order to the city's chaotic traffic. Rusted and stripped wrecks that had littered the roadside for months were hauled away, and huge red-and-white banners bearing slogans like "Mobutu = Solution" were being hung everywhere. The sycophants were busy and no amount of hype was being spared. If the Marshal was coming back, it was not merely to join the battle, but to win the war convincingly.

On December 17, 1996, six weeks after the Banyamulenge uprising began, Mobutu returned home. There is a venerable tradition throughout the continent of people lending their shouts and tears to celebrations and mourning in exchange for a fee. Mobutu's handlers had resorted to the trick countless times, proving just how effective the prospect of a few rounds of free beer or palm wine, or a bolt of printed cloth or some pocket change, could be in generating the appearance of enthusiasm.

As I rode out to the airport to witness his arrival, I thought skeptically at first that Kinshasa's hordes were just going along for the carnival ride. But as I watched tens of thousands of people pile into buses and every other manner of public transportation to gather at Ndjili airport, and line every inch of the twenty-seven-mile route into town at least four or five deep, my cynicism slowly began to crumble.

Still, there were certain fundamentals that no amount of popular excitement could change. The Marshal's army, never famous for its resourcefulness, had few means with which to fight a war. More ominous, the foreign friends who had repeatedly flown to the rescue during the Cold War were nowhere to be found. Government troops had scarcely engaged the enemy up to this point. As we waited for a sign from the sky of the president's arrival, it was tempting to wonder whether the funds required to print the women's matching outfits and hire the buses and bands would not have been better spent on bullets and bombs.

But at bottom, the army's problems had little to do with budgets. Rather, as with anything that involved money in this country, they could be attributed to a lack of accounting. Over the years, people had given Mobutu's famous Article 15, "débrouillez-vous," an increasingly literal interpretation. It had ultimately come to mean that it was okay to steal anything, even from him, and that is precisely what his generals had been doing, leaving the army unpaid and without ammunition. That is what the governors of the far eastern provinces had done, siphoning off money intended for the care of Hutu refugees and cutting private deals to rearm them. Undoubtedly, that's also what the organizers of today's sumptuous festivities were doing, and they would be presenting the president with bills for sums that far outstripped what they had spent.

This dazzling day, though, with a sky free of all but the highest, wispiest clouds, was not meant for settling accounts; it was a day for rallying the nation, for mobilization. At 3:10 in the afternoon, the president's white Boeing landed, and from his first wave to the crowds from the cockpit until late in the evening, Mobutu threw himself into the task with an eagerness that seemed scarcely diminished by his cancer.

Zairian popular music is famous for its bouncing bass lines and the lyrical staccato runs through the upper ranges of the guitar, sounds that ripple clear and perfectly formed, like the concentric rings of a stone tossed into a pond. The most famous style, soukous, had been invented decades earlier as an inspired response to the Cuban rumbas that were intently studied and lustily danced, as radios spread among the African population in the 1950s. By the 1980s, soukous from Mobutu's Zaire had become the most distinctive and successful pop sound in all of Africa, and like so much else of import in this country, the dictator had appropriated it subtly for his purposes.

The French word *liesse* hints at the effect of something very near to pure joy that this music seemed to produce so effortlessly. At the same time, the music became symbolic of Mobutu's rule and of the institutionalization in Kinshasa of Lingala, the trading language that originated in the president's native region, along the uppermost reaches of the Zaire River. Like a rape drug spiked into the nation's water supply, the music served to make the northern homeland of the president the cultural center of gravity of this vast and otherwise artificially conceived nation with almost no one the wiser for it.

The same formula of borrowing from abroad and making something imported one's own lay behind the mass mobilization and hero worship on display this day. Mobutu had carefully studied the personality cults of dictators like Ceauşescu of Romania and Kim Il Sung of North Korea as he set about crafting a cult of his own. By now, although one could still discern some of the inherited features—the use of uniform dress for civilians and mass chants of praise to the great leader—the product was as different from its communist forebears as the soukous heard in nightclubs all over Africa today is from Cuban son or salsa.

Manifestly, the Zairian people had nothing to celebrate, and yet here they were, gathered in huge, choking throngs to welcome home a president disowned by even his staunchest foreign backers. There were phalanxes of teenage girls whose smiles beamed as they bounced cheerfully on their toes, chanting welcome slogans in tight skirts and white tee shirts emblazoned with Mobutu slogans. Thousands of schoolchildren were arrayed class by class, standing under the sun in their uniforms waving fronds. Squadrons of hefty matrons trucked out by neighborhood sweated mightily as they bowed and swayed, laboring their way rhythmically through their dance steps. To top it off were the fighting bands competing fiercely to be heard over the din. The noise was such that there was no way to make out who was dancing to what beat. That could be done only by watching the bodies move and trying to link the motions to the distinctive strain of rhythm that every so often rang clear above the noise.

The music grew ever louder as Mobutu, carefully made up but quite pallid still, descended gingerly from the airplane, bearing his famous trademarks, the carved cane and leopard-skin cap, and strode onto the long red carpet laid out for the welcome. Walking at the same stately pace, but a deferential half step behind him, like a Japanese empress, was Bobi Ladawa, his richly overfed and bleached-skin wife, who, by dint of a queerly incestuous superstition, also happened to be the identical twin of another of the president's wives. One could not even call the relationship an open secret. Like the long name the dictator, baptized Joseph Désiré Mobutu, gave himself, Mobutu Sese Seko Kuku Ngbendu wa za Banga—"the all-conquering warrior who triumphs over all obstacles"—it was a chest-beating howl declaring the great man's prowess.* Mobutu's conjugal arrangements were the ultimate expression of keeping it in the family, but they also served niftily to keep friends and foes alike off guard. The sister often stood in for the first lady at official functions, just as surely as she did in the boudoir, and their resemblance was so great that only Mobutu could reliably tell them apart.

This dictatorship being a family affair, there was a suitable sampling of the rest of the presidential brood on hand as well. There were pampered daughters, women in their twenties, attractive to be sure, but in the preferred Central African way, meaning pleasantly plump. Although far less garish than their mothers, the young women seemed to aspire to the same sort of force-fed and overly dressed look. It was a style that gaudily married the de rigueur local costume of brightly colored African cloth with Parisian *griffe*—handbags, big gold jewelry and large-framed, face-concealing sunglasses, all conspicuously signed Vuitton, Chanel or Dior.

Then there was his son, the inevitable Kongulu, the twenty-seven-year-old army captain with the sparkplug build and scruffy beard whose nickname, Saddam Hussein, perfectly fit a man whose nocturnal death squad attacks on his father's enemies made him the terror

---

*Mobutu's full name has also sometimes been translated as "the strutting rooster who covers all the hens, going from battle to battle, leaving enemies fleeing in his wake."

of Kinshasa. With his perpetual scowl, Kongulu appeared to live on the edge of an outburst. On this day he was running the security for his father's arrival, and as Mobutu shuffled along the red carpet he exhorted his soldiers from the feared Division Spéciale Présidentielle to thrash anyone in the pressing crowd whose enthusiasm, or perhaps a push from behind, caused him to stray too close to the Guide.

Once Mobutu was atop the reviewing stand, the crowd fell silent for the national anthem, which he, while solemn, only seemed to mouth. To near-universal surprise, there would be no speech. Instead, after a few waves to the crowds, his guards hustled him into a black Cadillac limousine and sped off for the long drive home.

Gradually, as I moved along in the wake of Mobutu's long motorcade, the landscape mutated from the wide-open plains of the countryside to the cinder block and mortar of the dusty and overcrowded city. As we approached Kinshasa's center, and Camp Tshatshi revealed itself as the destination, the neighborhoods grew thicker with gawkers and revelers. Mobutu's outriders honked their horns furiously to announce his arrival and to clear the streets, and trucks full of soldiers doing their best to look fearsome in their sinister, wraparound sunglasses rumbled past just behind them.

Mobutu had remained invisible throughout the ride, hidden behind heavily tinted windows, but this seemed to have no effect on the atmosphere. Even in Matongé, the reputed bastion of the opposition, people choked the sidewalks and looked on from balconies and rooftops, many of them cheering, or rushing out into the streets a split second before the passage of the motorcade's first vehicles, in a daredevil gesture meant to show their excitement. Matongé was home to the famous *parlementaires debout*, or streetcorner legislators—ordinary, often unemployed folks, who gathered there to discuss the news for hours each day, usually condemning Mobutu and demanding a return to democratic rule.

Only a few days earlier, Zairian friends had told me it would be impossible to find a hundred people in Matongé to cheer for Mobutu. Now people were chanting his name wildly, and screaming things like "Papa's back, the price of beer will fall," while others, in a more direct reference to the war, shouted, "Kabila souki," or "Kabila's finished," in Lingala.

Mobutu had not lived in the capital since the first pillages had ravaged the city in 1991. When his presence was required in Kinshasa, he had shown his aversion to the place by staying on his luxurious white riverboat, the *Kamanyola*, named for one of the few victories his army had ever truly won. For his belated return, he had elected to establish residence at Camp Tshatshi, a vast, gated military installation that occupies a hilly suburb overlooking the Malebo Pool and the first cataract of the Congo River, which bars access to and from the sea 350 miles downstream.

With many grand residences to choose from, the choice of Tshatshi seemed rather transparently designed to suggest that the Marshal was returning to his military origins, that he had come back to lead the war effort. But with Kabila's rebels beginning to show signs of making good on their promise to cross the country and mount an assault on the capital, everyone understood that Mobutu felt safe only in a military camp, surrounded by troops from his own Ngbandi ethnic group. Mobutu had always boasted that he would sooner be a late president than an ex-president, but just in case he changed his mind, Tshatshi offered another comfort—powerful speedboats moored just above the cataract and ready to go. In a serious jam, the aging dictator could be hustled off to Brazzaville next door within minutes.

Passing through the base's heavy iron gates, one realized that Tshatshi also stood firmly for one other thing—segregation. Here there were no ragged masses. The city might be abuzz with excitement, but all here was tranquility and order. Selected visitors, including the accredited press, were told to park their cars in one of the sloping lots on the grounds and were conducted to the manicured gardens behind Mobutu's grand but sober mansion.

It was late afternoon, and the equatorial sun had finally lost its force and was beginning its ever-startling decline, its molten hues of deep orange and rust exploding as it swelled and then swiftly disappeared. I was jittery with excitement as I entered a scene as bewildering as if I had stepped through the looking glass. Gathered together were the leading representatives of the famous three hundred families, as Mobutu called the elite he had set out to build in the 1960s, after conspiring to take over a country left by the Belgians with a sole lawyer, a handful of doctors and not a single engineer after eighty-four years of colonial and imperial control. Mobutu's project was inspired, but in the end it had served only to prove the adage about absolute power corrupting absolutely. These were grabbers, not strivers. As they strolled through the gardens eating canapés and drinking cocktails served by waiters in black tie, their clothing and perfume revealed them to be a pampered and indolent lot.

Mobutu's rule had always depended on the clever manipulation of symbols, and most important was his splendor. Toward that end, the rapids of the Congo River served as a stunning backdrop. Peacocks and geese lent to the rarefied air, strutting freely around the periphery of the gardens, their cooing and cackling punctuating the smooth sou-kous of Koffi Olomidé, which was piped in on a sound system in taste-fully muted fashion.

Save for the birds and for the white noise of the river gurgling in the distance below, all went silent when Mobutu finally emerged from a knot of family members and appeared on the marbled balcony that looked out over the crowd. The Guide had chosen not to speak to *le petit peuple* at Ndjili airport, but rather to *his* people here. For the masses, impatient to know what lay ahead, their radios would have to do.

"No words, no verbal expression would be capable of expressing the depth of my gratitude and the contentment I felt when my feet touched the soil of Zaire," Mobutu said in a grave baritone that had suddenly gone tremolo with emotion. "Your warm welcome comforts me more than ever in my belief in our solidarity, which is the founda-tion upon which our Zairian fatherland was built.

"Recently, we have watched as the enemies of our people have cho-sen the moment when I was floored with disease to stab me in the back. They did this because they know that I represent the territorial integrity of our great Zaire, for which I have consecrated my entire life to the defense of its sacred values."

At that moment, Mobutu burst into tears, but after collecting him-self and asking people to pray for his health, he delivered what amounted to a call to arms. "I have never retreated, and once again, this time there can be no question of retreat," Mobutu said dramati-cally. "Zaire has become a victim of its African hospitality, and has been wronged. . . . But together we will restore the tarnished image of our beloved country."

Alas, the depths of this country's social fracture were too deep to be papered over, even amid a remarkable surge of patriotism. Zaire had the misfortune of having been ruled by the Belgians, a small, tribally divided European people who gave full vent to their pettiness as they set about colonizing one of Africa's largest territories. The Belgians imagined and enforced tribal distinctions everywhere they went. On the rear terrace of his colonial-era mansion in the old European quarter of Gombé, Cléophas Kamitatu, a onetime advisor to Mobutu, put it this way: "In every region of the country they favored one group over another. Here it was the Bakongo over the Bakaya. In Kasai it was the Baluba against the Lulua, the Baonge and the Bakete. In Shaba it was the Lunda against all the ethnic groups of the south. The Mongo enjoyed the ear of the Belgians in the north. But just as a precaution, they recruited their neighbors, the Bangala, to serve in the army.

"Our greatest misfortune was to be colonized by a country with such a small spirit. You will say that's all old history now, but the effects are with us still today. When I asked an official Belgian delegation that was here the other day if they were seeking investments in the country, they replied that Belgium would only invest once there had been elections. In the meantime, they said we are here to prevent anyone else from taking our place."

Kamitatu's quick history lesson was fine as far as it went. What he left out, though, was no prettier. Like almost everyone else in the political elite, in his own small way the weary old former diplomat, who somehow still managed to live quite well amid the country's ruin, had had his hand in Zaire's mess, too. It was said that he had sold the country's embassy in Tokyo while in residence there, and had simply pocketed the money.

Mobutu's generals were even worse than the civilian elite. During the first Shaba war, in 1977, when rebels from Angola occupied the country's southern copper belt, the chief of staff, General Eluki Monga Aundu, pulled off a train heist worthy of Butch Cassidy, robbing the entire payroll for the troops he was about to lead into battle. That he was quickly defeated was hardly a surprise. More surprising is that he was never punished, whether because of his kinship with Mobutu or because the Guide may have admired his audacity.

In the streets, everyone knew the code by which the country was ruled. But if Article 15 governed daily life, by no means did everyone subscribe to the degradation it wrought. Those who lived in roadside shacks and wore rags for clothes could not easily turn down a free drink or a bite to eat, and it was no different with a chance to party. But sobbing at a funeral or shouting hurrahs at a wedding for a few coins never made anyone a member of the festival, and the people rocking on the tarmac to the sensuous soukous or swaying in the streets cheering on the president's motorcade were no different. Theirs was little more than a dance of death for a country that was already on its way out of this world.

The truth was that Mobutu had no one to lean on anymore, least of all the vaunted masses that had turned out to salute him. For proof, with incomparably smaller means, Etienne Tshisekedi, the popular leader of the opposition and head of the Democratic Union for Social Progress, staged a return to Kinshasa that same week after a prolonged absence from the country and managed to draw crowds nearly as large as Mobutu's. More perplexing still, given that the two men were bitter political rivals, many of the revelers had turned out for both events.

"This is the Zaire we have become. The same youth that cheers Mobutu today will cheer Tshisekedi with the same fervor tomorrow, and eventually, why not Kabila, too," said Jean-Baptiste Sondji, a political activist doctor at Mama Yemo, Kinshasa's biggest hospital, which was named for Mobutu's mother. "That is the real legacy of Mobutu: the compromising of an entire generation of young people who have grown up without schools and without values."

The Great Man had chosen the practicable end of the Great River to issue his rallying cry. Ten miles or more across in places and almost unimaginable in its power, the Zaire River unfurls like an immense serpent whose tail lies in the deep south, its midsection running west along the equator, and its head basking at the shores of the Atlantic Ocean. It has not only given the country its name, but its very definition. But for all of its magnificence, for all of its much vaunted potential to light an entire hemisphere with hydroelectric power, it is a river impeded by huge boulders, broken in the image of the country itself, and sadly condemned never to fulfill its promise.

From the other navigable limit of the river, the end was already approaching for Mobutu. Though quiet still, Kisangani was about to assume the role that it had played so often in the short and tragic history of Zaire. Battles for the city had served as hinges slamming the doors on entire eras, helping close the book on every regime the country had known, from colonial rule to the *indépendantiste* struggle after Lumumba's assassination, and it would soon lower the boom on the famous survivor himself, Mobutu.

I flew into Kisangani aboard a Caravelle jetliner with the United

Nations High Commissioner for Refugees, Sadako Ogata. By that time, early in February 1997, the government had declared Kisangani a strategic zone, and hitching a ride on a relief flight was virtually the only way to get there. The UNHCR had promised the handful of reporters that it allowed aboard the flight a tour of a makeshift camp for Rwandan Hutu refugees at a place called Tingi-Tingi, and we were all expected to return to Kinshasa that evening aboard another chartered plane, or continue onward to Uganda with Ogata. I harbored a secret plan, however, to drop out of sight at the end of the day and make my way into the city by the bend in the river to report from there.

The scene at Kisangani's airport reminded me of the way split personalities were depicted in old Hollywood films. With an invisible line the only thing dividing them, fierce-looking Serbian and Romanian mercenaries leading Mobutu's war effort shared the tarmac with international relief workers who were running a major humanitarian operation. The foreign staffers from UNHCR and the World Food Programme winced as they acknowledged, just outside Ogata's earshot, that crated weapons and ammunition, along with uniforms and other supplies, were making their way into the bellies of the shiny old DC-3s, the aluminum-skinned workhorses that were ferrying sacks of food and medicines to the desperate Hutu. They insisted this was the price of cooperation from the local authorities.

It was unclear how much Ogata's aides knew of this piggybacking. But the surrealistic scene of mercenaries and aid workers sharing the same workspace led to equally surreal conversations when Ogata and local officials began exchanging greetings in the stifling hangar that served as the arrival lounge. Omar Léa Sisi, the potbellied governor of Manièma Province, either did not understand or was feigning confusion over the purpose of an international relief operation.

Dressed in a silk abacost, the buttoned tunic and pants outfit that Mobutu had once decreed as the only formal clothing fitting for Zairian men,* the governor spoke of obtaining UN help in winning back lost territory, and warned there would be stricter conditions on relief operations if such assistance was not forthcoming. Ogata, a handsome woman whose petite stature and crusty upper-class Japanese manners belied her toughness, stood her ground, and hammered away

*Abacost is a clever contraction of *A bas le costume*, or "Down with the suit."

at UN demands for safe corridors for the refugees and for the relief operations that were helping them.

The reality on the ground in this part of Zaire, where the war was quickly moving toward a defining moment, would yield to neither of these visions, although ultimately the governor's take would prove far closer to reality. East of Kisangani, the government was employing a few dozen Serbian mercenaries and a few thousand Hutu fighters to hold off the rebels, and just as they had done since the Rwandan genocide in 1994, the Hutu fighters were hiding among tens of thousands of Hutu refugees to shield themselves from attack.

Unfortunately for the governor, for Mobutu and, most of all, for the refugees, neither the human shields nor the mercenaries were of any tactical use in stopping the rebel advance. That is because what was happening, although unacknowledged, was more than a rebellion; it was the pursuit of Rwanda's civil war into the heart of Zaire, and in this struggle, moral complications presented no more obstacle to the invaders than the feeble military resistance they faced. Ethnic cleansing had always lain at the heart of Rwanda's civil wars, and if Kabila's AFDL had to exterminate 100,000 or more refugees in order to settle their score with the armed Hutu *génocidaires* hiding among them, so be it.

"African solutions to African problems," Washington's code name for the war, was an exercise in moral bankruptcy arguably more crass and even more complete than the failure to stop the Rwandan genocide. As it did in 1994, Washington pretended not to know the extent of the murder that was taking place in central Zaire lest it become a hot issue back home, drawing TV cameras and forcing action of some kind. By the time most of the dust had settled, six years after Zaire was first plunged into war, 3.3 million people had died in the eastern half of the country alone, more than four times as many people as had died in the Rwandan genocide.* Moreover, by some neat trick of misdirection, once Mobutu was gone, the worst of the slaughter and starvation went almost entirely unnoticed abroad.

Clinton administration officials often grew impatient with questions about the human toll associated with the Kabila army's seemingly effortless advance through the Zairian countryside. On a visit to Kin-

---

*Estimating casualties in conflicts anywhere is a rough and highly unscientific endeavor. This is especially true in Africa. The death toll in the Congo, although indisputably huge, is the subject of an ongoing and unlikely-soon-to-be-resolved debate.

shasa, David J. Scheffer, Washington's ambassador at large for war crimes issues, once angrily dismissed my concerns about the murder of Hutu refugees by Kabila's Rwandan Tutsi troops. Scheffer was far from alone in this attitude. Almost across the board, American officials had written off the Hutu as a pariah population, and no one had time for questions about their fate.

The U.S. ambassador to Zaire, Daniel Howard Simpson, ever fond of blustery talk, reduced the Hutu problem to a simple formula. "They are the bad guys," he once told me. This attitude would persist long after the war, as Washington ran political interference within the United Nations on behalf of Kabila as his new regime stymied all efforts to investigate mass killings that occurred during the AFDL's triumphant march from one end of the country to the other.

We in the press obligingly failed to cover what was arguably the war's most important feature, its human toll. We certainly didn't have the excuse of disinterest from the outside world, since Mobutu's demise had been on the front pages of newspapers for months. Some reasoned that it was too dangerous to trek through the war zones in the wake of Kabila's rebels, and in fairness the terrain was dangerous and unusually inaccessible. It still haunts me to think, however, that something far more insidious lay behind our failure.

Evildoing by the rebels fouled up an all too compelling story line. Mobutu was the villainous dictator, someone the press had loved to hate for years, and now even the American government had stopped propping him up. By contrast, Kabila had emerged as a jovial, canny foil. He had quickly learned how to keep the press happy with his blunt, boastful statements and colorful appearances before the cameras. He gave us the illusion that we were covering the war by allowing reporters to fly in briefly when a town had been freshly captured—that is, after any sign of atrocities had been carefully cleaned up.

As we turned the war into a black-and-white affair, with Mobutu and his Hutu allies playing the irredeemable bad guys, our most important failure was in suspending disbelief over the flimsy cover story of an uprising in the east by an obscure ethnic group. From start to finish this war had been nothing less than a Tutsi invasion from Rwanda.

The most powerful factor at work behind our self-deception was an entirely natural sympathy for the Tutsi following the horrors of the Rwandan genocide. From that simple starting point, emotionally overpowering but deeply flawed analogies with Israel and with European

Jewry and the Holocaust began to drive Washington's policies in Central Africa. Philip Gourevitch, whose compelling writing on the Rwandan genocide strongly influenced Clinton administration policy toward the region, wrote in *The New Yorker:*

> Despite Rwanda's size, General Kagame, who became the country's President in April, has built its Army into the most formidable fighting force in central Africa, and he has done so without recourse to sophisticated weaponry. Rather, what distinguishes his commanders and soldiers is their ferocious motivation. Having single-handedly brought the genocide to a halt, in 1994, the Rwandan Patriotic Army has continued to treat its almost ceaseless battlefield engagements as one long struggle for national survival. (The analogy that's sometimes made between Rwanda's aggressive defense policy and that of Israel—another small country with a vivid memory of genocide which has endured persistent threats of annihilation from its neighbors—is inexact but not unfounded.)

Americans are overly fond of good guy/bad guy dichotomies, especially in Africa, which for many already seems so unknowable and forbidding. But analogies like these paralyze debate over Central Africa rather than clarify it. Nothing could ever pardon the organizers of the 1994 genocide in Rwanda, yet it is no less true a fact that the wild adventurousness of the Tutsi leader Paul Kagame, who mounted a Rwandan insurgency from bases in Uganda in 1990, primed a country that had already long been an ethnic powder keg for a sharp escalation in violence and hatred.

The Tutsi, unlike Europe's Jews, were a small minority that had enjoyed feudal tyrannies in Rwanda and neighboring Burundi for centuries. In Burundi they had perpetrated genocide against the Hutu three times in a generation, and in both countries they were committed to winning or retaining power by force of arms.

There were no good guys in Rwanda's catastrophic modern history, and the same was true for Zaire's civil war. We in the press were far too slow in seizing upon the recklessness of Rwanda's invasion, and by the time the true dimensions of the tragedy it had unleashed could be discerned, almost no one cared.

On our way to Tingi-Tingi, our old DC-3, a shiny and unpainted model, probably built sometime in the late 1940s, flew low over the unbroken carpet of forest below, so low that the air inside the aged cargo plane never really cooled down on that blazing hot day. The handful of reporters allowed aboard were sweating in the aft amid the din of the airplane's propellers, and the jittering tambourine sound of ten thousand loose rivets rattling.

We were told Tingi-Tingi was 125 miles southwest of Kisangani, but the tiny settlement was too small to figure on my Michelin map. As we reached our destination, there was no airport below. There was not even a landing strip. What awaited our plane's rubber wheels instead was the pitted asphalt of a narrow, old two-lane highway, long abandoned to the jungle.

Throughout the flight my mind searched for images of what to expect at Tingi-Tingi, but in the end, nothing could have prepared me for what awaited us. When the fading drone from the plane's engines announced our imminent landing, I looked out the window as we banked for the descent and discovered a scene worthy of *The Ten Commandments*. On either side of this road, pressed to its very edges and sometimes spilling onto the highway itself, was a sea of refugees— 150,000 people or more, dressed in tatters and jumpy with excitement over the arrival of a special visitor bearing desperately needed relief supplies. Ours was the second of two identical planes to land. The first was loaded with aid, and, I suspected, with crates of guns as well. As we touched down, the sea of people parted in a feat of just-in-time reactions. I saw mothers reaching out to yank the shirts of overexcited children, and others sucking in their guts or feinting and skipping backward like skilled boxers slipping a punch.

Later we learned that someone had been killed during the landings, his head lopped off by the first airplane's wing. If true, the incident had done nothing to dampen the mood of joy for these people who had walked for seven weeks through some of the world's most inhospitable territory with killers in their midst and more killers on their trail. As we taxied, I was impressed by the way the crowd's eyes were fixed on the airplanes' glinting skins; from the looks of beatitude they doubtlessly imagined their salvation was at hand.

As Ogata began her tour of the camp, working the crowd and giving encouragement to the relief officials in the manner of a politician working a rope line, only far more dignified, I broke away from her party. There would be little time on the ground, and chances like these to encounter the wandering Hutu population were too rare to limit myself to a tidily arranged inspection tour.

Wide-eyed refugees swamped me as I plunged into the crowd. Many were desperate to tell me their stories, but could speak only Kinyarwanda. Others, their faces severely drawn, their ribs and shoulders protruding sharply through their flesh, held out their hands in hope of food. Others simply wanted to touch me, almost as if to confirm that this tall, well-clothed foreigner was not an apparition.

A thirty-year-old Protestant pastor named Thaddée Twagirayeza stepped forward to identify himself, and managed to quiet the crowd. "Like many of these people, I fled the combat in Rurengeri in July 1994, and lived in a parish in Bukavu," he said. "Most of the people here were living somewhere in South Kivu. When the war broke out in Zaire, we fled into the forest, moving westward, without clean water, without food, without medicine and without hope, in fact. Reaching here alive was the greatest trial of my life.

"Most of the ground we covered was uninhabited. Whenever we did find a village or a small town, the Zairian army had already passed through. Everything had been looted, and the villagers had fled."

I had little doubt that if I had allowed him to continue talking, Twagirayeza would have kept me planted there until it was time to leave. His story was powerful, but equally remarkable was the hold that he exercised over the people huddled around us. No one in the huge crowd interrupted while he spoke.

I recalled things I had read about the regimented and hierarchical nature of Rwandan society, a feature that had made the hundred days of door-to-door butchery perpetrated against the Tutsi possible. I was also wary because of what I knew about the role of church people in the genocide. How could I know whether this pastor had been one of the many Hutu men of the cloth who had called on his flock to go out and exterminate the cockroaches, as the Tutsi were called in the terminology of the genocide? There was simply no way to rule it out.

As I moved on through the crowd, I soon settled on a new interlocutor, or rather, he settled on me. Eugène Munyangoga, a thirty-five-year-old teacher from the Rwandan town of Ririma, introduced himself to me in as low-key a way as the surrounding crush of people allowed, proffering a piece of paper. They were credentials stating that UNICEF had selected him as a camp aide. As I read it, Munyangoga began to talk, his words spilling forth in a jumble that mixed personal history, details about the camp and stories about the extraordinary trek that had brought these people this far.

"The people you see here are survivors," he said with a clear touch of pride. "But we will have to begin moving again soon, and many are simply not in any condition to carry on. We will have to say goodbye to them. For them, Tingi-Tingi will be the end."

I told Munyangoga that I wanted to see children, and I asked him if he would translate for me. I was suffocating with doubt, not knowing whom I could trust or what I could believe, but my gut said that children beneath a certain age should be free of any taint from the genocide. Hearing their stories might deliver me from one moral conundrum—assessing the humanity of people who may have committed beastly crimes—even if it placed me before another: the helplessness of innocents.

Munyangoga told me the camp had its own makeshift orphanage. Some of its occupants were children whose parents had disappeared long ago, and others were children whose parents had only just succumbed to hunger, malaria or the unrelenting diarrhea that comes from drinking pond water.

The orphanage was nothing more than a tent, really, and as we neared it, three barefoot girls approached us. They wore simple muslin dresses, stained and torn from their walk through the forest, and one of them, Sophie, had a plastic rosary with a small cross that dangled on her bony chest. She and another girl named Marie-Claire were both twelve. Another girl named Edwige, feral and silent throughout, was said to be thirteen.

"We were separated from our parents in the forest," said Sophie, the smallest of the three, but by far the most self-assured. "Whenever I would ask someone if they had seen my parents they would either say that they had been left behind, or they would just shake their heads and say they didn't know."

Marie-Claire then spoke up and said that she had not seen her parents since the refugees in Bukavu broke camp in a panic after it came under attack from a rebel mortar barrage in the first days of the war.

Then, deeply suspicious, she asked me why the airplanes had landed here. Most of the refugees had seen the DC-3s as a portent of their salvation, but others clearly feared that something much darker was afoot, perhaps a forced repatriation.

I followed up my quick explanation of the visit with a question: How do you feel about going home? "We will never go back to Rwanda. The Tutsi will kill us," little Sophie said, her eyes widening and her voice suddenly aquiver. "If they try to put us in an airplane we will run away. We must remain here in Zaire, even if it means dying."

I caught a glimpse of the Ogata party in the far distance. They were wrapping up their tour and beginning to gather near the airplanes. My time was already running short. It was now or never for a frank discussion with Eugène Munyangoga. "There are fighters here, aren't there?" I asked him directly. His face froze, in a reaction that I immediately took for an admission.

"We don't call them fighters, but yes, there are former army members here among us," he said. "They have been receiving weapons from the Zairian army. Some of them were unloaded here today."

Munyangoga himself seemed conflicted. His job as a camp worker was the only thing that had spared him from forced enlistment in the Hutu effort to fight off their Tutsi pursuers, a fight he said he wanted no part of. Then again, he said, he knew that every day the mortar fire from the rebels was drawing closer. With no return fire, they were all as good as dead.

What does one say to a thirty-five-year-old Hutu man who, whatever his denials, might have had a hand in one of the century's great murder sprees? I thanked him for his help, and, sensing the humanity in both his person and his predicament, I wished him good luck. It was all I could do.

My last conversation in Tingi-Tingi was with Mike Deppner, a Canadian doctor who was the medical coordinator for the UN refugee agency. Mike had spent a lot of time on the ground here, and had a keen sense of the perilous fluidity of the situation. He also had a deep understanding of the military and humanitarian stakes at hand.

"Things are moving very quickly. Too quickly," he said. "Last week we were scrambling to set up a basic camp in Amisi. That has been destroyed already, and the people from Amisi are on their way here. It has been this way ever since Goma. The only thing that has changed is that the process is speeding up, and the deeper we get into Zaire, the heavier the concentration of the FAR becomes." The acronym FAR stood for the Forces Armées Rwandaises, and referred to the remnants of the country's former Hutu army.

Deppner spoke with a quiet anger that was altogether distinct from the smooth, well-worn diplomatic formulas of the visitors from UNHCR headquarters. They were international civil servants in both title and style; he was emphatically a man of the field for whom lives lost often meant stains on his own clothing, not merely digits in a statistical tally.

"In strict military terms, the rebels would be foolish to try to take Kisangani from this direction," he said. "Normally you just don't rush down the path of greatest resistance. But that is exactly what they are doing, and the reason they are pushing in this direction is the refugees. They were unable to make them return to Rwanda. Now it looks like they just want to kill them."

Events later proved Deppner right. Most of these refugees were indeed slaughtered. The killings occurred just days after my visit, and the bodies were buried so hastily that later they seemed to call out from the grave. Months later, after Kabila had been installed in power, he blocked UN human rights investigators from visiting the mass graves in Tingi-Tingi, and in many other parts of his country. The United States provided political cover, blocking condemnation of the regime in the Security Council and lobbying for the slimmest possible accounting of the massacres.

But the will to survive of some of the refugees had been more powerful than the bullets that rained down upon them. Quite by accident, the following year, in yet another refugee camp six hundred miles to the west, which they had reached almost miraculously by foot, I would encounter some of these people and hear their stories. But first, there would be a war of sorts.

I dropped the name of Guy Vanda, the closest aide of Mobutu's son Kongulu, and won quick approval from the Zairian general in charge of Kisangani airport to hang around for a few days. He even offered to give me a tour of the city's defenses. Ogata's Caravelle was taking off into the sunset, and with darkness approaching and no other contacts on the ground, I had to find a place to stay quickly.

As I set out from the airport on foot, a car full of foreigners stopped to ask where I was going. They were from the World Food

Programme, and after scarcely a minute of conversation they offered me a place to stay. It was one of those breaks that one thanks the stars for. I rode through Kisangani's heavily pitted streets for the first time as darkness fell on the equatorial town. At first blush, the city seemed as if it had little to recommend itself: On the riverfront, huge cranes sat rusted frozen, undoubtedly just as they had been for years. Downtown, meanwhile, was nothing more than a dust-ridden collection of miserable little cement-box houses with tin roofs.

This was the innermost river station, the scene of innumerable horrors since the days of Leopold II, the port beyond which no boats traveled. Kisangani had once boasted movie theaters and a bowling alley. There had been a Rotary Club and foreign consulates. People had attempted the grafting of Western culture here many times, but it never seemed to take. Outsiders were forever promising "progress," whether through industry, administration or Western religion, but seeing how it always involved violence and rape, the Africans who eked out a living here preferred to be left alone.

The diamond trade was the only surviving business in town, as was made plain by the cheaply stenciled advertisements on the walls of the storefronts. Rambo Diamond bore the image of a large gem and a machine gun. The next shop on the dusty roadway, Mr. Cash, strove for a slightly less intimidating image, with its picture of sparkling gems set off against a crudely reproduced $10,000 bill.

Although he named neither of them, Naipaul had gotten nothing so right in his acerbic book as his portraits of Mobutu and Kisangani. His words about the city hung in my thoughts as we bounded along toward the low, concrete villa of the World Food Programme representative, where I would sleep on the ground, on the front terrace, covered with mosquito netting and sweating and tossing through the night from the fierce, sawing attacks of the swarming insects that bred on the river nearby. "Valuable real estate for a while, and now bush again," Naipaul said of the city. "You felt like a ghost, not from the past, but from the future. You felt that your life and ambition had already been lived out for you and you were looking at the relics of that life. You were in a place where the future had come and gone."

CHAPTER EIGHT

Castles in the Sand

M y second visit to Mali came more than a decade after my first. In lieu of a goatskin sack and a battered tape player, I was carrying spiral notebooks and a mini cassette recorder. It was 1995, and I was returning to the African country that had first seduced me. Although I was no longer the footloose student-adventurer, I was every bit as thrilled by the prospect.

As a precocious democracy, Mali had come to occupy a special place in African politics. Like a latter-day echo of its early empires, the country was again in the continent's historical vanguard. Three years earlier, Mali had held one of West Africa's first competitive multiparty presidential elections, and ever since, it had been like a vast research laboratory on full public display. The highly experimental protocol being tested on African soil was an exotic notion widely known as Western-style democracy.

Alpha Oumar Konaré, the man who had emerged as president, enjoyed a reputation as a new kind of leader. He was an archaeologist who had given up a ministerial job during the country's long one-party era in order to join a growing civic movement calling for democracy, and he had spoken of democracy ever since as something that Malians deserved now, rather than in some hypothetical and distant future. Konaré's contemporaries among Africa's leaders imposed countless constraints on their adversaries, and used so many obfuscations when speaking of democracy as to drain the word of all meaning. The democracy that Konaré spoke of, though, was something that no Westerner would have trouble recognizing.

This was a region full of heads of state who had been guerrilla leaders, military men, stern founding fathers or faceless technocrats, who ruled at the pleasure of the so-called international financial institutions, or Iffys. To a man, they had sought to impose their persons, no matter how unattractive, on their countries. The evening news was a record of their day. Dancing troupes followed them everywhere to sing their praises. And their official portraits watched over workers in every government office. Konaré signaled his difference by exhibiting modest self-confidence with none of the oppressive props of the charismatic leader. He often drove himself around the capital, negotiating Bamako's dusty streets with a minimal security detachment discreetly in tow. He showed up at the funerals of ordinary people he had known way back when. And he had a generous enough sense of humor to laugh at himself.

For a journalist like me to see the president, all roads led through his director of intelligence, Soumeylou Boubèye Maïga, a man universally known by his middle name alone. Michel Kouamé, the editor in chief of Ivory Coast's state-owned newspaper, *Fraternité Matin*, had offered a bitterly cynical explanation for the fact that Mali's top spy controlled the president's agenda.

Michel came from a remarkable family of writers and journalists, but he had always remained committed to a model of African politics that had been under siege almost everywhere in the continent since the beginning of the decade: the one-party state. As an apparatchik of sorts, he had done well under Ivory Coast's authoritarian governments, and now that Mali was being touted as an example for the region, Michel wanted me to believe that Konaré, for all of his good press, was at heart no more of a democrat than any other African leader.

The proof, he said, would come when Konaré's second term expired, when the law would bar him from seeking reelection. "One way or another, Konaré will change the constitution," Michel told me with a patronizing chuckle. "You Americans are always looking for a horse to back, someone who reflects your own self-image; what you don't understand is that power works differently in Africa than it does in the West. Once you've got it, you can't just give it up." So I took note of Michel's skepticism, thanked him for the contact and headed off for Bamako.

Coventional wisdom holds that multiparty democracy can bloom only in a country with a large and prosperous middle class. And yet, in 1991, a citizens' movement made up of human rights activists, labor organizers, students and mothers whose children had been killed or imprisoned by the armed forces came together to overthrow a dictatorship that had been in place for twenty-three years.

An African coup, in itself, was hardly rare. What made Mali's revolution so special was the democratic spirit that had guided it, as unwaveringly as our own revolution more than two hundred years before it. "Give me time to make contact with the people, my people, for whom we have taken this action," Amadou Toumani Touré, the general who seized power, told the nation in his very first radio address, after several days of bloodshed during which soldiers killed scores of unarmed demonstrators. "We can say that this future action will involve the establishment of an unlimited multiparty system, social justice and total democracy in our country."

Touré held true to his word, ignoring the pressure to hang on to power that would come from clan and military colleagues alike. And little more than a year after the citizens' revolt, Mali had chosen Konaré, forty-six, as its first democratically elected president, giving him about 70 percent of the vote.

Like General Touré before him, Konaré had quickly shown that he was made of something special. Running what Americans would call a retail-style campaign in a country of parched badlands and tumbleweed as large as Texas and California combined, he avoided the temptation to pose as a rainmaker or to promise miracles. Instead, Konaré told crowds that his party did not have money to distribute right and left. Even more remarkable, once it appeared that he was the strong favorite, Konaré warned against the perils of a landslide, saying that a healthy democracy required a strong opposition. "We're here to identify the problems," he told an American reporter as they strode together down a dirt alleyway during the thick of the campaign. "What we guarantee is good management."

I was reporting in the Caribbean when all of this took place, and I can recall my sense of wonderment and pleasure when I first heard this news. If such things could happen in Mali, one of the world's ten poorest countries, where less than 20 percent of the population can read, they should be possible anywhere in Africa, I thought. I was reminded of a Creole saying favored by Haiti's president Jean-Bertrand Aristide: "Analphabète pas bête," or illiterate does not mean stupid.

As Robert and I flew from Abidjan to Bamako, I watched the landscape morph from dense rain forest to grassy savannah, and finally to an endless expanse of sere-colored sand and dust, relieved only by the lazy arc of the Niger River and the narrow, fertile band of green that hugs its banks. In the back of my mind, I was trying hard to picture Boubèye. In my African travels, I had dealt with more presidential goons than I cared to recall. However soft and gentle Mali's newly democratic face, there would always be some trepidation going into a meeting with a chief of state security.

I found a message from Boubèye waiting for me at my hotel, and the next day, at the appointed time, I went to the government office building where he had told me to meet him, and was surprised to find a slight man dressed unpretentiously in a loose-fitting two-piece cotton outfit. It was almost identical to the cheap casual clothing my brother and I had bought for our trip to Mopti years before. With his shrugging posture, he bore a distinct look of world-weariness, but I could detect none of the telltale signs of evil one's imagination associates with state security officers, whether the cold, squinting stare and skeptical interrogation or the clammy, forced friendliness meant to lower one's guard.

Boubèye received me in a windowless office and we talked for an hour or so. He asked me why I wanted to see the president, and then lectured me about a festering rebellion among the Tuareg, in the north. Finally, he surprised me with a question about American commitment to African democracy.

"Americans always say they have no strategic interest in Mali," he said, chain-smoking, as he pierced me with his indicting gaze. "Maybe that is true in military or economic terms, but whatever happened to political values? The extension and consolidation of democracy in Africa should be seen as a strategic conquest, a victory for humanity."

I was due to travel to Timbuktu after spending a few days in Bamako, and Boubèye offered to help expedite the laissez-passer that I would need to go there as a journalist. He gave me the names of some contacts among the local officials as well. Then, at the very end of our interview, he told me that my appointment with Konaré was set for four o'clock the next afternoon. "Try to be there a few minutes before-hand, please."

From my meeting with Boubèye, I drove to the American Embassy through Bamako's dusty grid of streets, which seemed to lie like a thin crust on what was still at heart a very large African village. I wanted to get Washington's view of the Malian experience. It would be wrong to say that there was no excitement about Mali among the embassy staff. In a continent where civil wars and authoritarian regimes were commonplace, many diplomats clearly considered democratic Mali to be a great posting. Still, there was a distinct undercurrent of defensiveness about American assistance.

The diplomat who received me, Michael Pelletier, hastily ticked off Washington's good works. There were 160 Peace Corps volunteers in Mali involved in health care, developing water resources, education and reforestation projects. There had been a proliferation of "democratization projects," too. These, he said, included support for a legal clinic for women, training for young lawyers and funding for civic education spots on local radio, urging people to vote and pay their taxes. Overall, Pelletier told me, the United States was spending $33 million a year helping Mali. "This has been one of the most important countries in our African aid program," he said. "Since democratization, funding has either stayed level or shrunken more slowly than in other places."

It was a game effort on his part, but there was no concealing the fact that the aid numbers were miserly for a country of this size. Across the continent, in fact, in Uganda, the government of a very different kind of new leader, Yoweri Museveni, was receiving nearly twice as much aid. And all the while, Museveni was virtually proclaiming multiparty democracy unfit for Africans, or at least for Ugandans, while fanning insurgencies that would spark genocide in both Rwanda and Zaire.

Washington's spending patterns were no mere abstraction. Africans saw them as a clear expression of the United States' deepest feelings toward the continent. Like the French president, Jacques Chirac, who had once proclaimed that Africans "weren't ready for democracy," Washington was still placing its biggest bets on "strongmen" who gave the appearance of maintaining order, while in reality sowing the seeds of future destabilization at home and in their surrounding regions.

Museveni was merely the latest in a long string of charismatic strongmen with whom the West had disastrously waltzed. The political bloodline ran through Mobutu, the infamous Idi Amin Dada, Hastings Kamuzu Banda of Malawi, Liberia's semi-literate Master Sergeant Samuel Kanyon Doe and the Angolan terrorist cum anti-communist guerrilla leader Jonas Savimbi, whom Ronald Reagan once toasted as Africa's Abraham Lincoln. Each of them was disowned only after the situation in his country had gotten frighteningly messy, or when America's interests had otherwise shifted.

As obvious as it may seem now, it bears repeating still, given their disastrous legacy, that we supported leaders like these for our own strategic reasons, and for those reasons alone, during the long years of the Cold War. Noble though our rhetoric may often be, democracy, indeed the welfare of Africans, had nothing to do with our choices. Tragically, for almost all of Africa, these years coincided with the formative period of the independence era.

Throughout the Cold War, the West had promoted what the French once called *vitrines du capitalisme*, supposed showcases of capitalism in Africa. These were countries like Kenya, Ivory Coast and even Zaire in Mobutu's heyday, where "pro-Western" dictators allowed the former colonials and settlers to play the leading economic roles, and to dictate broadly the thrust of their foreign policy. The skylines of showcase capitals often filled out handsomely with foreign-built office buildings and skyscrapers for banks, insurance companies and hotels. For many Africans, though, few of whom got to work in the shiny new towers, or even to visit them, this veneer of development seemed like a form of payoff to the regimes that banned their freedom of expression and deprived them of the right to a meaningful vote.

During Mobutu's reign, America's Export-Import Bank and its European counterparts found imaginative ways to fund economic monstrosities like the Inga Dam in Zaire, whose final cost of about $2 billion qualified it as one of the biggest white elephants of all time. America's overriding logic in an era of global competition with the Soviet Union was to control as many pawns on the African checkerboard as it could, and big projects, with their steep commissions and routine overbilling, were a good way to buy loyalty. As the Cold War ended, though, the need for African showcases ended as well. Many of the West's most obliging friends began to totter. Others, like Mobutu, who had served Western political interests unstintingly for thirty years while amassing personal fortunes (Mobutu's was $5 billion), were unceremoniously shoved from power by Washington's barely concealed hands.

A smaller circle of American friends soon emerged, and at its center was Washington's favorite new star, Museveni, who had managed to stabilize Uganda through force of arms in the mid-1980s, after years of chaos and ruin under two previous Western darlings, Amin and Milton Obote. As always, narrowly drawn questions of Western security, rather than considerations of Africa's longer-term development, were driving our choice. Our latest love affair with a Ugandan dictator stemmed mostly from Museveni's willingness to sponsor an insurgency in southern Sudan against that country's Islamic fundamentalist government.

Museveni would eventually win heavy praise for making Uganda a supposed beacon of economic promise for the continent. The country had posted 8 to 10 percent growth rates throughout the 1990s, but as with the bygone era of capitalist showcases, the growth reflected a self-fulfilling prophesy, because it was brought about largely through massive flows of aid from the United States, Britain, the International Monetary Fund and the World Bank. These almighty international financial institutions had become a virtual government in absentia for the entire African continent in the post–Cold War era. Through their tutelage, poor African countries were supposed to be mastering the mechanics of free-market economics, and absorbing vital lessons about transparency and accountability. The people who ran the Iffys understood implicitly that their own credibility required a few "success stories," and Washington, whose influence within the IMF and World Bank is paramount, annointed Uganda as the era's star pupil.

The whole process reeked of cynicism, though, with Western powers once again promoting a select few African stars for reasons entirely of their own. Moreover, though few bothered to examine the record, the advice of the World Bank and the IMF often proved disastrous, which is hardly surprising, given that poor countries were being pushed to compete with one another over commodities, driving their prices steadily downward, while rich countries protected their own farming and basic industries, like textiles, from competition. "The critics of globalization accuse Western countries of hypocrisy, and the critics are right," said Joseph E. Stiglitz, the Nobel Prize winner and former chief economist of the World Bank. "The Western countries have pushed poor countries to eliminate trade barriers, but kept up their own barriers . . . depriving them of desperately needed export income."

By the mid-1990s, Ghana, which for a decade had been held up by the Iffys as an economic example to other African countries, could hardly be said to be taking off. Rather than dwell on where their advice might have gone wrong, the Iffys began bad-mouthing Ghana while promoting Uganda as the fresh, new paragon. For all of the West's supposed moral superiority and intellectual firepower, its own commitment to accountability was proving as poor as that of any run-of-the-mill African dictatorship.

International assistance and political support for Africa has, to me, always borne more than a passing resemblance to horse racing, with Washington and its Iffys both playing and controlling the bank. In the 1990s three generations of horses were still on the track. Venerable old stars like Mobutu were being put out to pasture, and bets on recent "winners" like Ghana were shifting to Uganda, the shiny new horse, ridden by a not quite new but suddenly hot jockey named Museveni.

At the very moment when democracy was dawning across Africa, external assistance to the continent was drying up. With lots of democratic horses to bet on, the question that nagged was, Why were Western powers still placing most of their money on corrupt, authoritarian regimes held in the iron grip of charismatic dictators?

Leaders like Konaré, who were interested in providing electricity and clean drinking water to villages instead of building monuments to themselves, called for a New Deal with the West. What they got in reply was a clever new watchword, "Trade, Not Aid," whose catchiness could not conceal its mean spirit. In fact, there were few offers of better terms of trade. The United States and Europe stubbornly remained closed to the kinds of simple industrial products, like textiles, that classical economic theory says undeveloped countries should develop as the first rung in their climb out of poverty. Instead, in the guise of charity, the West was dumping cheap used clothes on African countries, badly undercutting local attempts to develop viable textile industries. The same was often true of food "assistance," with surplus American supplies of everything from grain to butter knocking the bottom out of African markets.

Without substantial bilateral assistance, Mali's leaders, like the leaders of all of Africa's other new democracies, were sent rapping on the doors of the Iffys, begging bowls in hand, and forced to swallow their economic medicine, which consisted of little more than austerity packages. Western powers, led by the United States, have always pretended that these programs promote economic growth and development, but those governments would be very hard pressed to prove it, which perhaps is why they have never bothered trying to. In this game, compliance with the prescribed treatment trumped everything else— even the survival of the patient.

Wherever I went in Bamako, ordinary people reminded me that the national debt, assumed during thirty years of Western-supported dictatorship, had surpassed the meager gross national product. Why, they often asked, did Washington and Paris cluck approvingly about Mali's political evolution, and then withhold the kind of sweeping debt forgiveness and other financial assistance the country desperately needed in order to dramatically improve its circumstances?

"We service our foreign debt on time every month, never missing a penny, and all the time, the people are getting poorer and poorer," said Amadou Toumani Touré,* the founder of Malian democracy. "For years and years, the West supported dictatorships like the one we had here for its own strategic reasons. Now that we are stuck, struggling with the enormous burden of the debts the dictators left behind, it seems that nobody is interested in considering the responsibility the West shares for our situation."

Such feelings of abandonment and despair were not Mali's alone. The misfortune of Africa's newly pluralistic countries like Congo-Brazzaville, Benin, Zambia and Niger was to have had their democratic moment at the very same time that communism was collapsing in Eastern Europe. Timing is everything. Now the West rushed in financial and political support to foster new democracies in Europe, and Africa drew nothing more than a long, indifferent shrug.

In the months after the fall of the Berlin wall, I occasionally tried to persuade colleagues in the press to cast the changes under way in Africa in the same epochal light that Europe was now bathing in. Africa's dictators had been supported for decades by East and West, and were often handpicked by outside powers. Their misrule had placed the continent in the deep hole it now found itself in, not some congenital incapacity for modern governance, as decades of shallow analyses about Big Men and "ancient tribal animosities" often insinuated.

*Touré was elected president of Mali in May 2002, succeeding Alpha Oumar Konaré.

Amid talk of a "peace dividend" at the end of the Cold War, I argued that the West had every bit as much of a moral obligation to try to undo some of the damage we had wrought in Africa as it did to help the Eastern Europeans. Needless to say, my arguments were ignored.

A senior editor I knew, a former Africa correspondent who had subsequently worked in Eastern Europe, told me bluntly that my ideas were a pipe dream. "Come on, Howard, we are talking about Africa, not real countries," he said. And with that, I was reminded that the roots of Africa's dilemma were far deeper than the mere fact that its democratic revolution was happening simultaneously with Europe's. Indeed, Africa's misfortune, where the West is concerned, has always been much deeper. How else to explain the ability of Europeans to rationalize the centuries-long slave trade, decades of forced labor for rubber and cotton, colonization on the fly and finally their abandonment of the continent to the very tyrants Africans were struggling to throw off? The answer lies partly in the fact that for Europeans, Africa has always been an irresistible "other." This may sound like a tautology, but that does nothing to diminish its truth. Like the indelible taint of original sin, the problem with Africa in the minds of Westerners is that it is Africa.

During an October 1996 visit to Mali by Warren Christopher, Clinton's secretary of state, I asked Christopher's top deputy for Africa, George Moose, why America had become so much less generous toward the new democracies than it had been toward the old dictatorships. Moose, an African-American whose tepid advocacy on behalf of the continent was typical of the few high-level blacks one found in the State Department, offered no apologies. "Virtue is its own reward," he told me unsmilingly.

It was a typical March day in Bamako, meaning incandescently hot. A small dune's worth of fine Sahara sand was borne on each feeble breeze, giving the sky the consistency of runny, cream-based soup. The sun's power was relentless, though, and it not only shone through the atmospheric sea of dust, it positively irradiated the city, making even late afternoon, when the heat is expected to abate in most climes, bleakly suffocating.

My taxi creaked slowly all the way up the long, gentle ascent of Koulouba, *la colline du pouvoir,* or the hill of power, as one of the five hills that rise above the city is known. I had taken Boubèye's warning about punctuality a bit too seriously, reaching the presidential palace almost twenty minutes early. Having time to kill, I asked the driver to park in the comforting shade of an acacia tree, and I listened to my little Sony shortwave.

Eventually, Boubèye emerged. He conducted me through the palace's cool white hallways and up a flight of stairs, past a huge wall-mounted map of Mali and, finally, into the office of the president.

The man who greeted me was tall and dressed splendidly in a voluminous, dark green boubou, but somehow he seemed shrunken and unmoored in his cavernous office, with its hand-me-down 1960s décor. Konaré's three years as head of state had been anything but a picnic. He wore something of a look of disappointment, frustration mingled with defensiveness, as he sat down to discuss African democracy with what seemed like a slightly forced casual "Mon ami French, comment vas-tu?"—using the familiar, not the formal, pronoun—spoken in his ever-hoarse basso.

He spoke like a battlefield commander reporting to headquarters about the tightening grip of a siege. "I am confronted with problems everywhere I look," he said grimly. "For the last two years, all I've been able to do is play fireman. Everywhere I look, there is a crisis."

The catalogue of troubles began with the low-level rebellion by the semi-nomadic Tuareg ethnic group in the north of the country, where the arid savannah of Mali's center gives way to the infinite dunes of the Sahara. Locusts had begun to hatch in the millet fields that hug the Niger River along its lazy arc northward, threatening the food supply and reviving fears of another great infestation, like the one that devastated the Sahel in the mid-1980s. The government was having trouble meeting its payroll. And lately, there had been signs of restiveness among the country's soldiers, who lived among the people in towns all over Mali; the government could not afford to billet them properly in barracks.

Konaré complained bitterly, too, about the opposition that he had once promoted. In his eyes, they were trying to manipulate the soldiers in the hopes of fomenting a coup. "I am practically in the position of the driver who must keep swerving to avoid running people over," he said. "I am trying to move the country forward, but the more I try to avoid colliding with the opposition, the more they throw themselves in my path. They pretend to act out of principle. They resemble crazy people, for whom power is everything."

No matter how difficult they had made life for him, though, Konaré distinguished himself by resisting the temptation to crush his antagonists, in the manner of so many other African leaders. "I have no illusions about the difficulties implicit in governing democratically, but there are no exemptions from the effort required to build pluralism," he said, speaking from the heart, but in the slightly wooden tongue he had developed as a student in the Eastern Bloc.

Rare for an African head of state, Konaré was also willing to openly criticize his presidential peers, people like Museveni, who had no patience for democracy. He did so in order to chide the West for its hypocrisy in Africa, and in the hopes of somehow persuading the rich world to reconsider the way it engages the continent. "I have lots of respect for Museveni, but I am not sure what value the Museveni experience will have for Uganda after Museveni is gone," he said in a carefully measured dig. "I am quite certain, though, that the experience of pluralism that we are living today will survive Konaré. And if I am correct, Mali will be a lot better off because of that."

Whatever Konaré's criticisms of African authoritarianism, though, his greatest disappointments involved the West. "They once spoke of providing a premium to assist young democracies, but we haven't seen anything remotely like that," he said, slumping low in his leather armchair. "Based on the patterns we have seen, it is not so difficult to predict the behavior of the aid givers. Rather than help us now, they will wait until the crickets have finished off our crops, and then they will send us food. They have promised to help finance a new power plant to replace the one that we have now, which is broken half the time. But they say the money won't be available for three more years.

"Three years might not seem like a very long time to people dressed in expensive suits who sit around conference tables and discuss the fortunes of countries like ours, but for Malians, three years makes all the difference in the world. The price of just one of the expensive airplanes that your country is always buying for its military could make a huge difference to Mali.

"Half of my population is unemployed. Democracy must be able to deliver some material progress in their lives, and to give them hope for a better future."

Hope still eluded the official statistics in Mali, as Konaré was painfully aware. Democracy had clearly not made the people appreciably richer in any measurable material terms—at least not yet. But like any people who have won their own independence through revolution or struggle, rather than having it simply granted to them, Malians exuded a feeling of ownership of their democracy. It was their baby, and while some people could already be heard to groan that the politicians of the capital were caught up in an Athenian fantasy, divorced from the everyday reality of the country's abject poverty, even among the most hard-bitten skeptics there was pride in the fact that the country's system was not a gift from any other quarter.

The living connection that Malians felt with their past was just as critical. "Our people have produced great empires," Konaré told me in parting. "Djenné and Timbuktu are there for all to see. People who know their own history, as we Malians do, develop a strong personality. That, more than anything else, is why I am confident in our struggle for democracy."

In sharp contrast to the Malian experience, for most Africans colonization had obliterated memories of self-government and cultural achievement alike. In places like Zaire and Nigeria, huge, populous countries that should have been the crossroads and anchors to entire regions, the confusion sown by arbitrary borders, by the abrupt and haphazard imposition of alien political systems, by deliberate Western destabilization and finally by the economic turmoil that logically ensued, had further undone any sense of hope or self-determination. The hasty amalgamations left behind by colonialism rendered the citizens of "independent" countries like these just as alienated from their governments and from their past as black America's urban underclass, and with similarly crippling consequences.

With a tolerant form of Islam nearly universal, and a dominant African lingua franca—Bambara—Mali, though, had become one of a select group of African countries that had succeeded in cobbling together its own cultural space, independent of Europe's colonial intrusion. And with the exception of the northern Tuareg, and a few other small minorities that hewed closer to the Arab-speaking Maghreb, Mali's ancient architectural treasures, still largely preserved in the country's arid vastness like dinosaur bones in the desert, remained a source of psychic strength for all its citizens.

Eager to see for myself what Konaré was talking about, I, together with Robert, drove to Djenné, setting out north along the same narrow strip of highway I had taken years before to Mopti. A few minutes after crossing the bridge that leads from Bamako's administrative heart to open countryside, the city vanished from view, as suddenly as the popping of a flash bulb. The immediate signs of change since my first, memorable visit to Mali were few, save for the expansion of the *bidonvilles*, sprawling squatters' camps that hugged the dusty edge of town like a tattered canopy.

Once we were clear of this wretched sprawl, though, the first thing I noticed was that the roadblocks, so common under the dictatorship, had disappeared. We sped along in our Toyota Land Cruiser on the open, single-lane national highway for what seemed like an eternity, only stopping a couple of times for gas. For hour after hour, the landscape was unrelieved flatness. Occasionally, a village popped up over the horizon, all circular, brown mud-walled houses with peaked thatched roofs that, from their appearance, might have been the inverted caps of some gigantic species of mushroom.

Anthills, baroque stucco structures the height of a tall man, were the only sign of animal life on these scorched plains. But the winner of the evolutionary race in these parts, hands down, appeared to be the giant baobab trees, whose stripped trunks and arthritic branches towered mightily over an emptiness of tortured bushes and dry, rough grasses. The trees mocked the termites with forms even more gnarled than the insects' mounds. They had resisted millennia of bushfires, and the cycles of drought, plague and pestilence that had emptied the Sahel's villages too many times to count meant absolutely nothing to them.

We arrived in Djenné late in the afternoon, and our exhaustion melted away at the sight of the great mosque, whose earthen walls glowed orange in the mellowing sunlight of the town's nearly deserted market square. It was the world's largest earthen structure, and although I had often seen pictures of it since standing in its shadow two decades before, I was floored by the creative genius that went into its design. The mosque wore its skeleton on the outside, like some huge, sculpted insect. Palm-wood pegs protruded outward in a geometric pattern of scaffolding so neat and regular that its function, which was to allow maintenance men to clamber up its sides every spring to spackle the walls with fresh mud, had been harnessed in the creation of extraordinary form.

At the summit of the rectangular structure, serrated panels with spiky peaks reminded me of the wooden Scripture boards carried around by young Islamic students, or *talibé*, to help memorize their prayers, which were written in Arabic. Three massive towers rose up from the facade, peaking into spires, with the wooden pegs projecting outward here, too, almost all the way to the top, lending the building the appearance of a proper mosque. Each of these peaks was capped with an ostrich egg, a symbol of fertility and purity.

The sight of the mosque brought to mind a dinner I had many years before in El Salvador, in a gathering of reporters and UN officials. After a couple of drinks, a colleague began to boast about his travels to India, Nepal and Tibet, and then sneered upon hearing that I was about to be assigned to West Africa.

"Has Africa ever produced anything memorable?" he asked. "Most cultures distinguish themselves through architecture. Have Africans ever produced anything more than mud huts?"

As the only African-American in the crowd, the comments came not just as an affront to the land of my ancestors and of my wife and children, but as a direct personal assault as well. But as feelings of resentment welled up inside, I was momentarily at a loss for a reply, and I let the conversation drift in another direction, after only a mild rebuke about his ignorance.

As I stood before the giant mosque, the shame I had felt at not answering this challenge more forcefully was replaced by a feeling of pity and anger at the arrogance of a Western world that has always denigrated Africa, ignoring its accomplishments and constantly emphasizing its ills. The building before me could comfortably stand comparison with virtually any of the world's great cultural monuments. It was an esthetic jewel, and at the same time, a functional masterpiece, made entirely from locally available materials, which were easily and perpetually renewable. The towering spires cleverly concealed ventilation ducts that carried away hot air. Its walls, sixteen to eighteen inches thick, depending on their height, absorbed the sun's blistering heat only gradually, keeping the interior cool by day and comfortably warm even on the chilliest of nights during the harmattan, or cool season.

Mali had its own cathedral at Lourdes, its own Taj Mahal on the Niger, a Pentagon made entirely of mud bricks, and yet the outside world failed to take notice of the very existence of this fantastic building. What is even more remarkable, I learned later, is that this great mosque is perhaps the least impressive of the three religious structures that have stood in the heart of this ancient city.

Koi Kunboro, a rich sultan who converted to Islam, created the first great mosque here in 1240 by converting his palace into a place of worship, but an early-nineteenth-century ruler deemed the structure too sumptuous, and built an entirely new mosque in its place in the 1830s. His name figures almost nowhere in textbooks, or in the annals of architecture, but a local master builder, Ismaïla Traoré, who was head of Djenné's guild of masons, designed the present mosque early in the French colonial period, at the beginning of the twentieth century.

The secret of this city's greatness, like the capitals of all of Mali's fabled ancient kingdoms, lay, in large part, in its location. Djenné sat astride a huge inland delta, nestled between the converging flows of the Niger and Bani Rivers. Its floodplains assured a steady supply of fish and abundant crops. Moreover, much like the cliffs of the Dogon to the northeast, the rivers and surrounding marshland shielded the population from easy attack by the invaders who had swept these plains through the centuries. For Djenné's settlers, as for those of Timbuktu, location was everything. The great fortunes that were amassed by individuals in each city were derived from their roles as brokers and middlemen in an ancient caravan trade of gold and slaves marched up from the coastal forests to the south, and salt and metalwares borne southward by camels from the Maghreb and Arabia.

What had drawn me back to Djenné was the work of Susan and Roderick McIntosh, two Rice University archaeologists who had begun excavating a site adjacent to modern Djenné that had distinguished itself with the title of sub-Saharan Africa's oldest city. Extensive excavations at the site had shown that the long-lost original settlement, known as Djenné-Jeno, was inhabited 250 years before Christ and mysteriously abandoned nearly a century before Columbus set out on his first voyage.

Roderick McIntosh had telephoned me in Abidjan with something close to panic in his voice to alert me to the ongoing plundering of long-buried artifacts from the ancient city. "What is happening is a looting of history on a scale not seen in Africa since Napoleon's armies looted Egypt," he said. He then gave me the names of several Malian archaeologists with whom he had worked for years, to act as my guides at the site.

One of the Malian scientists, Boubacar Diaby, met us in the unremarkable "modern" town of Djenné, a scorching, dusty place without electricity or running water, where tailors work their machines by pedal in the shade of mango trees, goats troop freely through the streets, bleating as they go, and the vehicular traffic is mostly two-wheeled, whether bicycle or scooter.

As we approached the site, what I could see of Djenné-Jeno above ground was little more than a low, mile-long mound that rose tear-shaped from the delta. But when we crossed the water and began to tread the mound itself, the history began to come alive, almost literally, in the crunching of a million shards of clay underfoot. These were fragments of a civilization that had created black Africa's first known city, a great walled agglomeration where perhaps twenty thousand people lived in the year 1000—bits and pieces from a broken figurine here, pieces of earthen burial jars there, iron fishing hooks, fragments of spears, pieces of bone from both humans and their domesticated animals.

Here and there, one could see eroded mud bricks, the traces of a massive wall twelve feet high and ten feet thick that had once surrounded the entire site. The McIntoshes and their team had dug twenty feet deep into the clay-bearing soil to meticulously document the story of Djenné-Jeno, proving that its inhabitants' ironworking technology, skill with pottery and finesse in crafting gold ornaments, which surpassed even the best of Bamako's contemporary jewelry makers, all predated contact with Arabic-speaking people of North Africa by four hundred years.

Djenné-Jeno's elite lived in spacious, rectangular mud-brick houses, whose design has been carried forward largely intact to the present day, as have sophisticated burial rites and ancestor-worshipping practices, at least among a handful of this region's smaller ethnic groups. Here was the past evoked so proudly by President Konaré—who had worked this site himself with the McIntoshes years before. In a world where the achievements of Africans get scant recognition, Djenné-Jeno's archaeological treasures resonate with the message that the people of this continent are capable of great things, and indeed always have been.

This city of gold traders, fishermen and farmers of the heavily silted Niger River delta was no mere spin-off from the cultures of the Maghreb, as many European historians once claimed, in a stroke depriving sub-Saharan Africans of credit for any genius of their own. Nor does it seem to have had any links with Egyptian civilization, as some Afrocentric academics have tried to claim, as part of a broader and longstanding effort to tie ancient Egypt together with other parts of the continent to the south. The truth is far more prosaic, and yet for Malians and for other West Africans who knew and understood it, potentially far more inspiring. A great culture had sprung up here locally, thriving for sixteen centuries before succumbing to a series of successor cultures that were driven by a powerful religious import, Islam.

Listening to the terrible crunching sound of the colored shards of clay underfoot as we surveyed the site, though, I realized there was also an awful irony at work here. Mali, one of the world's poorest countries, had sacrificed precious budgetary funds for more than fifteen years to help make this excavation possible. With so few means at its disposal for conservation, though, it was powerless to stop the pillagers and the steady erosion, which were working in unholy tandem to ravage the mound, along with dozens of satellite sites in the surrounding delta.

"There is no sign of fire, and there is no hint of war to explain why Djenné-Jeno suddenly died out," my guide, Diaby, told me. "It appears as if a devastating epidemic swept through the area and wiped every-one out. Today, you could say that the pillagers are the city's second great epidemic."

Vultures lurked on the few scrubby acacia trees that dotted the sur-rounding floodplain, creatures either already sated or, as seemed more likely, too lazy to bother to scavenge in the stifling afternoon heat. Here and there, peasants plied the river in their long pirogues. In the distance, a huge herd of cattle advanced slowly, pulling away at the sparse cover of fresh shoots of grass.

With each step, my tour with Diaby was turning into a seminar on the organized crime of archaeological theft, and at bottom, it all seemed remarkably similar to the diamond racket that was ravaging economies in Zaire, Angola, Guinea, Sierra Leone and Liberia, next door. In the badlands of the Malian Sahel, the rhythms of life have always been determined by the angle of the sun in the sky, and digging for artifacts, or what every villager in these parts called in French *les antiquités*, was no different.

With temperatures rising to 110 degrees or higher by early after-noon, Diaby told me, the sound of digging echoes across the flood-plains only during the early pre-dawn hours, when many people are still asleep. "The only thing that saves us here is that the thieves rarely dig more than two feet deep," he said. "The pillagers know lots of sites that we haven't discovered yet. In order to properly excavate them, though, you have to go down at least six meters [twenty feet].

"Many years of drought have made the people of this region extremely poor, and it is their pauperization that poses the greatest danger to these objects," Diaby said, invoking a combination that was basic to almost every African crisis: the misery of the locals and the greed of powerful outsiders. "As soon as Djenné's discovery was announced, the galleries and museums in Europe were paying agents to try to find them Djenné artifacts," he said ruefully. "That's what set off the digging, and it won't stop until the market is glutted with delta objects, and the interest shifts elsewhere."

Diaby was far more perceptive about the cultural complexities and consequences than his initial broadside against foreign dealers suggested. "The collectors will tell you that they are preserving the items, and helping spread knowledge and appreciation of our culture. But the very manner of procurement is fueling a market that feeds a whole underworld of looters who destroy the sites and pay pennies to the diggers.

"They tell us that we don't have any place to keep these artifacts in Mali. But if they have a real desire for promotion and preservation, let them come here and help us create a museum and educate our people. Instead, they collect the objects fraudulently, and their museums and galleries become laundering sites for the cultural products of our region. Honestly speaking, a few collectors may be profiting, but it is doing nothing but harm for Africa, and for Mali."

Poverty alone, Diaby knew, could not explain the ongoing rape at Djenné-Jeno. Indeed, with his mention of education, he had put his finger on another key to the problem, indeed to many of Africa's problems. Old, cracked pottery and ancient items of worship like figurines had no meaning and little intrinsic value to the poor farmers and herdsmen of this area. Most of them had no concept of the interest or value such items could hold for white people in faraway Paris or New York, either. To them it was all a little strange, but since digging for dusty bric-a-brac provided a means to survive, they were happy to dig. The only formal schooling that most of the men in these parts had received was in the bare little Islamic classrooms where, as boys, imams had taught them Koranic prayer.

Islam began to spread through this part of Mali in the eleventh century, and with it came a harsh rejection of ancestor worship, the use of masks and a rich tradition of other figurative art. Like Christianity, which arrived in West Africa much later, the new religious import meant a huge infusion of learning and, by implication, something we usually agree to call progress. But acceptance of the new faith came at a steep cost: cultural self-renunciation.

President Konaré's government had taken pains to plaster walls in towns and villages throughout the region with anti-pillaging posters. But to a thoroughly Islamicized population, moreover one that had recently lived through severe droughts and famine, and on top of that was illiterate, the effort was noble but ultimately meaningless. "To you it may seem paradoxical, but the people here don't feel the same connection to this history that the elites of Bamako, or maybe even an intellectual in Abidjan, does," said Diaby. "They have been taught to scorn their own art, and to revile their own culture. Saving Djenné-Jeno will require a lot of education. Museums must be built right here, so that tourists can come, and jobs can be created, and people can see for themselves how highly their own culture is valued."

CHAPTER NINE

Tough Love

The rains in Liberia had stopped as if on cue late one morning near the end of January 1996, and the sun was so strong that it required only a smidgen of patience to watch the puddles burn off. Madeleine Albright, Washington's representative to the United Nations, was due to touch down in a couple of hours, and even the weather had decided that it had better cooperate, clearing the skies for her Boeing 737. Liberians had long been accustomed to thinking of America as their all-powerful but, to them, inexplicably disinterested patron, and the disappearance of the clouds came like celestial reconfirmation.

Albright would be the highest-ranking American official to visit Liberia since George Shultz's visit eleven years earlier, and for anyone who still remembered, the precedent alone might have been grounds for concern. Like Shultz before her, Albright had chosen a sensitive time to visit. Against all odds, the country's main warlords had come together to form a transitional Council of State. Almost miraculously, fighting had ceased five months before, and there was serious talk of elections for the first time in recent memory. All of this would require money, however, and Liberia being America's West African stepchild, the international community was waiting to see what form Washington's commitment would take.

The Clinton administration had labored to keep Liberia's problems off the radar screen, and given the depressing grab bag of mediocre politicians and outright thugs who kept the country's pot boiling, it is certainly not hard to understand why Liberia was thought of as a headache when it was thought of at all. There were cheaper, faster and more secure ways for the world's most powerful country to transmit its intelligence and diplomatic messages, and just as surely as endless acres of oozing trees had become outmoded by the discovery of cheaper synthetic ways to make rubber, Liberia's antenna farms were now technological relics of the pre–global positioning satellite and pre-Internet past.

The ceasefire that greeted Albright in Monrovia interrupted what had easily been, on a per capita basis, one of Africa's most horrible civil wars. No fewer than 150,000 of the 2.6 million Liberians had died during seven years of mayhem. A comparable toll for the United States would be the loss of nearly 21 million citizens. Most of Liberia's survivors had been turned into internal refugees by the recurrent waves of fighting. In the capital there were no jobs, no electricity and no running water. After countless attempts to find a political solution to the conflict, Liberia's fighting had degenerated into a massive and chaotic asset grab, with each militia stripping from the land whatever of value it could get. And yet this time, somehow, West African diplomats had pulled out of their hats an agreement involving the leading warlords, which they believed just might hold.

But the country's neighbors, and Liberians themselves, knew that if the outside world did not inject emergency funds into the country, the fragile peace would not last. More than anything else, money was needed to help the corrupt yet indispensable 8,000-man West African peacekeeping force, ECOMOG, deploy throughout the heavily forested interior. Running a close second was funding for disarmament and job training for the thousands of boy soldiers who had the run of the countryside, and were now streaming into Monrovia. Without it there was certain to be another explosion, only the timing of which was in doubt.

Washington and its European partners were preoccupied with the crisis in Bosnia, though, and scarcely seemed concerned with what diplomats thought of as a messy, two-bit African tragedy. The United Nations was spending $25 million every week on peacekeeping in Bosnia in 1996, $4 million more than it spent in Liberia in the entire year. "It took the Americans one week to raise $1.8 billion for Bosnia,"

Victor Gbeho told me on the eve of the Albright visit. He was a senior Ghanaian diplomat in Liberia on behalf of the West African Economic Community, which had first fielded ECOMOG in August 1990. "If I were paranoid, I would say the Westerners' delays that we are always facing here are due to one simple fact: This is Africa."

For her curious little whistle-stop tour of Africa, Albright had chosen as destinations Liberia, Rwanda and Angola—all countries that figured squarely atop any list of places where the West in general, and the United States in particular, had failed the continent most spectacularly in the 1990s. Washington's client and ally Jonas Savimbi had kept the Angolan civil war going for sixteen years, using $250 million of American taxpayers' money and American-supplied weapons ferried via Liberia and Mobutu's Zaire, right next door, to thoroughly gut the country and leave a half million dead.

America's ostensible aim had been to force a Marxist government to hold democratic elections, which Savimbi was expected to win. When Savimbi was defeated at the polls in 1992, however, he began fighting yet again. The Clinton administration, feeling no sense of obligation to Savimbi or to a country that had hitherto been primarily the Republicans' obsession, simply turned its back on Angola, agreeing not to speak about the unspeakable in ways that only the truly powerful of the world can. Like the retouched May Day photos of old from the Soviet Union, where airbrushes magically lifted disgraced leaders from the reviewing-stand lineup, making them officially forgotten, the sacrifice of Angola on the altar of the Cold War would simply disappear from the news. Clinton decided to spend as little as possible on UN peacekeeping operations there, and the war America had helped create sputtered on for a full decade more, until Savimbi himself was killed in an ambush by the Angolan army in 2002.

By comparison to Liberia, the first stop on Albright's tour, Rwanda and Angola were both fresh tragedies. Liberia was a place where Washington's record of betrayal and disregard was already a depressing 174-year-old tale of recidivism, and yet no amount of bitter history could shake the Liberians' sweet and entirely genuine image of themselves as America's wards. The sentiment was a holdover from the very establishment of the country in 1822.

History had a way of serving up reminders to Liberians that their love of all things American was never meant to be requited. There had been the scandalously cheap price Firestone had paid for its plantations. There had been the singling out of the country by the League of Nations for sanctions over the slavelike work conditions, although European powers were using forced labor to grow cotton, rubber and cocoa all over the continent. Of much more recent note for most Liberians, though, was America's abandonment of the country in the early stages of its civil war, in June 1990.

Boy soldiers loyal to Charles Taylor were advancing on the city from one direction. What was worse, Taylor's insurrection, although it was not yet six months old, had already splintered, producing an even more fearsome force, a rival band of fighters from the National Patriotic Front led by an erratic, self-proclaimed field marshal named Prince Yormie Johnson, who were rushing toward the capital from another direction.

President Doe's peculiar means of fiddling while Rome burned had been to smoke marijuana and play checkers all day while barricaded in the executive mansion with several hundred loyalists from his Krahn ethnic group. When Johnson's irregulars reached the city, though, he roused himself from his stupor to order a merciless bout of ethnic cleansing against the Mano and Gio peoples, who he deemed were the rebels' main supporters. Doe, of course, was to be assassinated by Johnson's fighters in September 1990.

Liberia's horrors actually prefigured the atrocities that were to come in Rwanda, and America's instincts were identical in both cases. While churches full of huddling people were becoming scenes of unimaginable slaughter, 2,500 United States Marines who were part of a task force along with six navy vessels steaming off the capital's shore swooped into Monrovia to selectively evacuate the city's American residents, along with other Westerners and Lebanese traders. Liberians were left to their own devices, just as Rwandans would be four years later.

"We deployed a large marine amphibious force near Liberia to evacuate U.S. citizens, an operation accomplished with great efficiency," Herman Cohen, an assistant secretary of state for African affairs during the presidency of George H. W. Bush, told the journalist Bill Berkeley, speaking with deep regret, albeit years later. "A modest intervention . . . could have avoided the prolonged conflict." Cohen confessed, however, that throughout 1990 he had never once managed to speak to the president about the Liberian crisis.

On the ground in Liberia, American officials rejected all requests to provide protection for the skeleton staff that had managed to keep the city's main hospital functioning. In Washington, Richard Boucher, the State Department spokesperson, announced matter-of-factly in a statement read to reporters that "the U.S. military has no role to play in this conflict." "Somewhere along the way," an official told the *Washington Post* reporter in Liberia, "we just decided we weren't going to get involved. Period. My impression is that Washington and Congress are absolutely fed up with Liberia."

It did not take long for Liberians to understand that Madeleine Albright had not come bearing much of anything new. The new American dispensation that Liberians dreamed of was not in the offing, not even any aid for a transitional government desperate to make its cease-fire hold. What the American diplomat did deliver was the kind of bullish tough-love speech that was her trademark, and boiled down to its essence, it said that Liberians should help themselves first, and only then could American help materialize.

The weather may have bowed to an Imperial America, but in West Africa, Albright had decided to hold her news conference within the confines of tiny Spriggs Payne airfield, where the usual scrum of pickpockets, touts and sleazy immigration officials gave way to a pushy, sweaty crowd of journalists, nervous State Department security agents and Nigerian soldiers wielding big automatic rifles. America might have its high-flying rhetoric about being the indispensable nation, but on Liberian soil day-to-day survival depended upon Nigeria. Reinforcing this notion none too subtly, a Nigerian airlift into Monrovia of fresh soldiers and supplies continued throughout Albright's brief press conference, forcing the usually overpowering Albright to shout to be heard over the heavy drone of the Nigerian C-130s.

In her speech and in her brief give-and-take with the press, Albright had unself-consciously laid bare the fault lines that undermined American policy toward West Africa. The region supplied an important and growing share of American oil imports. U.S. trade with the region surpassed trade with all of the countries of the former Soviet Union combined. And millions of Americans traced their ancestry to the region. Yet the fervently held bottom line, one that resounded throughout her comments, was that America had no vital or strategic interests in the region.

The United States' top priority in Liberia was to avoid any direct involvement in the country's crises, and with the threat of an explosion ever present, it could pull this off only through moral compromises so ugly that they were better kept out of view. Washington rightly abhorred the Nigerian dictator Sani Abacha, but desperately needed his country to keep the lid on war-wracked Liberia and Sierra Leone. In Nigeria most citizens lacked electricity or safe drinking water, yet the country was propping up ECOMOG in these two countries at the reported cost of $10 million per month. Moreover, Nigeria was paying for relative peace in a currency that the United States had been unwilling to countenance in Africa since the 1993 debacle in Somalia: the lives of its soldiers.

Extending ECOMOG's writ beyond Monrovia's modest perimeter, however, required heavy trucks and communications gear, help with things like airlifts and spare parts, and in such areas America was indeed indispensable. The only consistent feature of Washington's policy toward Nigeria, whether we were censoring the country for its grave human rights abuses or cooperating in places like Liberia, however, was the emphasis on doing things cheaply. The United States had shown no stomach for serious human rights sanctions for fear of hurting American oil supplies or interests. At the same time, exhibiting a kind of hypocritical prudishness for which Liberians would pay the bill in lives lost, Washington was unwilling to work openly with Nigeria in regional peacekeeping efforts, even when they were well intended.

From all evidence, America's behavior was driven by appearances, not principle, and what counted most to the Africa policymakers was to avoid being seen to be cooperating with the Abacha regime. So in Liberia, a country desperately in need of international support for peacekeeping, the State Department devised a stingy bureaucratic solution that would satisfy no one. The idea was to hire American private contractors to perform essential tasks for ECOMOG, rather than to allow army-to-army cooperation with Nigeria's military regime. Soon, Americans were flooding the streets of Monrovia, driving huge trucks laden with food aid and other supplies, and building the odd concrete pillboxes that bored-looking ECOMOG soldiers would man at every major intersection.

Liberia was a country flat on its back, with unemployment high beyond measure and treasury reserves too meager to warrant counting. Washington's policy, though, would see to it that almost no jobs were created and that negligible funds were injected into the economy. For the cash-strapped Liberian Council of State, there was no alternative source of funds to the wildcat mining and marauding of the country-side that had been the main feature of the civil war in the first place. Those who knew the country best, from the senior Nigerian officials to the American ambassador, William B. Milam, understood implicitly that this situation could not hold. With occasional skirmishes in the bush over rich diamond fields, and lots of prickly jockeying for posi-tion among the warlords in the capital, it was only a question of time before Liberia's unstable concoction of an interim government would explode.

None of this dampened Albright's blustery oratory, though, as she gamely shouted to be heard over the droning engines of Nigeria's huge, camouflage-painted transport planes. "I can confirm to you that the president and his advisors are deeply committed to the future of this country and its people," she said. "The United States should take a risk for peace when we have the means to make a difference. The civil war is your war. The peace of Abuja is your peace. Either you take the courageous steps needed to secure it now or Liberia will again experi-ence tragedy. The future is yours alone to determine."

The next time I witnessed an American official holding forth in Liberia was barely three months later. Without warning, fierce fight-ing broke out in Monrovia over Easter weekend, when a large squad of men loyal to Charles Taylor had been sent to arrest his most voluble rival, Roosevelt Johnson, or better yet, to kill him should he resist. The undisputed kingpin of Liberia's warlords clearly thought he was apply-ing overwhelming force, but Johnson, a stubby, fast-talking man endowed with sleepy eyes and a preternatural cockiness, was blessed with another attribute that Taylor had not reckoned with: the kind of eel-like slipperiness in tight spots that feeds myths throughout this region about supernatural powers.

The tensions between the two men had been mounting powerfully for weeks, and after the civil war's seven years of attrition, Johnson was just about the only person left in Liberia who dared to match Taylor boast for boast and threat for threat. Although there was nothing in his background to recommend him for the title, Johnson had won a seat as minister for reconstruction in the country's volatile unity government. With members of his Krahn ethnic group approaching him constantly to solicit jobs that he had no power to grant, Johnson spent his days fuming in his third-floor walk-up office over not having been named one of Taylor's co-presidents on the Council of State. Still, Johnson compensated for his limited book knowledge with rare energy and cunning, and ever since his men attacked an ECOMOG position near Tubmanville earlier in the year, taking over the nearby diamond mines, his star had been rising among the idle and disgruntled boy soldiers for whom the war had long ceased being a matter of identifiable causes.

Johnson's men had been expecting an attack from Taylor's militia that Easter weekend and managed to slip out of the neighborhood unscathed. Heading northwest toward downtown Monrovia, they remained undetected by steering clear of the main boulevard that passes in front of the executive mansion and the gutted Foreign Ministry, home to hundreds of squatters. Instead, Johnson led his men stealthily through the narrow, fetid byways until they had wended their way toward their only possible redoubt in the city, the Barclay Training Center, or BTC, the headquarters of the mostly Krahn rump national army left behind by Samuel Doe.

The fog of war blew in on gale-force winds over the next few hours as rumors spread of an ethnic cleansing of the city aimed at eliminating the Krahn. In Monrovia, memories of the final days of Doe's rule, when the president's Krahn kinsmen were hunted down in the street and shot or dismembered, were still fresh. Indeed, Taylor's periodic sacks of the capital had only fed fears of renewed horrors. His two previous sieges had each been called "battles for Monrovia," which gave them more honor than they deserved. They had been horrific affairs, unencumbered by any rules of warfare, with civilians slaughtered, heavy weapons fired at close quarter, and rape and looting on a grand scale. No one could have known that battle number three was beginning in earnest, and that it would be the worst of all, but from the panic that coursed through the streets on this day, it was clear that no one was taking any chances.

It is said that forest fires start because of an abundance of dry brush lying around beneath the canopy. When the conditions are right, all it takes is a spark. Monrovia, too, was a blaze waiting to happen, and the fuel that ignited with a boom that day and burned fiercely for days had been blowing in from the countryside like tumbleweed for weeks—boys as young as eight or ten years addicted to drugs and armed with machine guns and rocket launchers. Years of rampaging by child soldiers had picked the countryside bare of everything it had to offer, and they were itching to use the blood feud between Taylor and Johnson as cover to relieve Monrovia's residents of whatever fancy, store-bought goods—or values, as they called stolen merchandise—they could snatch up.

Ever since the Abuja truce had gone into effect, seating their warlord bosses together in uneasy coalition, the boy soldiers, gaunt and hungry-eyed, their skin scabbed and scarred by every manner of wound and parasite, had been steadily filtering into the city to claim some kind of material reward. On my last trip to Liberia, I had spent several days interviewing the raggedy, atrocity-hardened country boys who had begun gathering on street corners, occasionally brandishing their rifles in broad daylight. To a Westerner, Monrovia may not have looked like much of a city, but to these hungry veterans of countless bush skirmishes and village looting raids, it must have looked like a huge, open-air shopping mall.

One of the boys I met, a gangly fifteen-year-old named Lawrence Moore, had forlorn eyes and gestures, full of flinches and false starts that bespoke both pain and guilt in quantities far beyond my grasp. Tentatively, he began telling me his story downtown on the median strip of Broad Street, where he had been loitering aimlessly on a hot Saturday morning. Lawrence's dream, now that he had reached Monrovia, was to work in Charles Taylor's personal entourage. Only those "lucky" few, he explained, could be sure of receiving any kind of payment at all, and it was usually in rice, not cash.

Lawrence had grown up near Kakata, a forgotten little town on the edge of the Firestone estate, and when he was eleven or twelve—he wasn't too sure—he ran off to join the infamous Small Boys Unit (SBU) of Taylor's Patriotic Front, following in the wake of an older brother and lots of other boys his age. There had been a few weeks of rudimentary training, and then, suddenly, it wasn't a fun child's game anymore. Lawrence said he had received a bullet wound to his foot in his very first firefight. Taylor's recruitment and indoctrination of young boy soldiers had rested on a few psychological keys, replacing the often missing father in the fighters' lives with a tough, mature commander, someone stern but caring, and Taylor himself loomed atop this guerrilla pyramid scheme as the *über*-father figure. Indeed, the boys were encouraged to call him Pappy, and most of them eagerly complied.

Lawrence's attachment to the Patriotic Front was sealed when he was evacuated from the front and treated in a bush clinic, given better care than he had ever known before and allowed to recover fully before being sent back into action. For most boys, though, other balms were required, and they were kept loyal and inoculated against fear through the copious supplies of drugs. "They were always feeding us opium, ganja and crack," Lawrence told me. "At first, I didn't want to smoke, but there was no way that you could refuse. We were forced to smoke those things, and after a while there was no way you could stop."

Soon enough, devotion to Pappy and the craving and fury induced by drugs had become life's two remaining motivations. "While we were fighting, there was plenty of food for all of us, there was opium and there was medicine if we got sick," Lawrence said. "When we weren't fighting, we had to fend for ourselves. So all we wanted to do was fight."

On two occasions, Lawrence said, his company was ordered to overrun his own village, and only much later did he bother to return to see whether his mother was alive and help move her to a safer place. "Our job was killing, and I've killed a lot of people . . . *plenty*," he added, stretching the word out for emphasis, like an exclamation point, as Liberians often did. "I've had lots of friends die right in front of my eyes, but I never felt bad. I said to myself, this is what war is, so I never stopped."

The battles that raged back and forth across the Liberian country-side became hallucinogenic blurs, of kids sky-high on drugs convinced they were shielded by amulets against enemy bullets, and getting ripped to shreds all the while. Fronts were ill defined and ground was rarely held for long, unless, that is, diamonds or iron ore or another rich source of a fungible commodity was at hand. For the boy soldiers, it was not readily apparent, but for their commanders, and for the war-lords whose groups had splintered into a score of factions, this was a war of spoils, and spoils alone.

Lawrence eventually tired of the war, and had come to detest the killing. Nowadays, he longed for his mother and sister, and as he weaned himself from the drugs during the recent ceasefire, he had begun to feel a crushing sense of remorse about his past. He had no notion of political science and could not read well enough to get through a newspaper, not even one of the skimpy and ink-smudged four-page broadsheets that circulated in Monrovia. For him, Pappy was still Pappy, though, and he remained loyal to him; the law of the jungle remained intuitive and natural. As the strongest, most feared and ruthless warlord, Taylor was Liberia's Little Caesar, and the only route to peace that Lawrence could conceive was that the country would render itself unto him. "If Pappy doesn't become president," Lawrence told me in his simple, heavily accented speech, "the situation in Liberia won't never be any good."

I heard the news of the Easter fighting in Monrovia on the BBC, and caught the next flight from Abidjan to Freetown, an even more war-wearied West African city and the capital of Liberia's neighbor, Sierra Leone. It was reported on the radio that the United States was planning yet another evacuation in Liberia, and by the time I got to the Mammy Yoko Hotel, a decrepit though once elegant resort complex built on a sweeping half-moon bay just outside Freetown, hordes of reporters had already gathered there.

I quickly learned that the marines, who had been sent to extract people from Liberia, were reluctantly planning to ferry into the country only a select few of us. Gathered with the other reporters who were to fly into Liberia with the marines, we chartered a rickety helicopter owned by Ukrainian mercenaries to fly us to Lungi, the mildewed, dilapidated airport located across the bay, on the far outskirts of Freetown, where the U.S. evacuation effort was already gearing up.

The Ukrainians had been hired by the Sierra Leone government to do battle against that country's own Taylor-style insurgency. With its thousands of loose rivets, their helicopter gunship sizzled frighteningly throughout our short ride across the bay, and the marines at Lungi watched with bemusement as the Soviet-vintage clunker landed. Later, as we prepared for takeoff in an American Huey, a marine expressed surprise that we would have risked flying in the Ukrainians' metal. "When you get in one of our birds, at least you know that the only thing that can bring you down by surprise is a direct hit," he said.

We were airborne again in a matter of minutes, and with our ears stoppered with plugs against the noise, the best we could do for communication was the hand signals we made in appreciation of the American bird's maneuvers as it swooped and wheeled, hugging the lush coast. We sped east by southeast for nearly two hours, zipping past abandoned lumber mills and mines, and the occasional forlorn village, usually little more than a modest clearing of red earth amid a sea of leafy green. The entire time, gunners peered out the bay doors, ready to reply with their impressively large mounted machine gun, in case anyone fired on us from below.

We landed in a huge open field, across the Mesurado River, a good ways from downtown Monrovia, which we were informed was entirely engulfed in combat and thievery. We were told to duck as we were hustled off the helicopter and quickly herded into a corner behind a high concrete wall.

Directing things on the ground was Ambassador Milam, a diplomat I had met many times before who had always impressed me with his hail-fellow decency. As he ministered busily to groups of people who had gathered here to await their evacuation, though, the relaxed smile that usually played on his open face was replaced with a look of deadly seriousness. The small crowd that had assembled on the grassy field that blistering afternoon contained a sampling of just about all the foreign residents who made up Liberia's heterogeneous international community.

There were doughy American missionaries dressed in clothing that looked almost as if it had been selected for its blandness; the families of the Lebanese traders who had been in this country for generations, running everything from the diamond business to petty commerce; a sprinkling of Greeks and Indians; and a handful of West Africans from Ghana and other nearby countries. Here and there, I could spot a Liberian family who had been allowed onto the field in preparation for evacuation. The diplomats said they were people who had lived in the United States or had some special claim to entry into the country, such as the birth of a child in America, which confers automatic citizenship to the infant. Even amid the crush and chaos, the Liberian families stood out. They had all somehow managed to put on their Sunday best, as if they had mistaken the marines' choppers for the church altar.

To my eyes, the presence of a few families like these only brought into sharper relief the ambiguous morality of the evacuation. The marines were doing their job with typical efficiency and even dignity, but there was no escaping the ugly fact that America was swooping into this country once again to conduct a triage, neglecting precisely those who were least able to fend for themselves. Ordinary Liberians were being relegated to a category of subhuman existence whose intimate workings I had first learned about as a young reporter covering police headquarters in New York. There, I quickly deduced how certain murders were automatically classified as nickel-and-dime cases—"jobs" that required little follow-up by detectives, and by inference, by the press as well. It was another insidious form of triage, and it took only a few days on the assignment to understand that the "garbage" cases almost invariably involved people of color.

When Milam finished attending to the evacuees, he told us that we had to wait until dark before we could fly onward to the American Embassy, where we would be put up, and where the evacuees would be ferried to a ship offshore. The embassy was a large, iron-gated compound located at seaside on a rocky promontory at Mamba Point. Like a good many American embassies in Africa, the physical setting provided for a defensive last stand, and quick escape from the country, if need be. Nonetheless, we had to land at the embassy under cover of darkness, flying in low and observing a total blackout, because Mamba Point had been overrun with militiamen and sobels—the clever neologism for the men who had first ripped Sierra Leone apart, and were now bringing the practice to downtown Monrovia. The soldiers by day, rebels by night in this particular frenzy of gunfire and theft were none other than the Nigerian and Guinean troops of ECOMOG, the dispirited "peacekeepers" whose job it was to preserve Liberia from just this sort of anarchy.

Our Huey came in low over the sea, ten or fifteen yards above the waves that crashed into Mamba Point in ceaseless, neatly spaced sets, and the smell of brine filled our cabin. Our little group of reporters was told that we would have to camp out by the embassy swimming pool. MREs, meals ready to eat, the army's shrink-wrapped rations, were handed out, and a long heavy-duty extension cord was strung to us from a generator that hummed in the distance. The embassy staff told us that we would have power for a couple of hours at best, because of the need to conserve fuel. I slept that night under the stars, poolside, stretched out on a chaise longue carefully enveloped in my mosquito net.

Hearing sounds from the compound and from the surrounding diplomatic enclave, I rose with the first light of dawn. Looking around, I could see that the large grassy grounds of the embassy had been turned into a huge waiting area, where hundreds of people were huddled, hoping for their turn to be flown out of the country.

An embassy officer gave me a tour of the compound. The ambassador's residence, which sat at the low end of the sloping grounds, had been turned into a sniper and machine gunner's nest for the marines, as well as a billet for the soldiers who worked in shifts to protect the perimeter of the compound from penetration or assault. On the second floor, a marine manning a tripod-mounted .50mm machine gun, aimed in the general direction of the Mamba Point Hotel, where I had always stayed, told me that he had already received incoming fire several times during his shift. "It doesn't really worry me too much," he said laconically. "I have faith in my training, and in my equipment. People who shoot at me tend to regret it pretty quickly."

I was led to the main embassy building, a piece of 1960s-era official architecture whose dull but imposing concrete facade would not have been out of place had it been an annex of the State Department. From a second-story roof I watched with another marine machine gunner as a band of rebels looted the nearby UN military observer's residence. One by one, the young fighters clambered out of the building carting off whatever they could carry: photocopier, fax, telex machines, computers. As they loaded up a stolen sedan, one of the fighters briefly waved his rifle at us and gave us the finger. The marine peered through his sight and unlocked the safety on his .50mm. I thought I was about to see an American demonstration of force. The scene was defused in an instant, though, when another rebel shouted from the car for the gunman to jump in, and he obliged. As the car sped away, the photocopier tumbled out of the overloaded trunk and crashed onto the pavement. The looters may not have noticed—their car never slowed down, much less stopped.

Ambassador Milam seemed worried and wanted to talk. Taylor and a rival, Alhaji Kromah, leader of the second-largest militia, had seemingly reached an understanding. They would overrun Roosevelt Johnson and his Krahn holdouts at the Barclay Training Center, and then dissolve the Council of State and simply take over the country. Taylor would be president, and Kromah vice president.

All along, the awkward and unacknowledged coalition between the United States and Nigeria had been working to prevent just such an eventuality. The Nigerian army had first arrived here during Doe's final days, and the West Africa superpower had created ECOMOG to prevent Taylor from shooting his way to power. In many years of trying, Taylor had never managed to beat the Nigerians on the ground, but little by little he had managed to cleverly undermine them. Most of the time this was simply a matter of cutting in ECOMOG's Nigerian commanders on whatever business the multimillionaire warlord was running, whether diamonds, logging, bauxite and iron ore, or cocaine.

The Nigerians had come from a country where corruption was as deeply embedded as any in Africa, and their president, Abacha, had set a particularly flagrant example. ECOMOG's discipline and esprit de corps had been steadily chipped away. Nigeria had received modest donations from the international community to help defray the costs of its operations in Liberia, but Abacha and his top commanders pocketed most of the funds and paid their soldiers a mere fistful of dollars each month. The Nigerians lacked transportation and walkie-talkies. Their rifles were filthy and rusted, and lately many of the men had even taken to selling their bullets to the rebels in order to make ends meet.

When hell broke loose in Monrovia on Easter weekend, the Nigerian peacekeepers made no pretense of carrying out their mandate. Instead, as I saw from the roof of the embassy, with their vehicles piled high with stolen goods coursing through Mamba Point, many Nigerians had wholeheartedly joined the rebels in the looting. When I asked Milam if the marines might have to be called upon to provide order, he shot me a look of pained resignation and answered, "Things would have to get pretty bad before we got involved." Then, a bit cryptically, he added, "There are rumors of a big attack on the BTC, and that could be one such incident. I do know the president [Clinton] has said he wants to do the right thing."

What was bothering the ambassador was not so much the lack of enthusiasm in Washington for any humanitarian intervention. After all, Liberia had been left to stew in its own juices plenty of times before.* It was the failure to do more to prevent things from reaching this point in the first place. "My view is that if we could have mounted some kind of economic program in time, we could have drawn a lot of these boys out of the militias and created some jobs, or started some schools," he said. "Now we are in just an impossible spot, having to

---

*And would be again in 2003, when George W. Bush procrastinated for weeks during fierce fighting in Monrovia, and the attendant humanitarian disaster, over sending U.S. troops to join an international force to secure the peace.

turn away mothers with crying babies wrapped around their legs because the whole country has come unraveled."

A battle had been raging for two days outside of the Barclay Training Center, where Roosevelt Johnson was holed up. In between the looting binges and torrential, blinding rains, which seemed to send everyone into hibernation, fighters loyal to Taylor and Kromah had been mounting sporadic but intense assaults with automatic rifles and rocket-propelled grenades. These spells of violence were as spectacular in their recklessness as anything ever filmed by Sam Peckinpah, and like a film they obeyed a certain choreography. By late morning, after the fog and hangover from the previous night's drugs and drink had worn off, a dozen or so gunmen, half naked or sometimes completely so, would rush the crumbling, bullet-pocked gates of the BTC, firing their guns wildly as they dashed forward. Roosevelt's men were badly outnumbered, but just as predictably, they would blunt the charge by taking cover and picking off a few of the enemy despite an abysmal quality of marksmanship.

Each round of this madness left half a city block littered with bodies, but those who survived more than a couple of them quickly became legends and were celebrated with names like General Housebreaker, General No-Mother, No-Father, General Fuck-Me-Quick and, most notorious of all, General Butt Naked, the commanding officer of Roosevelt Johnson's Butt Naked Brigade, who doused himself in a potion made from cane juice that he swore protected him from his adversaries' bullets. With his uniform of scuffed tennis shoes, Butt Naked truly lived up to his name.

Milam had told us that we were free to wander outside of the embassy compound, but that if we did so, we would be entirely on our own, and should not count on being rescued if we landed in trouble. Together with a couple of colleagues, I ventured gingerly down the hill and around the bend from the embassy to inspect the scene for myself, but saw nothing more than the occasional desultory round fired this way or that across the street. Here and there, though, uncollected bodies still lay in the street. These were not the corpses of the fighters, which each side dutifully hauled away after each skirmish. They were the remains of unlucky citizens, often men in their forties or fifties who had been caught in the crossfire, or executed during stickups. Despite the heat, none of them had yet reached an advanced state of decay. Their spilled blood was the best gauge of the freshness of their death. Small puddles glistened near the wounds of some, their faces fixed in agony. For others, the blood had long since dried up, leaving little more than dulled stains on the pavement.

When we got back to the embassy, Milam offered to take a few of us to visit a place known as the annex, a rocky patch of land owned by the United States, where hundreds of Liberians who had been forced to flee the fighting were living in the open. The distance was a mere stone's throw, and ordinarily one would have walked, but the diplomats were taking no chances, and we drove in an armed convoy.

The first person I met there was a family patriarch in his fifties, Simway Lattey, who had gathered his wife and children—from grade schoolers to young adults—around him. The Latteys had camped out next to one of the huge gray boulders streaked with black that gave the grounds, when they were empty, the foreboding look of an ancient geological formation.

"What kind of food have you had to eat these last couple of days?" I asked. "No food," Lattey said. "Nothing. All we've had is a little water." He held up a five-quart motor oil jug and a small sack of cornmeal, and added, "This cost me five dollars, and there are nine in our family." Lattey had brought his family to Mamba Point thinking the Americans would rescue them. "We walked here from Sinkor [a distance of two or three miles] overnight. Running, really, the whole way."

The marines flew me and the other reporters back to Freetown the next day, and while another group of reporters were getting their turn witnessing the American operation, I was trying to find a way to get back to Monrovia on my own steam. The transportation options were not great—taking the occasional aid flight, hitchhiking a ride with the never-too-press-friendly Nigerians aboard one of their C-130s or hiring the Ukrainians to rattle and roll me all the way back aboard one of their flying cymbals.

I had been holed up in the Mammy Yoko Hotel for a couple of days when I was paged as I was walking through the lobby. When I grabbed the phone at the grimy booth, it was Jackson, the *Times*'s Liberian stringer and the longtime Monrovia correspondent for the Voice of America. I had not heard him on the air for a couple of days, and without any other word from him, I had been worried. As Jackson spoke, I could hear the crackle of automatic weapons fire in the background. "Things are getting really scary here, Howard man," Jackson said. "I've got to get out somehow."

Jackson explained that he had been sheltered at the Mamba Point Hotel by its Lebanese owners. They had been hiding him in the basement whenever fighters came around asking for him. His car, which the fighters stole from the parking lot in the first days of the crisis, had given him away, though, and each time they returned, the demands that the hotel turn Jackson over grew more menacing.

A UN aid worker from East Africa named Jerry, who was somehow left behind in the stampede of foreigners out of Monrovia, was the only regular guest left in the hotel, and he and Jackson had become friends in their shared confinement. I urged Jackson to leave at once with the UN man, to head around the bend and up the hill for the five-minute walk to the embassy, where they could join the evacuation. "He can't leave because it is too dangerous to walk up the hill, and I can't leave because even if we made it, I don't have a visa," Jackson said. "The Americans have been pulling all kinds of people out of here who have no connection to the U.S., but they've told me I am not eligible for asylum, and they are adamant." Jackson said that he had pleaded with the embassy's information officer, but to no avail. The Voice of America had been of no help, either, he said.

For a long moment, I could not tell if I was more shocked or disgusted. I told Jackson I would call the Voice of America's headquarters to see whether that would help. I got the number from him and called, telling someone in the Africa Service that if anything happened to their Liberia correspondent, who was refused asylum despite facing a clear and present threat to his life, I would make sure it made the front page of the *New York Times*.

When I called Jackson back a few hours later to check, he told me that almost immediately after my call to Washington he had received a call from Dudley Sims, the embassy's spokesman. Sims told Jackson to sit tight, near the entrance of the hotel, promising that a diplomatic vehicle would arrive any moment to extract him.

I was relieved, but still incensed and filled with distrust. In the intervening hours, I had managed to hitch a ride back into Monrovia with some senior American officials whom I came across quite by accident. They would helicopter me back to the embassy compound, but once in Monrovia, I was on my own, meaning I would have to sleep somewhere else.

I called Jackson again to check with him just before jumping aboard the helicopter. No embassy vehicle had arrived, and the afternoon sun was about to begin its quick fadeout. Jackson was scared and depressed, and said he was going to return to the basement, where it seemed safer. I told him the only thing left to do was to try to reach the embassy on foot, and after several minutes of discussion, he agreed to try. I wished him luck and told him I hoped to meet him at the embassy when I landed.

There was a lot of scurrying about when our helicopter landed at the compound. Diplomats were busy sending off the last couple of helicopter loads of evacuees for the evening. I found Jackson standing in line. Sims stood sheepishly nearby. Jackson and I hugged briefly, and I could sense how troubled he was just by the look in his eyes. When I asked what the matter was, he told me that on instructions from Washington, Sims had ordered him onto the very first available helicopter. Jackson was to be flown to Freetown and then onward to Dakar, Senegal, where he was to board a flight to the States, paperless and penniless, and separated from his family.

"I want to stay here and report on the evacuation," Jackson protested. "I am a reporter. I want to do my job, but they won't allow it."

Then he explained to me how he and Jerry had followed the beach, clambering over boulders and being smashed by waves, rather than risking the road to the embassy, where even now gunfire occasionally rang out. The marines had grilled them at the gate, originally believing they were trying to sneak into the compound. Sims, who had told Jackson there was no way he could have asylum, and then later promised a van that never arrived, waved Jackson, dripping wet, through the security gate. "We are so relieved to see you," Jackson said Sims had exclaimed. "Now you have to promise me a good article about this in the newspaper."

CHAPTER TEN

Long Knives

The war in Zaire had begun to settle into a fatal rhythm by the early months of 1997. Each time the government announced a counterattack on a rebel position, it seemed to herald a fresh new advance from the east. Laurent Kabila's mysterious army was constantly on the march, and now all signs pointed to the imminent capture of its biggest prize yet, Kisangani. For over three decades, between long bouts of slumber, the city's vocation seemed to be to determine the entire country's fate. In Kinshasa, everyone knew that once Kisangani fell, a rebel victory would be inevitable. The details that remained to be decided would be as tedious as the running out of the clock in a lopsided football game.

In the last few weeks, the events on the ground had finally begun to force the Americans in Kinshasa to change their tune. The U.S. ambassador, the ever gruff Daniel Howard Simpson, had belatedly stopped arguing that Mobutu's regime could turn things around. To his credit, Simpson had worked feverishly at the outset of the conflict to seize Washington's attention about the unfolding humanitarian disaster in the east, where Rwandan Tutsi were hounding Hutu, and more urgently still, about the spread of political instability, lawlessness and refugee crises throughout Central Africa that the violent breakup of Zaire would engender.

Week after week, though, the American Embassy in Kigali, Rwanda, had been countering Simpson's view, issuing diplomatic cables that backed Rwanda's view of the war: No Rwandan troops were in Zaire, there was no refugee problem, there had been no massacres of Hutu, or at least no proof of massacres.

Mobutu had been America's trusty surrogate in Africa for so long that Simpson, a veteran of multiple tours in the country, had found it difficult to realign his thinking. The turnabout could hardly have been more stark, though. Rwanda and Uganda were now suddenly America's best friends in this neighborhood, and Washington was even courting its old enemies, the former Marxists who ruled Angola. Uganda was an eager partner in American policy to support anti-government rebels in its huge neighbor, Sudan, which was run by a dreadful group of Islamic fundamentalists. As I said earlier, Uganda had also become a much-touted "success story" of the World Bank. Support for Rwanda, meanwhile, had taken the form of penance by Washington for having turned a blind eye to the anti-Tutsi genocide.

This realpolitik flip-flop was dressed up with flashy slogans. The United States said it was promoting an "African renaissance" under a generation of new leaders. But whatever one made of the rationale, it was clear that America's longtime favorite African dictator, Mobutu, was being replaced as top dog by two newer, but by no means freshly minted, authoritarians, Museveni of Uganda and his former protégé, Paul Kagame, in Rwanda.

Just as it had done with Mobutu, beginning in the 1960s, when the young colonel was asked to fight a covert war on our behalf in Angola, Washington was beginning to entrust the new renaissance gang with the security of a vast swath of the continent. While Museveni walked the beat in southern Sudan, Rwanda was given the lead—and a free hand—in sorting out the nasty Hutu problem in Zaire. America was interested in Angola purely for its resources. The country has lots of oil, and most of its reserves are offshore, securely insulated from the region's chronic political instability. By comparison, Zaire's huge storehouse of mineral wealth is entombed not just by the country's red earth but by the country's horrendous corruption, interminable secession bids and political uncertainty.

Only gradually did it dawn on Ambassador Simpson that the argument in Washington was over, if there had ever been an argument. In an odd replay of the country's civil war in the 1960s, Mobutu had hired a couple of hundred Serbian killers, led by an international war crimes suspect named Yugo Dominic, from Krajina, to mount a last stand.

Thirty years earlier, Kisangani had been held by the Simbas, rebels who had been loyal to Patrice Lumumba, the prime minister Mobutu had overthrown and helped kill. Then, with help from the CIA, the ruthless young Mobutu hired Cuban mercenaries who were honing their skills for the failed attack on the Bay of Pigs to oust the Lumumbist faithful. This time around, the Serbs had three helicopter gunships and a couple of ground attack fighter planes, and the ambassador seemed to hold out some hope that the rebels might stub their toe for the first time, perhaps changing the war's course.

With the fall of Kisangani, though, Simpson, too, would make a full conversion, turning his thoughts and affections to Kabila. Compared to the ambassador, my best American intelligence source, a man I'll call John, had been far more closely attuned to Washington's true thinking from the very beginning. John knew or suspected that the American shift of African clients that was under way had been well planned, and he understood that the rebellion that was steadily building up steam like a tropical storm on its long route to Kinshasa was far too big a challenge for a few dozen mercenaries—even if they *were* Serbian war criminals.

"Do you know how many helicopters the United States lost in Vietnam?" he asked me over beers in a low-slung Kinshasa villa one evening. "Five thousand. The mercenaries might put up some resistance, but once the attack on Kisangani gets going, I expect them to commandeer whatever aircraft they can and get the hell out of there."

John couldn't get over the rebels' tactical proficiency. He knew Kabila's Alliance of Democratic Forces for the Liberation of Congo-Zaire, or AFDL, was no hodgepodge group of tribal fighters and child soldiers hastily thrown together and dressed in Wellington boots, as the official story would have it. "They've got an Eisenhower- or a Montgomery-type putting together a very impressive, very methodical campaign." The tactics, he said, even included sophisticated psy-ops, or psychological operations. One recent trick involved calling the confidential satellite phone numbers or radio frequencies of Mobutu's top generals and telling them the time to make a deal was running out.

As no American diplomat would, John acknowledged that this war was about one thing alone: counter-extermination. The Hutu had their day in 1994, killing the 800,000 Tutsi and Hutu moderates during the Rwandan genocide. Now, Rwanda's government, led by the small Tutsi minority, was butchering Hutu refugees in Zaire. The United States had eagerly avoided intervening in the first genocide, and its subsequent guilt over that decision kept it out of this campaign of slaughter, leading to the same kind of tragic results.

John maintained the diplomatic fiction that Kabila's army was mostly Zairian, or at least mostly the Tutsi pastoralists, the Banyamulenge, from the east of the country. All pretense ended, however, when it came to saying who was leading the insurgency, and what that group's aims were. "The original AFDL column came from Rwanda, passed through Burundi and entered Zaire near Cibitoké," he said. "They started taking on a lot of volunteers, but this was a Rwandan-trained and Rwandan-led force, and when they set out on the Walikale-to-Lubutu axis, it was with the express purpose of breaking up the Hutu camps and hunting down refugees.

"Some of the Hutu fought back, for sure. There was some very brutal fighting in the early stages, but the worst killing was in the mopping-up operations. Those forests out in the east have witnessed some real horrors, but luckily for the Tutsi, trees can't talk."

The official American line on the war effectively forbade anyone, whether diplomat or intelligence officer, to be quoted saying anything like this, not even on background. And for the most part, the media followed the official narrative. As Kabila's rebellion swept westward, almost no reporters made it to the front to witness actual combat, or to check the rebels' claims of victory or of popular support. Kabila or, more likely, his minders in Kigali were savvy enough to understand the paramount importance of controlling journalists' access. The peril of the war zone and the sheer impenetrability of the terrain also deterred most of those who might have been tempted to strike out on their own.

Even after the fighting had moved on—until the final stages of the war, at least—rare was the reporter who sought to determine the toll, or to dig into reports of atrocities, either. The death of large numbers of Hutu refugees was accepted with a journalistic shrug, as perhaps a sad but inevitable consequence of being on the wrong side of Central Africa's ugly history.

For more than three decades, Mobutu was not just America's best friend in Africa, he was a larger-than-life thief and scoundrel, a man who had bad guy written all over him just as clearly as the spots on his leopard-skin cap. Kabila's greatest public relations advantage, in fact, was Mobutu's incorrigibly negative image. To be sure, the sixty-something rebel leader sometimes seemed like a campy joke, roly-poly and all too jovial in his brief encounters with the Western press. But good and bad, or at least better and worse, had already been sorted out. The only story that mattered was the countdown to the overthrow of the mythical dictator in Kinshasa, and the inclination of the press to cheer the rebellion along only grew in strength as the weeks passed. There were plenty of well-informed sources on the slaughter of Hutu refugees that was unfolding in the east, but almost no one was listening to them.

As well as anyone else, Guillaume Ngefa, the head of the Association Zairoise de Droits de l'Homme, or AZADHO, understood what was happening on the ground. A slight man, he always spoke in careful sentences that reminded me of a clinician, except that even his weightiest thoughts were always eventually punctuated with an unexpected joke delivered absolutely deadpan, and followed up with a devilish grin. Ngefa was one of those almost recklessly courageous figures who had somehow proliferated and thrived—if intermittently—during the long, dark years of Mobutu's rule.

Ngefa received me late one afternoon in March 1997 in his office on Avenue Mutombo Katsi, and we chatted for a few minutes on the terrace, overlooking downtown Kinshasa in all its shabby glory. His description of what was going on was succinct and without appeal.

"You can call it a war, if you like, because there is some combat, and yet anyone who follows the itinerary of the rebels knows that this is a campaign to exterminate the Hutu refugees. The Tutsi thesis is that all of these people are Interahamwe [the Hutu militia that carried out the Rwandan genocide], and now, those who suffered a genocide are committing one in their turn," Ngefa told me. "The international community only sees one thing, the fate of Mobutu, so the rebels are free to kill whoever they like. The error here is that these crimes will not be forgotten. You can't march hundreds of thousands of people across the breadth of this country, killing them at every turn, and expect they won't seek vengeance someday."

For the relief agencies and for the refugees, the press had become a frail and final reed. On the last leg of their march toward Kisangani, the rebels had taken a telling detour at Pene-Tungu, a desolate jungle crossroads town, heading southwest instead of northwest, and they were going fifty miles out of their way to reach the Zaire River, within sight of Ubundu on the opposite bank. Awaiting them there was the largest surviving concentration of Hutu refugees still wandering the Zairian wilderness. There had been 150,000 of them less than two weeks earlier at Tingi-Tingi, but a third of their number had been picked off in machine-gun ambushes and artillery attacks during their desperate eight-day flight from a town where the United Nations had promised they would be safe.

The rebels were about to apply the brilliant military tactics that John had praised, executing the revenge genocide Ngefa had warned of. The only safe way across the river for the Hutu was in a rusty steamboat, an *African Queen*–style affair that could carry a few hundred passengers at a time, but even this ferry had been shut down by the government, which feared a flood of refugees into Kisangani, about seventy miles up the road. The river was unnavigable from here. Just downstream lay the tremendous cataract, where furious whitewater cascades and immense boulders had clashed without cease for an eon. In the invitingly calm tea-colored pools near the banks, crocodiles swam thick among the clots of water hyacinth, and were sure to devour anyone foolish enough to attempt to make it across.

The United Nations put on a flight from Kinshasa a small number of reporters, doubtlessly hoping that the pictures and stories of the scene at Ubundu would bring some kind of international action. Fifty tons of food were needed each day to feed the Hutu. There were five hundred tons, or a ten-day supply, stockpiled in Kisangani, but fighting in the area had rendered delivery nearly impossible. Even if the ferry service were restored, it would take three months of nonstop crossings for the creaky steamer to get all of the Hutu stragglers across the river. The only hope was a ceasefire. The Security Council was indecisive about the crisis, largely because of American and British resistance to any condemnation of Rwanda and Uganda.

The French called for an international humanitarian intervention, but they were virtually alone in clamoring for strong diplomatic action. Their arguments were weakened, too, by Paris's transparent preoccupation with its loss of empire. The only meaning the war had for the French, one sensed, was the erosion of their prestige and influence. In France, Rwanda and Uganda were seen as the spearheads of what Paris called Anglo-Saxon power.

From Kinshasa we flew to Kisangani, and the scene on the ground at the airport there could not have been more different from a couple of weeks before. The Serbian mercenaries had taken over the airfield, and here and there an advance team of French operatives were collecting intelligence and consulting with the Zairians about the defense of the city.

As we piled into a smaller plane to fly onward to the far bank of the Zaire River, beyond Ubundu, a French agent slipped in among us. I overheard him telling a French reporter that in a few days the foreign legion would be here, hopefully at the head of an international force, and the entire flow of the war would change. The French, he said, had already been building up their forces across the Zaire River from Kinshasa, in Brazzaville.

Twenty minutes later, after we had circled over Ubundu and done a quick flyover of the landing field, the plane plowed to a stop in a broad grassy field bordered by two thick stands of trees. After an exhausting day's travel from Kinshasa, we were told by UN officials that we had only forty-five minutes on the ground, because of approaching nightfall and the possibility of attack.

Piling out of the airplane, I immediately found myself surrounded by a sea of desperate faces. Incredibly, some of them had seen me in Tingi-Tingi and called out eagerly for me to acknowledge the extraordinary coincidence. This was a hopeless, broken population. Where there had been a proper settlement at Tingi-Tingi, carved out of the wilderness with the expectation of semi-permanence, and above all, of survival, the shattered people in the field near Ubundu saw themselves for exactly what they were: inmates in a death camp awaiting their summons to the chamber. Few had even bothered putting up makeshift shelters. Bundles of ragged clothing and whatever other belongings people had managed to bring this far sat in desolate piles. Babies tugged at the shriveled breasts of their mothers, who could do nothing but watch their children dying with downcast eyes.

"We are hungry and we are sick, but above all, we have lost all morale," said Imaculée Mukarugwiza, a widowed schoolteacher from Butare, Rwanda. She had walked eight days from Tingi-Tingi with her own two children and five orphans she had picked up along the way. With the sting of a summation, Imaculée asked me, "Are all of us guilty of genocide, even these little children?"

In the few minutes I had to wander in this desperate crowd, many of the refugees insisted on recounting the stories of their flight from

Tingi-Tingi. As they did so, they assumed an almost beatific air, and some of those describing the horrors glowed with the strange smiles of miraculous survivors as they spoke. Each concluded darkly, though, that he or she had only feinted death, not escaped it. "We heard the first gunfire around eight o'clock, and it just kept growing in intensity," said a thirty-one-year-old Hutu doctor from Bukavu, Zaire, who gave his name as Camille as he asked for my card. "Most people fled during the night, but there were nine of us and we stayed put. With sunrise they marched into the camp, and they shot at anything that moved. It was a total rout." Camille said he had survived only by playing dead alongside a pile of cadavers. When things finally went quiet in the settlement, he managed to find nine members of his extended family, everyone except his frail grandfather.

As he was a young man, the presumption of guilt for having participated in the 1994 anti-Tutsi genocide hung heavily over Camille, but after eight days of terrified flight through the forests, he had decided he would be better off going home to Tutsi-ruled Rwanda and facing his fate there. "All the world is willing to do is feed us, but that is of no use if we have to keep running like this. Take us home, but give us protection."

A man named Christophe stepped forward and spoke impassionedly to describe how he survived a previous ambush by Kabila's rebels, who, he insisted, were precisely what the Western diplomats were still denying—members of the Forces Patriotiques Rwandaises, Rwanda's Tutsi-dominated army. His first brush with slaughter, he said, had come in 1995 during an attack on his first refugee camp, in Kibeho, in southwestern Rwanda, where the United Nations itself had estimated that eight thousand Hutu were massacred.

"I was nearly killed in Tingi-Tingi because I took Madame Ogata at her word, that we would be protected. In fact, the world has done nothing for us," Christophe said. "They did nothing to save people in Rwanda and they have done nothing to save us here. But dying here at least has one merit. If people like you bear witness, sooner or later the international community will have to accept its responsibility."

I flew back to Kinshasa in an intensely dark mood. Kabila's fighters and the crocodiles would soon be sorting the refugees out, and whatever Christophe believed about the stories I and others would write, since there were no television crews here, the world, by and large, would be spared the disturbing images.

In the course of the war, I never saw fresh killing fields. But the faces of innocent people about to meet violent deaths stay with you. Having just been served up true desperation in crowd-sized doses, now I felt I truly knew what it meant to be haunted.

Mobutu had left the country again—this time, quietly—shortly after his faux-triumphal return from cancer surgery a few months before. For a man vain and depraved enough to sleep with, and then wed, his wife's identical twin sister, the hormonal castration that is a routine element of prostate cancer treatment was more than he could contemplate.

As Robert and I transited through Kisangani again after returning from Ubundu, Mobutu's commander on the ground exuded confidence, telling me that his defenses, bolstered by the mercenaries, were rock solid. "You can drive one hundred fifty miles out of town and you won't encounter any trouble," General Kalumé said. Kalumé, a tall, proud man whose warm, rounded features seemed to bespeak integrity and even kindness, may already have been working for Kabila. In any event, two days later, the rebels launched a well-planned attack on Kisangani.

Back in Kinshasa, I got a call on my satellite phone from a very well informed Catholic cleric late on the afternoon of March 15, just as the sun started its dappling descent over the cascades of the Zaire River. The river's beauty, which I could take in from my hotel room, was a rare comfort during weeks-long stays covering Zaire's downward spiral. The caller told me that a rumor was sweeping the city that armored vehicles and heavy weaponry—artillery pieces and Chinese-made mortars—were being rushed forward toward Kisangani, down the road from Bafwasendé.

By early evening, the smoke and dust of afternoon rumors had settled into a reasonably solid picture of what was happening, although the news was nowhere to be found yet on the news wires or the international radio stations. A UN relief worker in Kisangani who had given me mail for his family forty-eight hours earlier called to say that bombs and explosions could be heard going off here and there. A little while after that, all the aircraft controlled by the mercenaries and loyalists were ablaze, hit by artillery fired from as far away as seven or eight miles, according to John. As he described the scene, full of details about the operational range of this or that heavy weapon, he could hardly contain his excitement. The 24th Regiment of the Angolan army had joined the battle, which explained, he said, the unusual accuracy of the attacking gunners.

In the end, there was hardly a fight. The mutinous Serbs slipped out of town aboard their Russian-built Mi-24 attack helicopters, coming under fire from Mobutu's own 31st Paratroop Brigade as they flew away. The mercenaries put down in Gbadolité, Mobutu's fantasyland capital in the northern jungles. Mobutu's soldiers ran wild in Kisangani for a few hours, stripping off their uniforms and looting whatever they could. And then the invaders arrived.

General Kalumé changed his uniform but not his job, staying on as the local commander for the AFDL, and for a time, life went on just as it usually had in Kisangani, meaning nothing much happened and nothing much changed. In Kinshasa, though, nothing would ever be the same. "Everyone is making new calculations about their future," one of Mobutu's senior counselors told me. "The old game is up. The next few days will show what the new game is all about."

The verdict on the street was much the same. Overnight, the people of the capital had understood that Mobutu's days were now numbered. The only uncertainty was over what lay ahead. For years, in the political struggle for hearts and minds, Kinshasa—indeed, much of the country—had belonged to Etienne Tshisekedi, the stubborn and courageous leader of the country's democracy movement, and once and future prime minister. Though many in the capital cheered on the rebellion, people said they could not imagine a future under Kabila that did not also include an important role for Tshisekedi. The people of Kinshasa dreamed that somehow the democrats and the rebels would work side by side to finally deliver on some of their country's elusive promise.

In Matongé, the vast slum that had been the African quarter during the years of Belgian rule, the so-called *parlementaires debout* loitered around the newspaper stands to read the headlines and debate each day's momentous events. "We had been very worried for our brothers and sisters in Kisangani before the fall, because we all felt that Kabila was a killer and a puppet of the Tutsi," Patrice Makambu, a thirty-two-year-old electrical engineering student, told me. "But nothing bad has happened at all, and we can see that Kabila stands together with all of Zaire's forty-five million sons and daughters."

A cheer went up among the twenty or so people who had gathered at the newsstand, and then someone shouted a question about Tshisekedi, who, although he was sacked as prime minister by Mobutu during a previous crisis, many people still considered as their legitimate leader. The answer came swiftly. "Today, we are applauding Kabila, but if he thinks he can govern Zaire without our prime minister, we will drop him like a sack of rice."

Even the Kinshasa multimillionaires, the barons of the Mobutu system who fought Tshisekedi for years, had changed their tune. For men like Bemba Saolona, whose immense fortune from mining, agriculture and transportation had been built in connivance with the president-for-life, Tshisekedi's reputation for incorruptibility was a lesser evil compared to the sheer unpredictability of a revolution led by Kabila. "Tshisekedi is a strong personality, and that's exactly what we need in this situation," Bemba told me in his luxurious house, decorated with all the nouveau riche warmth of a four-star hotel. "If he is allowed to set up a national unity government, Tshisekedi can go and sit down with Kabila and ask him just what he wants."

The United States had other ideas, however, and was beginning to weigh in more and more heavily in favor of the rebels. With the fall of Kisangani, Ambassador Simpson was deep in the throes of his eleventh-hour conversion. He could now bring himself to say flatly that Mobutu was finished. Kengo wa Dondo, the mulatto prime minister whom Washington had worked so hard to prop up, was now suddenly, in Simpson's words, a "world-class crook," and Tshisekedi, the man designated to lead the nation by the people in the 1992 National Conference, the most democratic national event Zaire had seen in a generation, was a nuisance to be ignored.

The future envisioned by the United States was Kabila and only Kabila. "There is a consensus that we have to deal with Kabila," the ambassador told me, growing annoyed with my questions as we sat across a low table from each other in his chilly office. "Tshisekedi is an obstacle, and we don't see him as a player anymore. I just don't see any reason why Kabila at this point should deal him into the game."

Ironically, in the time it took Simpson to get with the Kabila program supported so enthusiastically by American embassies in East Africa, and ostensibly in Washington, too, strong doubts were cropping up within Simpson's own mission. John, for one, had early on applauded the rebels' pluck, but now that they had swallowed half of the country, and were girding for an assault on the capital, he was expressing serious reservations. "Mobutu destroyed Zaire militarily and politically, and brought this thing down on himself," John told me over beers at his home that same evening. "But now we have a guy taking over the country by military versus political means, and that is clearly going to debase political opposition movements all across Africa.

"We are welcoming Kabila without knowing who he is," he continued. "Is this a George Washington or a megalomaniac? Is this a period of enlightenment coming to Central Africa or a new dark age we've just signed up for? Personally, I have a hard time believing a man who trained at Nanjing University and who ran with Che Guevara can save this country."

John did not mention Tshisekedi by name, but implicit in his comments was a questioning of the betrayal Tshisekedi's supporters were already bracing for. It echoed a betrayal in the country's earliest independent history, when the United States preferred another strongman, Mobutu, over Lumumba, also a proud and democratically minded leader who was widely supported by his people. The United States had helped engineer Africa's first coup d'état, overthrowing Lumumba after less than ten weeks in power, over unsubstantiated concerns about his communist leanings. Lumumba was murdered less than a year later, in a political assassination that was also promoted by Washington.

With the fall of Kisangani, things were indeed moving quickly. Mobutu returned home for the third time from his coddled convalescence in the south of France. Once more, the crowds were carefully turned out, using all the old tricks of beer and pocket change, but from his airplane, angry, hurting and doubtless full of despair, Mobutu ordered that the festivities be called off, and slipped off to Camp Tshatshi virtually undercover.

In Kinshasa, the political significance of this sudden bout of camera shyness escaped no one. Albert Kisongo, the editor of *Demain le Congo*, captured the common feeling in a telling phrase. "We Bantus love a good spectacle, and that is why we have put up with Mobutu for over thirty years. Now he is telling us himself that the show is over."

That very same day, March 21, Kabila arrived in Kisangani. Thirty-two years earlier, in 1965, Mobutu's Cuban and Rhodesian mercenaries had defeated the Simba rebellion, and run Kabila, one of its leaders, out of Kisangani. This time, the mercenaries and their white magic had failed. Triumphant, Kabila was being greeted by huge crowds who turned out entirely of their own accord. Kisangani toasted him as its liberator, and the cheering crowds urged him onward to Kinshasa. To be sure, the old warrior had earned his credentials as a survivor, but he had to be as surprised as anyone else to be plucked out of his obscurity, more than two weeks into the supposed Banyamulenge rebellion, to head a creation of Rwanda and Uganda called the Alliance of Democratic Forces for the Liberation of Congo-Zaire.

The fall of Kisangani was followed a few days later by the fall of Mbuji-Mayi, lending added drama to Mobutu's predicament. Mobutu had now lost his last major source of income, the $20 million or so in monthly revenues from official diamond sales there. Deprived of cash, he now turned in desperation to his longtime nemesis, Etienne Tshisekedi, naming him as prime minister for the third time, in a stopgap gesture that had the distinct odor of a poisoned gift.

Tshisekedi responded with boldness, hoping to make the best of his weak hand with a series of dramatic gambits. He announced a new cabinet that included no Mobutu loyalists, and said that six positions would be held open for Kabila appointees. Infuriated by the slight, Mobutu moved to get rid of his rival even before his government could be formally seated. Security forces were told to prevent Tshisekedi from entering the prime minister's offices. Meanwhile, Kabila's response to Tshisekedi's olive branch dripped with contempt. "If Tshisekedi wants to pilot a ship that is going down, he must learn how to swim," said Kabila's uncle and close aide Gaëtan Kakudji. "Because this ship is going to sink."

Tshisekedi's Democratic Union for Social Progress (UDPS) boasted a large and disciplined network of activists in Kinshasa and throughout the western half of the country. In a three-way showdown in which the other two figures fielded men with guns, they were his only soldiers, and the time had come to call them out into the streets. If Kabila was to be prevented from storming Kinshasa, and if Zaire was to be spared a political takeover by force, Mobutu would have to be defied convincingly, through mass civil action. Tshisekedi's final option, in effect, was to have his own legitimacy validated by the people.

For two days, Kinshasa boiled with tension, and it seemed impossible to tell how things would unfold. Mobutu enjoyed some residual support in the parliament, largely as a result of payoffs from his ruling party, and Tshisekedi loyalists—mostly students and other young people—set up roadblocks using burning tires and the chassis of abandoned cars on the roads leading to the building, and roughed up many of Mobutu's supporters. Mobutu responded by calling out the army, and the green trucks of the feared Division Spéciale Présidentielle, or DSP, rumbled through the streets of Kinshasa, smashing the students' barricades and breaking up demonstrations. The street scenes were passably reminiscent of Beijing in 1989, during the Tiananmen protests. Young people armed with nothing more than their courage stood in front of armored personnel carriers and trucks full of troops, lecturing Mobutu's soldiers on the need for democracy and peaceful change until their drivers, whether convinced or merely discouraged, changed course.

Students rode around the city banging on the sides of the decrepit minivans that were the most common form of transportation, or formed clusters, ready to disperse at the first sign of a threat, and chanted slogans like "Mobutu, don't you know the name of the people's prime minister? It's Tshisekedi." Others warned the soldiers to be on guard when Kabila's forces arrived, treating the matter as an inevitability. Above all, they urged, the military must protect civil authority. "Once Mobutu has fled into exile, let Kabila come. Don't resist him," said Didier Bitini, a twenty-seven-year-old student. "The only thing you must insist upon is that Tshisekedi be given a free hand as prime minister."

It was a tall order, too much, in fact, even to dream of from an army that had known only dictatorship, an army that was disintegrating wherever there was combat. I asked a soldier who was looking on impassively what he made of the demonstrations. "Let them do whatever they want," he told me. "Politics is none of our business."

If what was left of Mobutu's army could not conceive of fighting for Zairian democracy, the outside world was not much moved by the idea, either. Setting aside the continent's immense natural resources, for the West the only reliably compelling subject in Africa is the theater of misery and suffering. In such a universe, scenes like the peaceful uprising of Tshisekedi's supporters simply did not compute. No statement of support for Tshisekedi would be coming from Washington. There would be nothing even resembling a strong call for a freeze of the fighting on the ground so that a civil solution could be found.

On Capitol Hill, George Moose contented himself with stating the obvious, while avoiding the essential: the future stability and integrity of Africa's third-largest nation. "It is clear," he said, "that Mobutu, the Mobutu regime, is a thing of the past."

In late April, Tshisekedi decided to step personally into the fray. The international press had been alerted that the renegade prime minister would lead his supporters on a march along the broad avenues that led from his home in the leafy Limeté district to the seat of government in Gombé, to assume his office by popular force.

Pierre drove me to Tshisekedi's house that morning in his dilapidated Fiat, together with Robert and a couple of other colleagues. The crowds were already impassably thick for many blocks surrounding the prime minister's villa. Militants from the UDPS acted as lookouts on every corner, and for extra measure, large trees had been cut down and laid across the streets leading to their leader's residence.

After two days of muscular street demonstrations, and a huge turnout of supporters that morning in Limeté, Tshisekedi's lieutenants exuded confidence. One advisor, Martin Tshibanga, bragged to me that the boss was still sleeping. "He hasn't even gotten up yet. He hasn't lifted a finger to call people out. They have come of their own accord."

Later that morning, in sweltering heat, Tshisekedi finally emerged from the office in the back of his home to discover a thick crowd of reporters who had been allowed into the courtyard. With a wan little smile, and a simple "Bonjour," he turned on his heels and disappeared. There would be no press conference, we were told. "Toujours énigmatique," Tshibanga said, nodding approvingly. I was far less sure. A few minutes later, though, Tshisekedi reemerged before the large crowds that choked the surrounding streets and suddenly the march looked as if it was on. Just moments after setting out, however, the scene erupted into total panic with the arrival of Mobutu's shock troops.

Trucks full of DSP troops had completely surrounded the area, and when the order was given, they began firing off tear-gas canisters and shooting live rounds, sending people scurrying for their lives in a terrified frenzy. Pierre had taken the precaution of parking on the heavily shaded carriage lane on the road leading to the center of town, and not on one of the narrow side streets that were now completely blocked off. Dodging rifle butts as we ran, Pierre, ever trusty, got us out of there.

Working my cell phones on the ride into town, I quickly learned that Tshisekedi was safe. The huge army trucks that had besieged his neighborhood now began appearing in Pierre's rearview mirror. Cars were being forced off the road, and reporters were being pulled out and beaten. Pierre went back onto the carriage lane to park and wait out the storm, while Robert set off to take pictures of this menacing convoy.

Pierre and I sat in the shade for what seemed like an eternity as the huge green military vehicles passed by, and just as we began to fear that something serious might have happened to Robert, he showed up. He was filthy and looked pained and crumpled. He had been hurt somehow, but most of all he was piping angry. "Fuck. Fuck," he kept repeating. "Those bastards stole my cameras."

Robert had been shooting dramatic compositions of the trucks rolling down the avenue with angry, rifle-waving soldiers leaning from the sides, when a driver suckered him, opening the door to the passenger's cabin just as he pulled up alongside him. Robert had been knocked senseless, and the next thing he knew, the soldiers were striking him with their rifle butts and stripping him of his cameras and other valuables.

When we reached Mandela Square, a dusty traffic circle on Boulevard 30 Juin, where the UDPS was telling its supporters to mass, Tshisekedi's supporters were already there in the thousands, chanting, "The power is in the streets. Mobutu and his ragged prostates are finished." It was as if they had walked there faster than we could drive. The circle is bisected by several avenues, and without forewarning, Tshisekedi soon materialized at the head of a cluster of close supporters. The air was already electric, and the crowd roared its approval and fell in behind Tshisekedi, who bore the grim expression of a man who knew this might be his last act.

Mobutu's thuggish son Kongulu entered the circle from another boulevard, heavily armed and accompanied by his close aide, Guy Vanda. Guy, who was hoisting an automatic rifle, had become one of my best contacts inside the Mobutu entourage and had even become a friend of sorts. He saw me and beckoned, and when I approached him he warned me to leave the area. There might be violence. People could be killed.

I thanked him for the advice and wisely or unwisely ignored it, getting as close as I could to Tshisekedi, who was blanketed by chanting supporters like a queen bee surrounded by her drones. A clutch of Mobutu's agents, all armed with machine guns, moved to cut off the march, blocking Tshisekedi's forward progress. The enigma then began to speak. "This is a dictatorship in its final agony that refuses to die. A fraction of the army is trying to prop it up. But it goes without saying that in the days ahead, we will maintain our pressure until the results of the National Conference are respected."

At that moment, a beige Peugeot split the crowd, and there was a lot of desperate, panicked pushing and shoving. The air crackled with gunfire, and people were again scattering frantically as the shooting grew wild and sustained. Tear gas thickened the air. I hid behind a tree and could see Tshisekedi being forced into the car, which sped off quickly. Soldiers were savagely beating whomever they could grab hold of.

Amid the mayhem, I was separated from my colleagues and jumped over a wall into someone's garden. I raised Ofeibea Quist-Arcton, a reporter and close friend from the BBC, on my cell phone. We had been standing together moments before. She was okay, and we agreed on a meeting place. Other friends called to say they had taken refuge inside people's houses. Robert, already injured and without cameras, had returned briefly to the hotel.

Later we learned that Tshisekedi had been placed under house arrest. He was not seriously hurt. The hope of civilian transition in Zaire was dead, however. And the American Embassy was silent.

In his hour of greatest need, Mobutu turned to another powerful man he held in high distrust. Dictators whose primary mode of operation involves slithering tend, it seems, to feel most comfortable with other reptiles.

In Mobutu's entourage, reptiles were in great supply, and he named one, General Likulia Bolongo, to replace Etienne Tshisekedi. The nomination was at best legally questionable, because the parliament was bypassed, but Kabila's forces had reportedly reached Bandundu Province, whose capital, Kikwit, 370 miles southeast of Kinshasa, was where the Ebola outbreak had occurred not long before, and with the democracy movement broken, few were in the mood for arguing.

"The accent of this government is particularly on patriotism," Likulia said, dressed in full four-star uniform and straining to put a brave face on things as he introduced his government on the steps of the prime minister's office, surrounded by other senior officers. "One of the prime missions of these ministers, outside of peace and the defense of territory, is the restructuring of the army. Please note the presence of generals from great military academies and professors and researchers from different university disciplines."

Men of valor were practically unheard of in the senior ranks of the Zairian armed forces. Mobutu, who counted on foreign powers for security and feared being overthrown by his own aides more than he feared attack from abroad, had always wanted it that way. So as Likulia spoke, all eyes were on General Marc Mahélé Lièko Bokungu, who after being kept out of action for most of the war was now being made deputy prime minister and defense minister, along with his previous title, army chief of staff.

Mahélé was that rarest of Zairian species, a professional soldier who had earned his stripes. He had proved his bona fides during the two brief secession wars in Shaba, where he was the only commander who could be counted on not to steal, and again during the pillages in Kinshasa, when he ordered his men to fire on rioting troops. Distinctions like these would have made him a national hero in most countries. In Mobutu's Zaire, though, where he had the further demerit of not belonging to the president's Ngbandi ethnic group, they made him a marked man.

As the regime cracked, Zaire was opening up like a crocus. Suddenly, it seemed as if everybody, from the innermost insiders to the foreign powers who still wielded tremendous influence from the shadows, wanted to reveal their most closely held secrets to me—everybody, that is, but Mobutu himself. I was selfishly pleased with Likulia's nomination, because his aide-de-camp was already a valuable source, and had long ago given me details of the corrupt dealings of the army's top generals, including his boss. Mobutu's new interior minister, a former general named Ilunga, was also a good source, and he told me not to pay attention to any of the new government's rhetoric. People in high places were already sending their families out of the country. Even Likulia knew the game was over, he told me, and had accepted the job only to steal what was left to be grabbed. Guy, who was in and out of the presidential palace every day, told me that Papa Mobutu, as he called him, knew about all of the stealing. Guy also said that Mobutu had taken precautions to prevent General Mahélé from ever enjoying a truly free hand, however many titles he accumulated.

Mahélé knew what needed to be done to fix the Zairian army. But like Tshisekedi, he had been called upon too late to make a difference. Unlike Tshisekedi, though, he would not be easy to shake. Quite unexpectedly, the general summoned me to a private residence in Kinshasa one afternoon shortly after his "promotion" for the first of several secret meetings. The first key to getting the army to fight, he said, was surprisingly simple: Pay the soldiers. Even as Kabila's fighters swept across the country, Mobutu's relatives, Ngbandi generals like Baramoto and Eluki, were stealing the army payrolls.

The worst of the general's scorn, though, was reserved for Kengo wa Dondo, Mobutu's prime minister for the last three years, and along with his contempt came a potent dose of suspicion of the West. "The more I think about things, the more I wonder if the West didn't use Kengo to eliminate Mobutu," Mahélé said, choosing his words slowly and with great care. "This calamity isn't so much the reflection of Kabila's achievements. Before Kengo we had one country. Now we have two or three. Before Kengo we had one national language, now we speak English and French. It is a complete disaster."

Mahélé reeled off financial figures as he recounted for me one dirty affair after another. "Kengo ran things during the best years of Gécamines [the world's largest copper mine], a six-year period when the company's revenues ran to a billion dollars," he said. "His biggest coup was pocketing the surplus when the world price of copper sky-rocketed. The profit was in the order of four hundred million dollars, and the proceeds were split between Mobutu, Kengo, Seti Yalé [former chief of security and financial advisor to Mobutu] and a few others. When the president visited Kengo's villa, Le Refuge, in Marbella, [Spain,] even Mobutu was impressed. With a smile, he told Kengo, 'You have foreseen everything.' "

The range of Mahélé's knowledge and the resentment that burned in him proved that Mobutu was not altogether wrong to hold him in suspicion. Yet Mahélé had little interest in mounting a coup against his commander-in-chief. He was rather like a son who had never enjoyed his father's favor, desperate to prove his worth. He would do his best to repulse the coming offensive on Kinshasa, he vowed, but his efforts were meant to buy time for a peaceful, orderly and hopefully negoti-ated transition that would spare Kinshasa violent destruction, secure a place for some elements of the elite in the new order and even assure a dignified departure from power of the great dictator.

The long white Cadillac pulled up to Mobutu's Camp Tshatshi resi-dence surrounded by a large security entourage. At the steps of the slate gray two-story palace, out jumped Bill Richardson, President Bill Clinton's personal envoy and representative to the United Nations. During seven months of civil war, through the savaging of refugee camps and massacres of their fleeing inhabitants, to the rout of Zaire's third city, Kisangani, the United States had been content to remain offstage. American diplomacy was activated only to stop others, like Canada at the beginning of the war and France ever since, from impeding the rebellion's progress. Now, with Kabila's capture of Kinshasa only weeks or perhaps just days off, Washington decided it was time to jump in with both feet. Mobutu, dressed in a blue abacost and leopard-skin cap, looked as elegant as ever in his own distinctively outrageous way, but he was conspicuously frail and leaned heavily on his carved cane. His face was so drawn that it lent a cartoonist's emphasis to his hooded eyes and pouty lips, but still he managed a weak smile to greet Clinton's man of special missions. A few formalities were pronounced to the large press contingent gathered in the peacock garden, and then, just before 11 a.m., the two men disappeared inside.

On his arrival in Kinshasa earlier that morning, Richardson had publicly announced his visit in these terms: "The United States strongly believes that there can be no military solution to the crisis, but rather a negotiated settlement leading to an inclusive transitional government, and fair and free elections. I am also here because of our grave concerns about the plight of several hundred thousand refugees and displaced Zairians."

Amid the high-sounding rhetoric, though, the one key objective was to engineer Mobutu's departure and a "soft landing" of the capital. After the talks here, I was told, Richardson was flying off to Lubumbashi, Zaire's second city, which was also now in rebel hands, where Kabila was waiting to meet him. Richardson's aides said there was space in the plane for me and that I was welcome to come along.

Nearly two and a half hours after they had begun, Richardson and Mobutu appeared on the terrace again. The American party looked nervous but visibly relieved, like little boys who had unexpectedly pulled off a prank without getting caught. Mobutu, on the other hand, wore a mournful look, and his entourage, composed mostly of immediate family, like Nzanga, the fleshy-faced son who bore the strongest likeness to his father, appeared stricken and utterly deflated.

"President Mobutu assured me today that he is prepared to meet

Mr. Kabila immediately under Organization of African Unity or UN auspices," Richardson announced. Then he repeated much of his earlier language about the need for "an inclusive transitional government," peace and reconciliation. Throughout the encounter, Ambassador Simpson had served as interpreter.

Aboard the small State Department jet en route for Lubumbashi, Richardson described the discussions with Mobutu, dropping the sterile, lapidary formulae of diplomacy, which he had learned on the fly in his UN job, and lapsing into a more familiar guttural mode, part Bronx, part Santa Fe. "Mobutu," he said, was "alert, but a bit frail, a little debilitated. I told him you are living in a dreamland, pal. You've got a bunch of advisors who are not telling you the truth. You are out. Do you want to leave with dignity or as a carcass?"

The American team he headed had purposely included all the relevant agencies in order to leave no hope of a back channel to Washington for the wily old dictator, friend of American presidents, millionaires and spymasters. They informed him that Kenge, the last major town on the road to Kinshasa, was in rebel hands and had not been recaptured by his army, as Mobutu's aides had assured him. Ashen-faced, Mobutu had lapsed into emotional pleas, reminding the Americans of loyal but long-past services in the war against communism, and complained to Richardson, "You guys have not been loyal to me."

"I said the mess you are in is not our mess," Richardson said. "You didn't govern your country." Given the thick ropes of complicity that had tied Mobutu's Zaire to Washington's Cold War agenda in Africa, these were self-serving half-truths at best. Already, the superpower was writing history, and Richardson had crafted a bluntly effective epitaph for America's longtime erstwhile ally.

"You've got about a week," Richardson told Mobutu, handing him a letter from Clinton asking him to bow out quickly, gracefully. There were oral assurances of a continuing role for the president's political party, the Mouvement Populaire de la Révolution. "I told him you are about to be overrun. What's it going to be?"

We landed in Lubumbashi late that afternoon, reveling in the cool, dry air and the golden and ruby tones of the high plateau that made the light magical just before sunset. Lubumbashi, situated deep in the south of this huge land, is as far from Kinshasa as Miami is from Baltimore, and one of the sublime pleasures at this African latitude is the gentle, lingering evening, so unlike the abrupt shift from day to night that one experiences near the equator.

The last time I had been here I had spent the better part of my stay under interrogation by SNIP, the National Service for Intelligence and Protection. This time, in wild contrast, I was getting VIP treatment, and from the look of the apron at the airport, jammed with the corporate jets of the big mining companies and diamond merchants who had come to cut deals with Kabila even before he could grab power, the rebels were getting some practice in such treatment as well.

On the flight down from Kinshasa, Richardson said he needed to convince Kabila to accept a face-to-face meeting with Mobutu. This, he hoped, would produce a ceasefire, along with the inclusive transition and free elections that he had announced in Kinshasa. "Kabila has to decide whether he wants to be accepted in the international community or he wants to be a renegade," he said. Richardson also stressed that he would tell Kabila that the mounting reports of massacres of Hutu by the rebellion's Tutsi forces were hurting him. "It will be very difficult for him to gain acceptance if those reports are true," he said gravely.

Just days before, the United Nations had reported the literal disappearance of 100,000 Hutu from several makeshift camps that had come under attack from Kabila's army in the dense rain forest near Kisangani. "They are scattered. We found nobody," said Carlos Haddad, a World Food Programme official who overflew the area on a UN reconnaissance mission and found nothing but billowing smoke and three clusters of about a hundred people each where large camps had once stood.

Many of the victims of this rout in the forest near Kisangani were survivors of the group I had recently met in Ubundu. Lashing sections of bamboo together to build rafts or selling their last belongings to pay for passage on small boats, they had managed to cross the Congo River. Many hundreds, perhaps thousands, of others drowned.

UN Secretary-General Kofi Annan said the Hutu appeared to be "victims of a policy of slow extermination." Even if the Clinton administration remained much more guarded, politically it could not afford to appear to be indifferent, and State Department spokesman Nicholas Burns said the situation in the refugee camps was "bordering on humanitarian catastrophe."

In our conversation aboard the aircraft, however, Richardson was already polishing the flagstones for a diplomatic "out" should Washington decide it needed one. "We don't really have a stick, to be honest. There is already some feeling [within the rebellion] that if the international community doesn't want to work with us, that's fine, because international business is lining up already," he told me when I pressed him about what the United States would do to oblige the country's incipient leader to respect his commitments with regard to democracy and the fate of the refugees. "Zaire is an important country and we are going to have to deal with whoever is ruling it. Obviously, we can be more or less cooperative."

I was left unsettled by the sudden talk about Hutu refugees. I was one of only a few reporters who had written frequently on the subject, and when I did so, the weight of the *Times* meant that other media could not ignore the issue completely. It disturbed me deeply to think that this belated flourish of attention might be more clever public relations than substance, part of a sophisticated effort to buy me off with extraordinary access and co-opt me by appearing to share my concerns.

Other interpretations were readily available, but they were equally troubling. Kabila had tremendous wind in his sails, provided by a broad coalition of African powers—Rwanda, Uganda, Burundi, Angola, Eritrea and others. Investors were indeed rushing in. Perhaps, just perhaps, Washington was wielding the human rights card to maintain its leverage and remind Kabila who keeps the keys to the club.

Together with the other members of Richardson's traveling party, I had been picked up at my hotel in Lubumbashi by Dennis Hankins, an American diplomat whom I had previously known as a political officer at the embassy in Kinshasa. For weeks now, Hankins had been quietly acting as Washington's liaison to the rebellion. We pulled up to a Dutch-style mansion to meet Kabila just as the last light was failing. Appropriately, given the rebellion leaders' early zeal to trade on the country's vast mineral wealth, the residence had belonged to the director of Gécamines.

We were made to wait for a while in a green-carpeted room that looked out onto a columned atrium. The diplomats fidgeted like sleepless kids on Christmas Eve dying to see their new toys. Finally, a smiling Kabila emerged, looking jaunty and relaxed in a white sports shirt that contrasted sharply with the business suits of the men he was greeting. "You are welcome in Congo-Zaire," he blustered, speaking in a booming voice in English heavily tinged with an East African accent, picked up during years of exile. Richardson's face, and those of his party, spoke volumes at their first sight of Kabila. The moment of truth in this blind date had arrived, and they were yearning to be alone, to finally get to know each other. The party disappeared into an ornately chandeliered dining room furnished with a large round table, and someone shut the door. I waited outside, together with a handful of local reporters.

Three hours later, the American team reemerged, looking as if they had gotten well beyond first base. Judging from the anxious, slightly guilty smiles, perhaps they felt they had even hit a home run. Looking far more sober, Kabila chose not to address the press. He no longer seemed to have any use for the easy, swaggering charm that he had exploited, together with the ambient sympathy for Rwanda's Tutsi, to win generally uncritical coverage from the international press through nearly seven months of war.

That task was left instead to the rebellion's foreign minister in waiting, Bizima Karaha, a rail-thin man whose grim, toothy face, which never evinced a smile, recalled Dracula. Kabila would meet Mobutu, Karaha announced, to discuss the dictator's departure, and that alone. By training, Karaha was a medical doctor; by countenance, he was a humorless and edgy man of Tutsi ancestry, who appeared to be in his early thirties. He spoke in a reedy, almost adolescent voice that strained for gravity but managed only to grate. "The end of the war can only come when the person who is its cause has gone."

Karaha then tried to explain away the ongoing atrocities against the Hutu refugees. "As the numbers of people who want to be repatriated has diminished, the ex-FAR* and Interahamwe, who don't want to be repatriated, are growing desperate. They are creating these incidents to block the orderly return of others to Rwanda."

At this point, Dennis Hankins whispered to me, "I've been telling them they should say this all along."

Richardson briefly looked annoyed, but like the political pro he is, he focused on preserving the air of accomplishment. Later that evening, Richardson would tell me what he had said undiplomatically to the neophyte foreign minister. "You've got to get rid of that Maoist shit," he

---

*Forces Armées Rwandaises, or FAR, the acronym for Rwanda's formerly Hutu-dominated army.

said, referring to Karaha's stilted, vintage 1970s revolutionary-style speech. "You've got to learn something about foreign affairs, too. Maybe you ought to be the health minister."

For the small gallery of reporters who had waited for the meeting with Kabila to end, though, Richardson had this upbeat message. "It was a discovery on both sides. It was a good meeting," he said repeatedly, again trotting out some of the boilerplate he had used earlier in the day about the transition. "Mr. Kabila assured me that any Alliance soldiers involved in human rights violations would be punished."

Vitally, Richardson said, Kabila had dropped his sixty-day deadline for the Hutu refugees who remained in Zaire to leave the country. Henceforth, this would merely be a goal. Meanwhile, UN relief workers were to be allowed back into rebel-held zones, including areas where there had been reports of atrocities.

After we left the villa, Richardson shared his personal take on Kabila. America's newest African friend was "a street-smart, charismatic person with a quick intelligence but a very narrow vision and perspective, simply because he's been in the bush all these years," he said. "I told him that if he wanted a relationship with the United States, democracy, human rights and free-market economics were going to be important. I told him that he had taken a huge hit on the human rights issue, and that this was going to be important for us. 'Clean up your act, because you'll be a pariah if this stuff continues.'

"I told him you're going to need us, and that's when the breakthrough came," Richardson continued. "We established a tie, and the ambassador [Simpson] even got his fax and phone numbers." In the tense and dramatic days ahead, I would come to realize that of all the talk, the exchange of phone numbers would be most important.

As a parting gift, Richardson said he had given Kabila a New York Yankees cap.

Our traveling party checked out of our hotel early the next morning, and I grabbed a coffee and croissant on the veranda, where I found Ambassador Simpson looking crisp and distinctly satisfied in his tan Brooks Brothers suit. He did his best to brush me off, but when Richardson joined us and behaved with his customary friendliness, the ambassador was obliged to play along.

We were to fly to rebel-held Kisangani, where we would make a brief stop so that Richardson could demonstrate his concern for the plight of the Hutu refugees and meet with the local authorities. Once we were airborne, Richardson's confidences continued briefly. He told me he had addressed Kabila as "president," and that this had disarmed him. "Kabila told me that he was surprised to get a visit from somebody like me. He said, I thought you Americans were still tilting toward Mobutu."

At first blush, Kabila's reported comment seemed ordinary enough. After all, the United States had helped Mobutu knock off Lumumba, and had supported him unstintingly until now. Moreover, if the outside world knew little detail about Kabila's life, the American intelligence agencies undoubtedly knew much more, and the closer one looked, the uglier the picture became.

There was good reason the Kabila strut we saw on CNN, an endlessly replayed clip showing the rebel leader reviewing his young boot-clad troops in Kisangani or Goma, resembled that of a streetcorner hustler. He had perfected it the old-fashioned way, as a genuine thug. He was a survivor who had never given up on his dreams of wealth and power, even if his ideology, a utopian Marxism much influenced by China's Cultural Revolution, had long ago lost its fervor.

For years, Kabila had the merit of running the only armed opposition to Mobutu. His own obscure little rebellion had begun in October 1967, when the young, would-be revolutionary traversed Lake Tanganyika at the head of a band of sixteen men and set up camp in the mountains of Zaire's South Kivu Province, armed with a total of three revolvers.

Che Guevara, who had come to the Congo with a detachment of Cuban revolutionaries to bolster the Simbas in their fight against Mobutu's mercenaries, had all but written off Kabila two years earlier. In the very last lines of his Congo diary, *Pasajes*, he said of the then erratic young man that "he has not yet developed an ideology or displayed the seriousness and spirit of sacrifice necessary to be the leader of a revolution. . . . He is young and may change, but I . . . have very great doubts that he will be able to overcome his deficiencies."

Kabila's life story bespoke extraordinary determination, but in service of what? Any attempts to answer that question quickly lead into extraordinarily murky territory. In the early days, Kabila had once preached that all of the country's wealth would be placed at the disposal of the people. Money would be abolished, and liberated Zaire would function through some kind of magical accounting system where every citizen would be given chits and "people's stores" would provide for their needs in food and clothing.

For a few years, at least, this evocation of paradise seemed to appeal to the Bemba ethnic group that predominates in the Fizi area. The rebel leader's delusions of grandeur soon spun out of control, though, even as the territory under his group's dominion stagnated and shrank. Eventually Kabila accumulated more titles than Mobutu himself, claiming to be president of the republic, head of his Popular Revolutionary Party, commander in chief of the Popular Armed Forces, president of the Popular Assembly and foreign minister, and when the number two and number three officials in the revolutionary hierarchy died, their posts were simply eliminated.

Kabila's propagandists hailed even the smallest skirmish as a major battle, although many of the clashes with Mobutu's army were staged. It was convenient for local commanders to have a threat like the evanescent Popular Armed Forces around, if only to keep the salaries flowing from distant Kinshasa.

By the mid-1970s the rebellion was not looking so promising, and Kabila turned toward outright hustling, poaching elephants for their ivory, selling leopard skins and dealing himself into the underground gold trade that has long been a feature of life in Zaire's eastern hinterland.

Ultimately, Kabila forced his way onto Washington's radar in 1975 by kidnapping three American students and a Dutch researcher. They were released by his rebels sixty-seven days later, after an undisclosed sum was discreetly paid to the rebellion. By 1979, he had morphed from a localized incarnation of Mao into Kurtz, Conrad's monster in *Heart of Darkness*, and was ruling the zone under his control through sheer terror and atrocity. With his unpaid fighters deserting and local populations rebelling against him, he organized a bizarre purge of suspected sorcerers, poisoning an estimated two thousand elderly people in a modern-day version of the Salem witch trials. "Toward this end, he made a concoction of roots and herbs," writes William B. Cosma. "It was a very strong potion, so strong that any physically weak person would go dizzy if he swallowed it or had it splashed in his eyes. Dizziness, though, was a sign of sorcery, and any person showing signs of it after this test was branded a sorcerer and burned alive."

Not long afterward, Kabila reportedly came to the attention of the United States in yet another way. In the late 1970s, an American emissary, Henry McDonald, reportedly visited him in his Fizi redoubt to persuade him to end his rebellion and join the Mobutu government. Kabila is said to have thought favorably of the idea, but in the end he found Kinshasa's price wanting. "Since he was not satisfied, he decided to remain in the opposition, in order to make his presence felt and to enrich himself by exploiting the riches of the region, even if his party was declining," writes Cosma.

Through most of the 1980s, Kabila could boast only a tiny band of men under arms in the mountains in Fizi, perhaps eighty at most. For himself, he preferred a nearly invisible exile, mostly in Tanzania, usually operating under the pseudonym Francis Mutware. That was, until the Rwandans came calling in 1996 with a plan to invade Zaire.

Since the mysterious start of Kabila's 1996 rebellion, Washington had been unable to escape suspicion that it had secretly been the uprising's sponsor. The "evidence" was fragmentary at best, but given its history in the region, the United States had only itself to blame for the blend of skepticism and outright cynicism that observers manifested toward its every step in Zaire.

In the months immediately prior to Kabila's rebellion, the United States had trained hundreds of Rwandan troops in everything from psychological operations to tactical special forces exercises. Paul Kagame, Rwanda's president, had trained at the U.S. Army Command and General Staff College at Fort Leavenworth, Kansas, and could be presumed to have made many valuable American contacts. And in any event, Kagame had visited Washington in August 1996, just six weeks before his country launched its invasion, to discuss the threat his regime faced from Hutu refugees massed across the border, in Zaire.

Senior officials from the American Embassy in Rwanda reportedly had been sighted leaving Kabila's residence in Goma, the eastern Zairian city that was the rebellion's first headquarters, in November 1996. By April 1997, Dennis Hankins had been posted to Goma. And there were persistent reports of American troops spotted in Rwanda even after the war began.*

---

*In August 1997, three months after Kabila's victory, a U.S. Defense Department chronology revealed this rumor to be true, but said the American troops were trainers for land mine removal, civil affairs and public information instructors.

As our white State Department jet soared over a dense, dark and immensely wet world of endless green, Richardson's Kabila anecdotes petered out and I was left to chat in the cramped quarters with a cluster of other Clinton administration officials. These ranged from the CIA's man aboard to Sean McCormick, who ran African affairs on the National Security Council. The conversation quickly turned to the theme of the rumors linking Kabila to the United States, and over the next hour or so, a thumbnail official narrative was spun. The bottom line, I was told, was that because of the attacks on Rwanda from Hutu refugee camps in Zaire, Washington had known that trouble was coming to East Africa, but was caught entirely by surprise by Kabila's sweep across the country.

"I was on the April 1996 mission with [then Deputy CIA Director] George Tenet to Zaire, and he told Mobutu that if he doesn't take care of this situation it is going to come back and bite him in the ass," McCormick said. "We came up with a plan in July to get the refugees to return back to their country, gradually reducing the camps. The Rwandans and Ugandans felt good about this, but nobody in the international community would accept it. We were out there alone, and finally, the Rwandans threw up their hands and said we're fed up."

There was an uneasy moment of silence, and I felt as if I was being sized up by a bunch of very eager salesmen. Should I press ahead with my most serious reservations, fed by the ache that still haunted me from seeing the faces of innocent people tracked by death in places like Tingi-Tingi and Ubundu, or should I let their story unfurl all of its own energy, limiting myself to pro forma questions to show that I was engaged?

The CIA man, who had lived up to the secretive image of his profession throughout the trip, sharing the merest scraps of dialogue with me and then tuning me out before I could pin him down on anything, including his name, suddenly piped up. "We didn't know about [plans for a rebellion]. We weren't informed about it. We didn't have any intel on it until the attacks first started in the Uvira region," he said. "We knew that at a minimum [the Rwandan army] wanted to push the refugees back from the border, and at a maximum, in my view, they would want to kill them.

"When the rebellion took off, we were caught playing catch-up, and the Zairians got steamrolled. There is no wink and a nod. There was never a wink and a nod."

We were running against the clock in Kisangani. There was an absurd proposition behind the stopover: a photo-op amid a holocaust. In the forest less than thirty miles away, extraordinarily unspeakable things had been happening. According to the latest reports, the AFDL had blocked access to one of the last refugee-gathering points south of Kisangani, a place of horrific death with no more descriptive name than its distance marker, Kilometer 42. Bulldozers had been sighted heading south down the road from Kisangani, and relief agency officials who had passed nearby on a train said the area reeked of incinerated bodies. Stories were spreading from Zairian villagers of daily roundups of the emaciated and diseased Hutu who straggled up the road toward Kisangani. Mini-massacres had become the routine, and women and children were given no more mercy than the men, who were ostensibly suspected of carrying out the anti-Tutsi genocide in Rwanda three years before.

Mocking Kabila's promises, UN officials were being turned back by Tutsi soldiers every time they tried to venture down the road that leads south out of town. The pretense for their refusal to allow forward passage was that they had never received any orders to that effect. Each night, meanwhile, under the cover of the equatorial forest, the bonfires and the bulldozers continued to do their work.

Reports reached us of a fresh arrival of refugees into town, and soon after our landing we rushed to one of Kisangani's river ports to witness it. Our timing was perfect. With a sweeping arcade of flamboyant trees framing the scene in red against the silver-hot sky, Richardson approached the docks with his party bunched closely around him. Aides quickly ushered him toward a distraught mother who carried an infant swaddled in a colorful scrap of indigo cloth. Someone whispered something in Richardson's ear about the baby needing urgent medical care. Richardson's face bore the most basic expression of human sympathy and recognition of life's fragility, and his pity appeared entirely genuine. Nonetheless, as he spoke a few words of sympathy to the mother, there was an inescapable feeling of an American electoral campaign stop. Then, at the very moment he reached for the baby, its short life expired.

It took us all a few minutes to gather our composure, but soon enough the caravan was in motion again. We went to see the local governor, Jean Sitolo, freshly appointed by the AFDL, and from wrenching pathos we segued seamlessly into pious sermons. "It is too bad you were not able to visit Biaro. Our alliance has been accused of massacring refugees, but whatever incidents have occurred are things that have happened between the refugees themselves. Don't forget, because of hunger, because they have been walking for two years [*sic*], many of them are dying."

"We in the international community will be watching very carefully," Richardson said, a bit stiffly. "Today you have been very cooperative, and we appreciate that. We must also ask you to give free access to journalists. That is the meaning of a free society."

After witnessing the baby's death close up, it was impossible for me not to be underwhelmed by the sentiments expressed. Richardson never insisted that we be allowed to travel down the dirt road that reportedly led to the killing fields. Whether it was the United States or the United Nations, no Westerner would ever push hard enough to lift the veil over this crude little Auschwitz. In fact, just a few months later, Washington would be pushing to make sure that no Western investigators ever made it down that road.

Tacitly, America had already made common cause with Rwanda's Tutsi-led government, which was counting on the thickness of the bush at the heart of the continent to hush the agonized cries of the massacred, just as it was counting on the unending rains that fed the great river to wash away the ashes, along with every last drop of blood.

Over the next few days, tragedy turned to farce, but this being Zaire, it was never more than a reprieve. Richardson had obtained agreements from Mobutu and Kabila to meet at sea aboard a South African ship—an icebreaker no less—named the *Outeniqua*.

Mobutu may have been clinging to power, but this was no ordinary procrastination. By now, he could barely stand up, and with one glance at the *Outeniqua*, he said there was no way he would be ascending the thirty-one-step gangplank to get on board. Copious amounts of time were wasted trying to devise a backup plan. Someone suggested the dying leader be hoisted aboard by crane, but the cancer had done nothing yet to diminish his vanity, and the idea was quickly discarded. In the end, a special ramp was hastily put together, allowing Mobutu to drive up the steep incline in his black limousine. He even managed a smile as he waved through the window at the mass of journalists gathered at the scene.

Kabila was already affecting the haughtiest of airs, and decided to keep people waiting for him well beyond the scheduled time for the talks to begin. When it came time for the two men to finally meet, however, his monumental arrogance did nothing to conceal his deep insecurities. Kabila was now on the verge of overthrowing Mobutu, mostly by virtue of the fact that he was the last opposition figure remaining of any historical note who had never cut a deal with him. As the two men stood on the prow of the ship, though, it was clear that Kabila, like almost every other Zairian, was in awe of the old man, sick or not. Mobutu turned toward his rival on several occasions to try to engage him, to work some combination of his immense native charm and the universal African sense that one must respect one's elders.

Kabila, dressed in a dark blue safari suit, mugged for the cameras like an African Mussolini, but he dared not look Mobutu in the eye, not even for an instant. The man who had organized a witch hunt and pogrom back in Fizi years ago seemed deathly afraid that Mobutu, who supposedly possessed the mythical attributes of the most revered forest animals, the leopard and the eagle, would pull a sorcerer's trick on him, perhaps transferring his disease with a magical wink and denying Kabila the victory he himself had never completely believed in.

Nelson Mandela and Richardson jointly oversaw the shipboard meeting, acting as shepherds and facilitators, but it produced nothing of real substance. The ice had been broken, but barely. There was talk of a freeze of forces on the ground, and conciliatory words from Kabila about seeing to Mobutu's safety. The two sides said they would meet again soon, but when each departed, it was to prepare very different endgames. Mobutu wanted more than anything to avoid handing the country over to a man he believed unworthy of succeeding, never mind overthrowing, him, and thought he had a few final tricks up his sleeve.

There were 3,500 Western troops just across the river in Brazzaville. Most were from France, but the United States had sent 1,150 soldiers, and there was a smattering from other countries as well. Rumors began to circulate among usually well informed Zairians that Mobutu was secretly hoping for—or perhaps even planning—another grand bout of pillaging and that that, combined with the murder of a few white people, would draw the troops across the river to stabilize Kinshasa, at which point Kabila would not dare attack.

Whatever he had promised aboard the *Outeniqua*, Kabila's forces never stopped their advance into positions around Kinshasa. The Zairian army had blown up a major bridge just south of Mbandaka, three hundred miles to the north, upriver from Kinshasa, to slow the AFDL's approach along the river. The rebels had long ago become adept at fording rivers, though, and the only thing that detained them at Mbandaka was the need to dispose of a large population of Hutu stragglers, who by that point had walked a thousand miles, traversing the entire breadth of Zaire on foot, and were now hoping to cross into the Congo Republic next door.

Mbandaka became the next scene of the horrible, rolling massacres. The city was a major river port and border crossing, and, unlike places like Ubundu and Kilometer 42, was not entirely lost to time or smothered amid impassable roads and forests of elephant grass and bamboo. Local Zairians who had initially applauded the rebels' arrival were soon horrified by the scale of the killings by Tutsi troops, and word of the atrocities spread quickly.

While Washington remained low-key, in Lubumbashi Kabila brushed off questions about the fate of the Hutu, calling it a "petit problème." But Emma Bonino, the European Union's humanitarian aid commissioner, qualified, saying that the zones under Kabila's control had become a "slaughterhouse," and international human rights networks were already beginning to insist that whoever came to power in Zaire must address what had happened at Mbandaka.

In Kinshasa, people were too concerned with their own survival to think about something as distant and abstract as massacres of foreign refugees. This was the fall of Saigon brought to Central Africa, and scenarios of disaster and dread played in everyone's mind. Few thought that Mobutu's army would actually make a last stand in the capital, turning it into a battlefield. Most people were fixated, instead, on the random danger and sheer chaos that another bout of pillaging would surely bring.

Hearing Elie Noël, a forty-five-year-old carpenter whose heavily varnished beds and other furniture he made cluttered the Matongé sidewalk in front of his shop, recall the last pillage, it was easy to understand the horror people feared would be repeated. "It began at six a.m. with the sound of bullets penetrating the rooftop and walls," he said. "I heard the soldiers enter my neighbor's house and then they were beating on my door. They took everything of value they could find, even my clothing. I was lucky that my wife and daughter had slept somewhere else the night before. Next door they raped my friend's daughters, ten years old and twelve years old, and they made him watch.

"People denounce our soldiers as savages, but this was all done on Mobutu's orders. The rapes and the pillaging were meant to punish us for supporting the opposition. They say he wants another round now to save himself."

The diplomats were still pushing the idea of talks to avoid this kind of scene from transpiring. Mobutu and Kabila were to meet aboard the *Outeniqua* one more time, and with people in the president's entourage sending their families out of the country, talk was spreading that if no agreement could be reached between the two men Mobutu would opt to fly off into exile. Kabila, sure of victory, chose to stand everyone up.

Mobutu took a short flight back to Kinshasa the next morning, cutting short the speculation about whether he would return. In the meantime, I had again spoken to General Mahélé. He was furious that Kabila had not shown up, and equally frustrated that Mobutu was showing no sign of leaving. His priority, he said, was to negotiate a peaceful handover of Kinshasa. "If I make contact with the other side I will be regarded as a traitor. But otherwise, what will tomorrow be like?" he asked, agonizing over his predicament. "Make contacts today in order to spare the city and you risk being executed. If you do nothing, there will be a great tragedy here, and you will be marginalized in the end, and perhaps executed anyway."

I thought Mahélé was merely rehearsing his thoughts aloud for me, but the coming hours showed how far and how fast things had moved. The following day, on May 15, I was summoned to army head-quarters along with a group of colleagues, ostensibly to meet with General Mahélé. Clearly, everything was in play, but we were to be given only the narrowest, most sanitized version. Mahélé's aide, Colette Tshomba, a woman whose conspicuous elegance suggested other special missions on the general's behalf, sternly warned us that the moment was grave, and told us to be responsible in our handling of information. "We in the government are doing the best we can do to give negotiation a chance. We do not believe in war for war's sake. That is nonsense. We can all imagine what would happen if fighting broke out in Kinshasa." Later I learned that Ambassador Simpson had urged Mahélé to speak directly with Kabila in order to negotiate the so-called soft landing for the city, and making use of the telephone numbers he had obtained in Lubumbashi, the ambassador was proposing to personally broker the telephone call.

The next day, Mahélé and the other top generals jointly petitioned for an urgent meeting with Mobutu to tell him bluntly and for the first time that the situation on the ground was hopeless. In a scene that brought to mind the meeting of Dorothy, the Lion and the rest of their merry band with the Wizard of Oz, Mobutu's top generals, many of them his in-laws, and most of them perfectly useless figures, were ushered in to meet the badly diminished president at 5 p.m. The group promptly lost its nerve, or perhaps, as some suggest more skeptically, they strategically deferred to Mahélé, allowing him and him alone to stick his neck out, deliberately leaving their rival, a man Mobutu had always distrusted, way out on a limb.

Mahélé spoke forcefully, even raising his voice on occasion, straining to convince Mobutu that his survival depended upon his abandonment of power. "Vous devez partir," you must leave now, he pronounced boldly, but with an air of loyalty. "We can no longer assure your security." Mobutu fumed, listening silently throughout, and when Mahélé finished his soliloquy, Mobutu curtly pronounced, "Give me an hour and you will have my reply."

One hour later the generals were summoned anew, and Mobutu intoned gravely, "I will not leave." At that point, and for the very first time, Mahélé lost his composure, and as the generals filed out, he slammed the door. At 4 a.m., Mobutu called his generals and told them that he had changed his mind and would leave that morning. He ordered a plane to be readied for a 10 a.m. departure.

I had taken to sleeping with my cell phones by my pillow, and received first word of the second generals' meeting with Mobutu in a late-night phone call from the aide-de-camp of General Likulia, the prime minister. He told me Mobutu would fly off the next morning for Gbadolité.

A few minutes later my phone rang again, and the news was confirmed, mournfully, by Guy Vanda. It would keep ringing through the night, as the rumor of the Leopard's departure swept the city. There would be no public announcement, Guy told me, but if I wished to witness the president's final flight from Kinshasa, I should be at Ndjili airport at dawn.

I shared what I knew of the situation with my friend Ofeibea, who had heard as much from a foreign airline manager who seemed to be in the know whenever something important was about to happen. The airline man generously offered us a ride to Ndjili in one of his company vans. It was about the only sure way to get near the airport on a day when anything else moving was likely to be shot at.

A half dozen or so of us crammed into the van and drove the sixteen miles through Kinshasa's dusty, potholed streets. Zairians knew better than to be out and about, and the route was absolutely deserted. Soldiers had already been stationed at regular intervals along the route, and we could see a few photographers being attacked and arrested as they attempted to stake out positions to capture Mobutu's motorcade on film.

Ndjili airport was deserted. There would be no pomp for Mobutu today. Our airline van deposited us at a side building a hundred yards away from the VIP entrance that the president would surely use, and as the BBC-TV people I had shared the ride with began setting up their equipment, we heard the wail of sirens, faint at first, but clearly drawing near. At the very moment Mobutu's motorcade wheeled into view—identical black Cadillacs, a bleating ambulance and scores of outriders—a handful of soldiers who had been posted at the VIP entrance came to life and began waving at us, signaling that we should put away all of our cameras. Then some of them began running in our direction. There had been all too many moments like these during the last seven months of war in Zaire, when I did not know whether my face was going to be smashed in or indeed if there would be a tomorrow.

The streets had been absolutely clear of vehicles during our entire drive to the airport, but at that instant, as if by magic, a lone, shabby taxi appeared, and with the soldiers closing in on us, I managed to discreetly wave him to a halt. "Ofeibea, Ofeibea, come on, let's go," I urged my friend, but she was too valiant to allow herself to be separated from her BBC colleagues, and I jumped in the car and drove away, not knowing what would become of them.

On the long ride back to town I worked my telephones, calling Guy, who had often saved me from the SNIP and the DSP in the past. I called the British Embassy and the American Embassy, too, and told them that a news crew at the airport was in peril.

Mobutu had fled, and in a final act of vanity he had prevented anyone from filming it. The war was all but over. All that remained now was to await the rebels, whose forward positions were said to be scarcely a few miles beyond Ndjili.

Guy called me back at the hotel that afternoon to tell me that Ofeibea and her crew had been released unharmed.

Late that Friday evening, as I sat in the Memling Hotel writing about the final day of Mobutu's thirty-two-year rule, my telephones started to light up again. Likulia's aide-de-camp told me to expect the general/prime minister to go on television at 11:30 that night to announce an agreement stipulating in part that the ten thousand theoretically loyal troops who remained in Kinshasa would lay down their arms. Another confidant, General Ilunga, Mobutu's interior minister, told me that Mahélé had urged Likulia to cross the river to Brazzaville, to wait there in safety; in case of a foreign intervention, Likulia could then be called upon to rule as an interim leader. "Both of us will be marked for death; at least one of us must remain alive," Mahélé is reported to have said.

In the instance, neither man was leveling with the other, but Mahélé's objectives, at least, had a partial purchase on honor. Likulia had already been selling himself to the French as an eleventh-hour alternative to Kabila, whom Paris, paranoid as ever, imagined to be an American battering ram wielded to shatter the last vestiges of French influence in Central Africa. Mahélé had taken Ambassador Simpson up on his invitation to place a call to Kabila's satellite phone, and may have envisioned himself as a future commander of the army or perhaps one day even president. The bottom line, though, was that Mahélé truly wanted to avert a catastrophe in Kinshasa, while Likulia's only hope for advancement depended on one.

Yet another call came. The caller, who was with Mahélé, said that Mobutu's son and dreaded enforcer Kongulu had called the general from Camp Tshatshi. Few words were spoken, but the air of emergency was unmistakable. "We have a situation here," Kongulu said. "I need you to come right away."

Mahélé understood this to mean that a revolt was spreading through Camp Tshatshi among the troops from Equatoria Province, who were Mobutu's ethnic relatives and the final rampart against the rebels. With the AFDL closing in and Mobutu gone, the troops from the Division Spéciale Présidentielle feared for their lives. It was as if Mahélé's worst nightmare were coming true. All that remained was for the men at Tshatshi to break out of the barracks with their weapons and rampage through the town, looting while the looting was good.

In fact, it was another of Mahélé's nightmares, the fear of his own assassination, which he had confided to me a few days before, that was coming to pass. Mobutu's generals had spread the word that he was a traitor, and the word of an uprising at Tshatshi was little more than a trap, one that the general, true to himself and to his uniform, fatally could not resist.

Not long after his first call to my informant, who even today insists on remaining unnamed, Kongulu called again. "Mahélé is dead," he announced starkly. "The situation is extremely dangerous. Tell me where you are." Alarm bells were going off in my informant's mind, but for some reason he answered truthfully. "I'm at the Intercontinental." My informant then fled the hotel, taking refuge in a mansion nearby, in the ritzy Gombé district.

Next came a call from Guy. "Howard, Mahélé is dead. I saw the whole thing. They killed him while he was trying to address the troops. Soldiers from the DSP began denouncing him as a traitor and tried to arrest him. Mahélé's bodyguards tried to push him into a car and rush him away from there, but somebody ran up to him and shot him in the head, point blank."

I told Guy that I felt sure that Kongulu was the killer, but he insisted that was not the case. "We had arrived when this happened. It happened before my eyes. We could have been killed ourselves."

The early editions of the *New York Times* were already coming off the presses with the news of Mobutu's departure emblazoned across the front page. I needed to update my story with this latest drama, but by the rules of the trade, in order to state Mahélé's death as a fact, one eyewitness was not enough. I required a second source.

I called Ambassador Simpson on his private number and insisted that he come to the phone. "I have it from eyewitnesses that Mahélé has just been murdered," I told him. There was a long silence. "Mr. Ambassador, can you confirm that?" Simpson told me to call back in a few minutes. When I reached him the second time, he told me that all he could confirm was that Mahélé "had been detained" at Camp Tshatshi. Hours later, the U.S. military attaché confirmed the news of his death.

Dawn came after a brief and fitful sleep. Artillery could be heard far away, its low and muffled boom like the slamming of a distant door.

Soon my phones were ringing again, and with the calls came details of Kongulu's marauding all-night rampage through the city, culminating with a visit to the Intercontinental Hotel, where he searched for traitors, real and imagined.

Word came of an SUV abandoned in the middle of the road that ran alongside the river in Gombé. A small, clandestine pier sat half hidden in the overgrowth nearby. By all accounts, Mobutu's most dangerous son, the one who had nicknamed himself Saddam Hussein, had fled into the neighboring Congo Republic.

Nervous and excited, the press gathered by the hundreds downtown to share impressions and exchange snippets of information in the lobby of the Memling Hotel. A carload of Mobutu's generals had stopped by and urged the reporters not to wander the streets. Then they zoomed off with a loud screech.

I returned to my room on one of the upper floors, and within minutes a call came from Guy. "Stay in your room because a death squad is going to pull up to the hotel and spray it with machine-gun fire, and maybe launch a grenade or two," he warned. This was the last gasp of the regime, the long-dreamed-of scenario whereby death or danger to foreigners draws the French army, and perhaps the Americans, too, across the river from Brazzaville, preventing a Kabila takeover of Kinshasa.

The elevators crawled with traffic, so I ran downstairs to the lobby as fast as I could and shouted to my colleagues to clear the area and go to their rooms. Someone asked what I was talking about, and breathlessly, I explained the substance of the telephone call. For a moment, it was absolute pandemonium as the lobby cleared.

I waited in my room for over half an hour, and nothing happened. The only noises were the rumbling of the artillery, which had grown steadily closer, and the occasional clatter of small-arms fire. Ofeibea and I then summoned our nerve and set out onto the streets, against the advice of our colleagues, who were now warning *me* of the danger. Sticking close to the walls of buildings for cover, in almost comical mockery of a police movie, we headed for Avenue 30 Juin, the city's weed-filled Champs-Elysées. The only other people about were glue-addicted street children, a scruffy young teenage boy and a couple of little girls, perhaps child prostitutes, their barely formed breasts half exposed in their grimy, tattered clothes.

At 5 p.m. the first Kabila troops came marching into the city center, in parade fashion: neat and orderly. Conspicuously, they were not, for the most part, Rwandan. The columns seemed to stretch without end as the troops marched, dripping sweat and visibly fatigued, chanting in the humid late-afternoon air, kicking up dust from the fine riverine soil they trod underfoot.

Once it became clear that the shooting was over, huge crowds began descending into the streets and leaning from the balconies of the central city buildings, cheering, "Congo! We are free! Congo! We are free!" as they watched the would-be liberators file by.

Bantus love a spectacle, and now it fell to Laurent Désiré Kabila to provide it.

CHAPTER ELEVEN

Le Roi Est Mort *(Long Live the King)*

M obutu's homecoming in Gbadolité turned out to be little more than a hasty stopover. Neglecting to pay the troops can be a costly mistake, even if they are from your own ethnic group. Knowing the game was up, the Ngbandi garrison in the city heeded Mobutu's old watchword—pay yourselves—and commenced looting. In better days, Mobutu had flown off to vacation from here with his large clan in tow aboard specially chartered Concordes. For his final departure from Gbadolité, only his innermost circle would clamber aboard the Soviet-built Ilyushin cargo plane loaned to him by his longtime protégé, the leader of Angola's UNITA rebellion, Jonas Savimbi.

As Mobutu's plane gained altitude, though, even these rudely downgraded travel plans went sour when members of the Division Spéciale Présidentielle, irate at being left behind to face advancing rebel armies, opened fire on the jet. Thus went the departure of Mobutu, molder of nations and tamer of men.

Laurent Kabila's very first act as president, on May 17, 1997, would be to restore the name Congo to the country—Zaire became the Democratic Republic of the Congo. Washington wasted no time in recognizing the new reality. "We will no longer be calling this country Zaire," State Department spokesman Nicholas Burns announced.

"Zaire went away on Friday afternoon with Mobutu. That country has vanished."

Mobutu had changed the name from Congo to Zaire in 1971 in a bid to overcome Lumumba's enduring legacy, but only with time would I realize how carefully Kabila was stealing from Mobutu's playbook, although sometimes, as with the name change, he was doing things in reverse. It was not long, too, before extracting criticism of the new regime from the American Embassy would become as difficult as it had once been under Mobutu and his serviceable prime minister, Kengo wa Dondo—that is, before Washington designated them, respectively, a "has-been" and a "big crook."

With the change in regimes, I moved across town to the Intercontinental to watch the new elite as it settled into residence in this ritzy hotel, built by Mobutu in the 1970s as one of the proudest monuments to his own glory. Breakfast and cocktail hour were the best times to observe this motley crowd—Kabila's ethnic allies from Katanga Province, who formed his inner circle, and the Tutsi officers from Rwanda who eyed them carefully from beneath ten-gallon hats, or as some observers already whispered, pulled the real strings. Exempted from paying any bills, the Congolese piled their plates high, and wined and dined a parade of mistresses new and old, who grew ever more gaudily dressed as the weeks went by. The Rwandans, for their part, affected fatigues or sober business suits and were far more modest in their tastes, or at least more discreet. This cast was filled out by the kadogo, the pint-sized boy soldiers with AK-47s, who would crowd into the elevators, excited to be riding in them for the first time, and the carpetbagging foreign businessmen, here to cut quick and sleazy deals with a government in need of cash.

As I said, when Kabila and his sponsors entered the city, they had been careful to keep the Rwandan forces who constituted the brunt of the rebel army out of the picture. But when it came to taking charge of the country, and of the sprawling city of Kinshasa, there was no hiding the identity of the men who owned the guns. The first signs of trouble came early in the new regime, when Tutsi soldiers launched an ill-advised crackdown on moral laxity and roughed up some downtown streetwalkers. The new government then issued an edict banning miniskirts, and began rounding up women—including my driver Pierre's girlfriend, Nounou—who had failed to comply.

The rebels may have won some good press early on by straightening out the bedlam at border crossings in the east, but we were in a city that lived on beer and soukous and reveled in its Gomorrah-like image. All it took to realize this was to listen for one hour to the hip-churning tunes that played on the radio. But the Rwandans and their handpicked new president, with his long years in the bush, were way out of touch.

I had no idea of its importance at the time, but the flap over miniskirts helped seal Kabila's image as a man totally out of sync with "his people" and, even worse, in the eyes of the Kinois, residents of Kinshasa, who soon invented a zombie-like dance in mockery of Kabila, known as the "dombolo," a man held prisoner by his sponsors. The warning signs multiplied steadily. Severe-looking Tutsi agents took over security at Ndjili airport. Kabila's son, Joseph, a shy, boyish man in his late twenties,* was named to lead the army, but *everyone* answered to a Rwandan officer named James Kabarebe. Though burly and mightily prepossessed, Kabila himself soon appeared to be imprisoned by a wiry phalanx of Tutsi bodyguards.

Kabila and his minions contented themselves with the illusion of power, dividing up the spoils from regimes past by setting up a Bureau de Biens Mal Acquis, or Office of Ill-gotten Gains, to parcel out the spacious villas built by the Belgians in the breeze-conditioned hills of Binza. Meanwhile, schools and health clinics were not yet opened, and Congo, a vast and proud, albeit disheveled, country of 45 million, was being reduced to a satrapy by Rwanda, a tiny and cramped land of 7 million.

The first serious headaches, though, came from the United Nations, which was demanding access to Mbandaka to investigate reports of mass killings of Hutu refugees there. Kabila had been toying with the organization for a long time, as the United States ran interference in the Security Council, just as it had done at the outset of the war, when Washington had blocked calls by Canada and France for humanitarian intervention.

Here again, Philip Gourevitch, the chronicler of the Rwandan genocide whose writings had deeply influenced the Clinton administration's thinking on Central Africa, helped supply the rationale. Gourevitch's marked sympathies for Rwanda's Tutsi often led him astray on the Congo, and he played an important role in selling Laurent Kabila in Washington, ironically by restoring him to the Lumum-

*Joseph Kabila became president in February 2001 following his father's assassination.

baist tradition of respectable nationalism. In his writings, Gourevitch curiously airbrushed the old Congolese highwayman and mountebank, minimizing his ideology and avoiding unpleasant details of his dodgy past.

"Oddly, a number of recent reports have called Kabila's qualifications for leadership into question by noting that Che Guevara, who visited the Congo in 1965, found him wanting in Marxist-Leninist fervor—as if Che's regard had suddenly become a credential for statesmanship," Gourevitch wrote in one of a series of articles on the fall of Mobutu. Subsequently, he downplayed the importance of the massacre of Hutu during Congo's civil war, accusing the United Nations of "cavalier, imperial irresponsibility" in Central Africa, and ridiculing its demands to be allowed to investigate and account for the dead.

"For weeks now, the U.N. sleuths have been stuck in Kinshasa, waiting for government travel approval, which appears more unlikely each day," Gourevitch wrote in *The New Yorker*. Rwandan Hutu, he said, had formed the core of Mobutu's defenders, and were perceived as "future génocidaires by *Kabila's forces*, and this population was the main target of the massacres that Kabila's government is denying ever happened." A bit later, Gourevitch said of international calls for an investigation of the alleged atrocities: "It's hard to imagine that anybody in the Congo stands to benefit from this test of wills."

With a new strategic vision wheeling into position in Washington—one based on fighting Islamic radicalism in Sudan, securing the lion's share of Angola's petroleum reserves for American oil companies and atoning for its criminal negligence during the Rwandan genocide—the White House anointing of Kabila as one of its newly designated group of African renaissance leaders was an act of expiation meant to soothe Tutsi-led Rwanda. Long rumored, Gourevitch's influence in Washington became explicit during the visit of Madeleine Albright to Kinshasa on December 12, 1997, and for Kabila, a man who had lived a life of such little consequence, it was an undreamt-of consecration.

Kabila's breaking out in Mobutu's leopard's spots had accelerated alarmingly in the weeks before the Albright trip. His government had banned opposition parties and begun ruling by decree. It had successfully forced the United Nations to replace the head of its forensic investigation team, effectively sacking Roberto Garreton, a renowned Chilean lawyer and human rights investigator, after he produced a preliminary sixteen-page report that identified forty sites where Kabila's AFDL was suspected of having committed atrocities. The worst stories centered around Mbandaka, where the government had banned visits by journalists, and had repeatedly disrupted UN attempts to commence field work, as Gourevitch wrote.

Etienne Tshisekedi had been silenced by house arrest, and anyone else who challenged the government was being thrown into prison. "We thought we were getting a sweet orange and we ended up with a bitter lemon," one of the streetcorner parliamentarians told me in Matongé, speaking with the deft and playful allusiveness typical of Kinois. "Maybe our country is just cursed."

But if the Congo was cursed with dictators, it was also blessed with a resilient civil society, and articulate new opposition figures willing to risk their freedom to fight for democracy were sprouting up as fast as Kabila could eliminate them. One of them was Arthur Zahidi Ngoma, a former UNESCO official, whom I first met in August 1997. "In our countries, dictators establish themselves by two methods, by creating fear, and when that no longer works, by corrupting people," Ngoma told me. "We have seen it all before under Mobutu. Kabila has been jailing people. Now he is going to move to the next phase."

Pinned down in the capital covering Mobutu's fall, I had been unable to get to Mbandaka or any other flashpoint during the final stages of the rebels' advance. Thus I could not assess for myself the proliferating charges of the massacre of innocents. But Robert Block, a South Africa–based reporter for the *Wall Street Journal*, had somehow managed to visit Mbandaka in early June 1997, about two weeks after Kabila's triumph, and the accounts of fresh atrocities by the Tutsi troops that he brought back were bone-chilling. "Townspeople say they little suspected what was in store when the rebel troops strolled into town on May 13, virtually unopposed," Block wrote. "The people of Mbandaka were on the streets eager to welcome the soldiers of Kabila's army as liberators. . . . As soon as they arrived [the soldiers] said they were looking for the place where the refugees were kept. . . . They said that their first enemy were these refugees from Rwanda, not the population and not even the Zairian soldiers of Mobutu's army.

"What happened next beggared belief, say those who were there," Block continued. "The soldiers approached the refugees near the harbor. When they arrived, says Justin, a local Red Cross worker from the nearby village of Wendji, the soldiers had someone shout in Lingala, the local language, 'Zairians get down.' The Zairians dropped to the ground, Justin says, while the Rwandans remained standing. 'They shot them. They shot them. They shot them,' Justin says, trembling."

In the end, the UN human rights team was never allowed to do its work in Mbandaka, where two thousand or so people were gunned down or beaten to death, and given testimony like that quoted by Block, it is little wonder why. I never made it to Mbandaka, either, but with Madeleine Albright's visit to Kinshasa approaching I came very close to the truth of the killing fields there nonetheless.

By August 1997, the stalemated UN investigation had become the biggest story in the Congo. All around, Central Africa was coming apart at the seams, and Kinshasa's most interesting diversion, as depressing as it was, was an invitation to dine on the balcony of a tony downtown high-rise to watch the fireworks across the river. Brazzaville could be reliably counted upon to deliver a breathtaking sound-and-light show every evening, as militias loyal to the present and former presidents slugged it out savagely with heavy artillery, helicopter gun-ships and anti-aircraft batteries. Just a few miles and a monster of a river away from wherever we might gather by evening over Chardon-nay and canapés, a half million refugees were on the march, almost completely ignored by the world.

"You have the French ambassador living in his bunker, protected by thirty gendarmes, and you have the oilmen who work in Pointe Noire, who live in a heavily protected enclave, and you have us watching from up here," a diplomat remarked to me over cocktails at a UN dinner party in early September. "Other than that, this is a war without witnesses."

With that, someone asked if I was interested in going into the "other" Congo with a UN human rights team to visit a refugee camp a day's boat ride downriver from Mbandaka, where 4,800 Hutu lived more or less stranded. I answered yes.

I showed up at Kinshasa's junk-strewn, inner-city airfield early on the appointed morning. It was the same place I had flown to Kikwit from to report on the Ebola epidemic two years earlier, but that already seemed like a lifetime ago. There was a small crew of UN refugee officials, yet another banged-up old DC-3 and a hold full of food and medicines. With minimal fuss we were airborne, and after a short flight that followed the course of the river northward, until it reached a great fork—the junction with the Sangha, a huge river in its own right—we put down. I expected to spend two nights in Loukolela, the little town where the refugee camp was located, and had brought a minimal kit: my briefcase-sized satellite phone, a laptop, my Sony shortwave radio, one change of clothing, spiral notebooks, a novel and some magazines. There was also a medicine kit stuffed with something for almost any tropical eventuality.

The resident staff in the camp wore the hardships they endured like badges of honor. In their neat little tent city, temperatures soared to well over 100 degrees every day, and the humidity seemed to surpass saturation. In greeting me, their eyes appeared to be saying, We're just waiting to watch you wither.

I headed out almost immediately for the nearby camp. Within a few minutes I was sweating heavily as I made my way along a trail, but soon enough I came upon the little Hutu refugee city that I was looking for. The camp was draped across an expanse of hillocks and lush green vales, and was spacious and orderly—a world apart from the besieged settlements I had seen in Tingi-Tingi and Ubundu. But just as in those forsaken places, in an instant I was surrounded by young camp denizens who wanted to know who I was and what I had come for.

We enacted a little impromptu skit that on my part conveyed, "Take me to your leader," and in no time, I was introduced to a man who enjoyed some kind of special standing in the camp. He agreed to give me a tour. As we descended a hill into a little depression where women were washing clothes in a stream, someone yelled out, "French! Monsieur French!" I turned to see a man running toward me with a broad grin and a look of disbelief that matched the one that was now on my face.

It was Camille, the doctor who had accompanied me so enthusiastically as I strolled through the camp at Tingi-Tingi during my visit there with Sadako Ogata of the Office of the United Nations High Commissioner for Refugees. He grabbed me by both hands and shook me, disbelieving his eyes, wanting to confirm that this was for real. I too felt as if I had stepped into a dream. How had he survived the string of massacres that had laid a trail of blood, tears and bones across Zaire? How had he ever survived the walk—more than a thousand miles had it been in a straight line but certainly far more since the route had wound through some of the world's densest rain forest?

This was no surprise reunion of old friends, but the improbable way that fate had linked us made the experience just as powerful. We stood there in the deathly mid-afternoon heat and exchanged pleasantries. Finally he got around to asking me why I had come, and I told him I had come for the same reason that had brought me to Tingi-Tingi months before: to see what had become of these people.

I was beginning to feel unbearably hot, and became aware that I was sweating profusely. I toted it up to the fact that I had risen so early to get to the airport, and had not had a real meal yet that day. Camille brought me to the camp's medical clinic, where he said I could sit in the shade and interview people who came for care, or simply passersby.

The first person to come along was a twenty-year-old woman named Odette Mporayonzi, who said that on May 13, 1997, she had been in Wendji, the scene of some of the worst massacres from the end of the war, judging from the stories that were being told. "My husband had gone to fetch firewood, so I was all alone when it began," said Odette, who was seven months pregnant and had come to the little clinic—nothing more than a clapboard shack, really—for a checkup. "The bullets were falling on us like the rain in a storm. I ran until I fell, and then I just watched what happened.

"Two soldiers summoned me to halt. They grabbed me, and I just pretended I was deaf and mute, and when they let go of me, I just continued walking. The soldiers kept shooting and shooting, and so many people were dying. When a Zairian soldier stopped to rummage through the belongings of people who had been killed, an officer shouted to him in our language, 'That stuff can wait until our mission has been accomplished.' "

Odette never saw her husband again. She wandered the forests after the gunfire finally died down, and was eventually taken in by a Zairian family, who told her that she looked enough like the local people not to arouse too much suspicion. They told her to wear a white bandana, just as the local townsfolk were doing, in a show of support for Kabila and his rebellion. And they warned her not to talk to strangers.

The next day, while she stood outside the house where she had taken refuge, Odette said a truckload of troops rumbled up and stopped nearby. This, she thought, would surely be the end of her, but instead the soldiers grabbed a teenage Hutu boy who happened to be walking by. As they began beating him, Odette said the soldiers yelled, "Here is another son of Habyarimana," invoking the name of the former Hutu president of Rwanda. "Right there in the road the soldiers swung the boy by his feet and beat his head against a tree trunk until he was dead. I had to squeeze my eyes shut to keep from screaming."

As Odette spoke I began to feel ill. My stomach was queasy. I felt faint. Her story was one of the most disturbing I had ever heard, and yet by now I was struggling to keep my eyes open. Although I was sitting in the shade, the air felt as if it was coming straight from a furnace, only it was dead still. Sweat cascaded down my brow as if poured from a cup, and yet my skin felt incredibly clammy.

Camille asked me if I was okay. He offered me a Coke, which I gladly drank as Odette's story continued, thinking that the sugar would give me a lift. "A couple of days later, a sergeant and a young man from town came to eat dinner at the house where I was staying. They had just participated in a mass burial, and one of them said, 'Ah, Kabila has really killed a lot of people here, hasn't he?' The other man replied, 'Yeah, but the worst thing is that they are burying people twenty to a grave, and all they can think to tell us is to work faster.' "

I did a few more interviews in the camp, but soon I felt too ill to work. Camille offered to escort me back to the UN workers' encampment, but I excused myself and trod back through the heat alone. "I'll be back for more interviews tomorrow, early, before it gets so hot," I told him, though I knew I was falling seriously ill. I already suspected malaria and wondered if I would ever make it back there at all.

I retired immediately to the tent I had been assigned, and took a triple dose of Fansidar, one of the strongest medications available for acute malaria. I had already been taking daily doses of a prophylactic drug, but I knew it was not 100 percent effective in Central Africa, and I counted myself lucky for never having come down with the disease before.

Dinner was still a couple of hours off, and I felt too sick to do anything but lie down on my cot and listen to the radio. There was a small fan, but as soon as I turned it on I went from boiling heat to maddening chills. I joined the UN folks for dinner and tried to force some food down, but had to excuse myself halfway into the meal. I wanted to call my father in Virginia on the satellite phone, since he is a doctor with extensive experience in Africa. When I called, it was comforting to hear from him that I had already done all that I could.

As the night wore on, though, it became apparent that my health was getting far worse. I could not stop shaking, even with the fan off. I went through fits of violent vomiting and diarrhea. My cot was soaked through with sweat. At dawn, I crawled out of my tent and summoned the UN staff. I was too weak to walk, and my vision had gone blurry. "There's no doctor here," someone said. "The nearest medical help is the Médecins sans Frontières doctor who is working a few villages away from here. We'll try to get her on the radio."

My teeth chattered as I lay on a cot outdoors in the morning sun, trying to get warm. I overheard someone say that fighting in the area had prevented the doctor from coming. Later, I could hear the sound of gunfire. Then, when I had all but given up hope, the doctor appeared, like a vision in a dream, a beautiful Colombian woman, and we spoke in a mixture of Spanish and French. She told me that I probably had cerebral malaria. "Your condition is very dangerous," she said, injecting me with a dose of morphine to settle me down. Then she gave me a fistful of quinine tablets, which she said I should chew until they were gone. "They are going to make you feel even sicker, but it is the only thing that can break your infection."

The doctor said I should be near a hospital, if not in one, and urged the UN people to call in an airplane to fly me to Kinshasa, and then she was off. Her warning about the quinine proved right, but she had told me only half of the story. Soon, my ears were ringing as if I were trapped in a belfry. The medicine, which was originally derived by Native Americans from the bark of the cinchona tree, was the most bitter thing I had ever tasted, and although my stomach was empty, it made me retch even more violently than I had the night before.

I ducked miserably in and out of consciousness for the next few hours. In fact, the passage of time completely escaped me. Eventually someone from the UN encampment roused me to say that a small plane had arrived to pick me up.

I reached the Intercontinental Hotel late that afternoon and saw my Reuters colleague and friend William Wallis exiting the huge copper-trimmed doors of the reception area as I arrived. Why had I mysteriously disappeared for a couple of days? Where had I been? he asked. Perhaps he suspected I had a big scoop. But as he took a closer look at me, the banter quickly ended, and he helped me into the elevator.

William must have called the UN offices to tell them I was gravely ill, because as another equatorial sunset exploded gaudily over the Congo River, my phone began ringing with inquiries from concerned officials and friends. In the morning, the United Nations sent someone to take me to its Kinshasa clinic, where a blood test was ordered to see if I had been cured or not. The UN doctor looked at me in shock as he took my history, when I told him the dosage of quinine the Colombian doctor had given me in the field.

"Are you sure of that?" he asked. I produced the little white envelope upon which she had written her instructions. "That is enough quinine to stop someone's heart," he said. It was apparently not enough to kill the parasites still circulating in my bloodstream, however. When the test results came back, the infection still rated a three out of four on the simple scale used to measure the presence of falciparum malaria, meaning that I was still in serious condition.

The doctor gave me a new drug, Malarone, and ordered me to stay in bed. I promised to stay put in my hotel room and call him if I felt any worse.

After years of bad roads and horrible flights, separation from family, arrests, unsafe water and contaminated food, and finally now malaria, I began to conclude that Africa was starting to kill me. So many loves had kept me going here: the beauty and the unfussy grace of the people, the amazing food—yes, the food—music rich beyond comparison, the sheer immediacy of human contact, the pleasure of living by my wits. But the grim truth was that a single mosquito bite had contained enough deadly force to lay me very low indeed, and left me feeling seriously weakened and vulnerable as never before.

I had decided to return to Africa as a journalist in 1994 because I wanted to dig into the kinds of stories about African people and culture that do not often get told. In the beginning of my tour I had done a fair bit of that, but then Nigeria exploded, followed by Liberia and Ebola and the Kabila invasion, and too many smaller crises to recount. In short, I became something of a glorified fireman, despite my best intentions. In the process, though, I came to appreciate more than ever why it is wrong for us to push African news—and not just the riotously colorful features that one editor once described to me as the continent's "oogah-boogah"—to the margins.

The chances for the kind of pure discovery that had lured me back to Africa had dwindled, as had my energy. But I did make it a point to get to Cameroon as soon as I had recovered sufficiently from my illness. The subject was pure magic, a mountain kingdom that dated back over six hundred years, whose king, Ibrahim, a renaissance man who reigned early in the twentieth century, had commissioned an original, indigenous written script called Shumom in order to modernize his culture. Ibrahim designed his own printing presses and built one of sub-Saharan Africa's first museums. He wrote a poetic treatise on esthetics, which included nearly two hundred criteria for the appreciation of feminine beauty. He produced an elaborate written history of his kingdom, and he commissioned a pharmacopoeia of local plants and traditional medicines.

Then, with the advent of World War I and the takeover by the French of a zone that had been a loosely administered German protectorate, French was imposed as the official tongue, and Ibrahim, suspected of harboring sympathies for the British, who ruled in Nigeria next door, was sent into exile.

The Congo dragged me back down to earth from my Cameroonian idyll soon enough. Madeleine Albright was coming to town, and I had to get to Kinshasa. There had been a last-minute invitation from the State Department to join her on her inaugural trip to the continent as secretary of state.

I was immediately struck by the itinerary, which I fancied as the "renaissance tour," because it included most of the gang the Clinton administration was touting as Africa's new leaders. The choices filled me with skepticism and even chagrin, but my reasons for declining to travel with Albright were rather more practical. The notice was simply too short. Physically, I could not countenance another zigzagging marathon around the continent, and deep down, I felt I had seen far too much hypocrisy and wrongheaded diplomacy in Africa already, too much suffering and neglect, and too many hollow slogans and broken promises to be cooped up in a small airplane and slathered in spin.

It grated on me how thoroughly we had come full circle, renouncing an old guard of "Big Men" only to embrace a brand-new crop of them. The renaissance leaders Albright was visiting were Africa's new soldier princes, men who had come to power not through the ballot box but at gunpoint. The Clinton administration was, in effect, endorsing a supposedly enlightened authoritarianism as just what Africa needed to close some of the yawning gap that separated it from the rest of the world.

Albright made a formulaic stab at promoting democratic values before leaving for Africa, saying that "in our efforts to help post-conflict societies, we should always bear in mind that democracy provides the best route to long-term reconciliation." The message, delivered as a statement rather than in a high-profile speech, made her words seem more like a fig leaf than a heartfelt declaration.

On her first stop, in Ethiopia, Albright made a go at apologizing for the Clinton administration's failure to halt the 1994 Rwandan genocide. "Let me begin that process here today by acknowledging that we—the international community—should have been more active in the early stages of the atrocities in Rwanda in 1994 and called them what they were: genocide," she told the Organization of African Unity, whose headquarters is in Addis Ababa, the Ethiopian capital. Bill Clinton used much the same tepid language in the apology he delivered in person in Rwanda in March 1998. But what, I wondered, is the worth of an appeal for forgiveness that avoids acknowledgment of the original transgression? "In reality the United States did much more than fail to send troops. It led a successful effort to remove most of the UN peacekeepers who were already in Rwanda," said a minutely researched critique of the Clinton administration's behavior during the Rwandan genocide that appeared in *The Atlantic* magazine. "It aggressively worked to block the subsequent authorization of UN reinforcements. It refused to use its technology to jam radio broadcasts that were a crucial instrument in the coordination and perpetuation of the genocide. And even as, on average, 8,000 Rwandans were being butchered each day, U.S. officials shunned the term 'genocide,' for fear of being obliged to act. The United States in fact did virtually nothing 'to try to limit what occurred.' Indeed, staying out of Rwanda was an explicit U.S. policy objective."

In her speech to the OAU, Albright denounced a "culture of impunity that has claimed so many lives and done so much to discredit legitimate authority throughout the region," yet she said nothing publicly about the roundup of journalists there days before she landed in Ethiopia, or the banning of the local rebroadcast of news from radio stations like the BBC and Voice of America. "Africa's best new leaders," Albright said, "have brought a new spirit of hope and accomplishment to their countries. . . . They are challenging the United States and the international community to get over the paternalism of the past, to stop thinking of its Africa policy as a none-too-successful rescue service and to begin seizing the opportunities to work with Africans to transform their continent." These words were being spoken a week before she landed in Kinshasa to embrace Laurent Kabila.

If getting over paternalism meant such patronizing speeches, Africans could probably do just as well without them. America's choice of African friends—countries that were not only not democratic but, for the most part, had no plans of ever becoming democratic—was bad enough. That the Clinton administration was endorsing this new authoritarianism at the very moment when vibrant but fragile democracies were taking root here and there across the continent was more than a pity. It was a disgrace.

Joseph Kapika, a senior aide to Etienne Tshisekedi, put it best to me a few days before Albright touched down in Kinshasa. "It is America that has decided that Paul Kagame is a great leader, and that Yoweri Museveni is a great leader. And now they want us to consider Kabila as a great leader. What we want to know is why it is that what was bad for the countries that lived under Soviet influence should be good for the Congolese?"

Albright's party arrived in Kinshasa on December 11, 1997, and immediately plunged into private meetings with Kabila and members of his government.

Two days earlier, UN investigators had arrived in Mbandaka hoping to finally begin their investigation into the reported massacre there, only to be surrounded by a hostile mob and forced to take refuge in their hotel. The following day, 271 Tutsi, refugees who had fled to Congo to escape the strife in Rwanda, were slaughtered near Bukavu by marauding bands of Hutu militiamen armed with rifles, grenades and machetes. Later came reports of another anti-Tutsi attack inside Rwanda. Clearly, in Central Africa there was more than enough evil to go around.

On the morning of the twelfth, after Albright delivered a speech to a polite audience at the Intercontinental Hotel, I ran into her spokesman and closest aide, James Rubin, in a corridor nearby, and he seemed unusually eager to deliver his talking points. "The feeling is that we have to take a risk in Congo, because the danger to the entire region of chaos in this country is so great. Rather than wait until Kabila does everything we want on democracy, on inclusion, on human rights, the feeling is that he is a clear improvement on Mobutu, and [Albright's] feeling was that we should emphasize the positive. The secretary believes that as the Congo goes, so goes the region, and this region matters, and so therefore does the Congo."

Rubin was on such a roll I could scarcely get a word in. "If you look at Museveni, you look at Meles [prime minister of Ethiopia], and you look at Kagame, they are not saying they want huge amounts of money from us. They are saying they want us to help them work through their problems.... We want to show that this is a region where we can do diplomatic business, and hopefully a place where businesspeople can do business. Our best intelligence info tells us that this group of leaders is not personally corrupt, so that gives you an added sense of confidence.

"Actually a lot of my take comes from an even better source, and it comes to me directly. Philip Gourevitch is my sister's boyfriend." And with that, Rubin said he had to run. Albright was rushing to the Palace of the Nation, where she was to meet Kabila, and then give a joint news conference. I rode over to the palace a little while later with Pierre in his battered and wheezing Fiat. Kabila's security detachment would not allow him to drop me in front of the gates, which give access to the large grassy grounds that surround the coldly formal Chinese-built presidential offices. I had to hoof it the last hundred yards or so, and as I turned the corner and crossed the street, nearing the entrance in the morning's soupy air, I stumbled upon a beating. Uniformed soldiers with black truncheons were furiously laying into a handful of would-be protesters. When a couple of the soldiers turned toward me with what looked like hostile intent, I held up one of my collection of press cards and shouted repeatedly in Lingala, "Ba journaliste!" (I'm a journalist), to which they shrugged and returned to whacking the victims at hand.

The press had been asked to assemble early, and we found ourselves in a large marble hall, a clutch of American reporters who were traveling in the plane with the secretary and me off to one side, and several dozen Congolese and other African reporters across a small divide of empty space. I had been told that there would be time for only one or two questions each from the foreign and the Congolese press, so I tried to work with some of the traveling press on devising questions that would get at the heart of the human rights crisis in the country.

I felt certain that the news of the day would be dominated by the massacre in Bukavu. It was yet another monstrous crime, like so many atrocities before it in the eastern borderland with Rwanda, but in a way it made for a softball of a question, guaranteed to produce ringing condemnation but little new light. I wanted to make sure that Albright and Kabila faced a question about the arrest of opposition leaders in the Congo, and if time permitted, about the government's failure to allow the forensic inspection team to set up operations in Mbandaka.

The traveling press was unaware of the arrest, beating and detention without charge of Arthur Zahidi Ngoma a couple of weeks earlier. This reflected a structural problem that afflicts any traveling press corps. There is rarely time for much advance preparation when they travel. They are moving about in lockstep with the president or the secretary of state, and have little time to report anything on the ground for themselves.

Working quickly, I filled in the reporter who seemed most intrigued by the political situation in Congo, Roy Gutman, then of *Newsday*, focusing on Ngoma's arrest. Gutman asked me if I was sure of my facts, and I said I was, producing a printout of an article I had written about it in the *Times* a few days before. Ngoma had ran afoul of the Kabila government when his group, Forces of the Future, organized a political forum at the Memling Hotel. Kabila had pledged to hold "free" elections two years after seizing power, but in the meantime, only his ruling AFDL was allowed to function openly as a political party, and function it did, flying its blue flag outside the little storefront offices it opened in nearly every neighborhood of Kinshasa.

Kabila's secret police had ordered Ngoma to cancel the forum, but a determined group of activists set up bunting downtown announcing the meeting, and distributed flyers on street corners urging people to come. On the second day of the meetings, security forces cordoned off the area around the hotel and began arresting people. Ngoma, who had not yet arrived, was tipped off and urged to stay away. Bravely, he sent word back to his lieutenants that they should invite the participants to his house, where the meeting could continue in the privacy of his courtyard.

When Ngoma's compound began to fill with activists, journalists and curious passersby, Kabila's police smashed the iron gate and began firing off live rounds and saturating the air with tear gas. Nearly everyone present was arrested. Once in detention, activists and journalists alike were stripped and beaten, one by one, some receiving as many as forty lashes.

A few days after that, I received a call from Arthur Ngoma's brother, Kitwanga, who asked to meet me. Arthur had managed to send me a handwritten note from jail that he wanted published. It read, in part, "we have been subjected to illegal detention, physical and moral torture, and inhumane conditions of detention. But if this is the price we must pay, it is worth it for democracy."

Albright's press conference got off to a bad start when a Congolese reporter, picking up on Kabila's own bitter comments in an interview published a few days before, asked why the United States was pledging "only" $35 to $45 million for the country's reconstruction, "because we need billions and not millions of dollars." Before Albright could respond, he put an equally plucky question to Kabila, asking him to explain the massacre the day before of "more than 200 DRC* citizens on Rwandan soil."

"I believe that the package that we have proposed was actually quite a generous package that has a number of positive aspects to it," Albright said, arching her hawkish eyebrows, immediately on the defensive. "We believe that rather than dispensing large sums of money through that kind of assistance, we should supplement our assistance with trade and investment."

Kabila had glowered impatiently throughout Albright's answer, as if he had just emerged from his twenty years in the bush and was getting his first real taste of the spotlight. "I will answer the two questions that I was asked," he said, his chest puffing with eagerness. "In Bukavu, I can say it was a rearguard fighting of those who still believe—in the name of Congolese revolutionaries—in the management of the republic. . . . The killing of refugees—they are not two hundred; they are over eight hundred, and we have heard nothing from the international community. When we kill one Interahamwe, an assassin, people cry out for a commission of inquiry. I don't have anything more to say on this."

A few moments later, another Congolese reporter ventured farther onto controversial ground, asking, "Mr. President, there are reports that this morning the UN mission of the massacre of Rwandan refugees was blocked at the entrance to Mbandaka. How credible is this information?" For the space of a single answer, Kabila recovered his poise, even if what he was saying was an outright lie. "I should be

*Democratic Republic of the Congo.

informed of this issue before I can answer the question correctly. I am not aware that they were barred from doing their work. I do not know what happened there, because I was not there. I will wait until the minister of rehabilitation, who is in charge of this issue, makes a report to me. I know that they are in the field. We must know what is happening in the field; if they were barred or not."

Kabila knew how tough African journalists could be, which is why he had been locking them up. Now it was Albright's turn on the hot seat. "Ms. Albright, your government regrets having created and supported President Mobutu," began Mwamba Wambumulamba, an editor from the Kinshasa newspaper *Le Potentiel*. "During your visit to Kampala, you showered praise on Ugandan president Yoweri Museveni. Some media reports even said that you presented him as the strongman of the subregion. Since Uganda is not an example of democracy and respect for human rights, is it possible that you are in the process of creating another Mobutu, just to regret it later?"

I fought to repress a smile, and felt a deep professional pride—joy, even—to hear such a foreceful question about America's relationship with African democracy being asked. "First of all," responded Albright, "let me say that there are many people here who are responsible for the existence and the development of Mr. Mobutu, and who still share the responsibility for that." She was arch and seemed so surprised by the challenge that the best she could do was to recycle some stale tidbits from her OAU speech and from other "talking points." She was rambling, almost incoherent. "I do not exactly know what comments people have been making about what I said about President Museveni. I made it quite clear, as I also did in Ethiopia with Prime Minister Meles, that Africa at this stage is fortunate to have a group of strong leaders who are interested in regional cooperation. I also spoke of the same subject in Rwanda during my visit there, and I am still speaking about it with President Kabila by telling him that he is one of these leaders. These presidents have the responsibility to work together and promote economic development, democratization and cooperation in this region of Africa."

Finally, the foreign press's chance to ask a question arrived and the moderator chose my colleague from *Newsday*, who stepped forward a little bit uncertainly, carrying his notebook and a little piece of paper upon which he had written Zahidi Ngoma's name. "Madam Secretary, since you said that you favor freedom of association of the political opposition, some of the political leaders you might have wanted to meet here are all in jail—they have been jailed in the past couple of weeks. Have you asked President Kabila to release anybody who is in jail now for political association? Has he given you any assurances there will be general freedom of political association? Is there any link between U.S. aid to Congo and the freedom of political association?"

He had asked a tightly constructed series of questions, and had left Albright almost no wiggle room. "Yes, President Kabila and I had a lengthy discussion about the importance and effectiveness of elections and the importance of dealing with numerous different political groups," she answered, shifting her body in a way that seemed to express both self-righteousness and annoyance. "And in fact, I think I can say that the bulk of our discussion was about the importance of building a civil society, freedom of association and, generally, the importance of building democratic institutions in a country that had been run in a dictatorial way and full of corruption for several years, and let me say that during the course of these discussions with President Kabila, we established what I believe to be an excellent relationship and I decided that we will give each other telephone numbers so that we could discuss problems that may come up."

Kabila looked as if he were going to rupture a blood vessel while he waited with visible anger for Albright's long, errant answer to finally wind down. "With the permission of the U.S. secretary of state, I would like the journalist who asked the last question to mention the names of the politicians who were arrested for their political affiliations," he said, with an air of challenge. My colleague shot a glance downward at his tiny note, and then pronounced the name Zahidi Ngoma.

"He is not a politician," Kabila said, furiously stabbing his finger in the air and nearly shouting. "He was writing pamphlets and calling on the people to take to the streets and kill people. How can someone who divides the people be a politician? Is this the work of a politician? He was writing pamphlets. Moreover, he was drafting them in the embassy of a foreign country just to divide the people, so that people would resort to force. Do you call this person a politician? Are such people not arrested in your countries? Are they left free? Ngoma is not a politician. I am sure he [referring to the correspondent] has seen the leaflets drafted by this notorious Ngoma. Well, there will be many of them to go to prison if they incite the people to resort to violence. Long live democracy. Ha-ha-ha!"

My colleagues and I shared looks of astonishment. Albright was visibly embarrassed. Her eyebrows arched ever more severely as Kabila spoke, forming italicized question marks on her deeply knitted brow. Diplomatic moments like the one arranged for her were not meant to include such ugly surprises. As the press conference broke up hastily, I imagined the secretary of state was fuming that she had not known more about her Congolese counterpart in advance, starting with a curriculum vitae, which would have read like a rap sheet, before personally stamping him with Washington's seal of approval.

Back in my hotel room I received a call from Susan Rice, Albright's thirty-two-year-old African-American assistant secretary of state for Africa. Her party was already on the road to the airport, and Rice seemed angry and rattled. The Clinton administration and its secretary of state were keenly image conscious, and their high-profile tour of Africa was suddenly turning into a public relations disaster. Rice's voice had an accusatory tone even as she urged me to make haste to Ndjili airport to join them. I sensed she suspected I had somehow engineered all of this. But whatever my role, they had walked into this mess themselves. Indeed, it was of their own making.

James Rubin, operating in deep damage-control mode, issued a statement after the news conference explaining that Albright was unfamiliar with Ngoma's case but intended to find out about it. "Obviously every government has the right to counter those who would incite violence," Rubin said. "But basic to freedom of speech and freedom of association is the right of individuals to state their views freely and openly to others. On this issue, clearly the government of the Congo must improve its record."

Three years later, long after Rwanda had turned on Kabila, invading Congo a second time, this time with the hope of unseating him, Philip Gourevitch wrote in *The New Yorker* what Washington must have already known but chose to ignore. The Clinton administration had subordinated reason and principle to their wish to atone for their past sins in Rwanda by supporting that tiny country's bid to impose a man under its control as president of a neighboring country ninety-five times as large. "It was true that from 1967 to 1986 [Kabila] had managed, as a rebel warlord, to hold out against Mobutu's forces in a tiny redoubt in the mountains of eastern Congo. But his record there was grim enough to make Mobutu look almost benign by comparison. Kabila, preaching a crude sort of Maoist doctrine, had ruled with an absolute hand, and what he called a 'liberated' zone rapidly descended into the sorriest state of dystopia."

Historians decide where the beginning of the end for any regime lies, but for my money the Kabila-Albright press conference was the high-water mark for Mobutu's successor. After her trip, Albright aides and supporters lashed out at the human rights "establishment" for misunderstanding her African diplomacy, but Washington would never again show ardor for the new government in Kinshasa, though another couple of stabs at keeping Kabila in the fold were made over the next few months. Jesse Jackson showed up in Kinshasa a few weeks after Albright's trip in his capacity as "special envoy for Africa." The visit had an unmistakably remedial air, with Jackson meeting Etienne Tshisekedi and other opposition figures whom Albright had snubbed. In a fit of pique, Kabila declined to meet with Jackson, and after the special envoy's departure, he sent Tshisekedi into internal exile "to till the land," forcing the sixty-six-year-old lawyer to live in a village in his native East Kasai region.

In March 1998, Clinton himself made a historic and carefully planned trip to Africa. The president wanted to hit all the right notes—democracy in South Africa, economic revival in Ghana, the emergence of a vibrant civil society in Senegal, where he would make a famous non-apology for slavery. At Entebbe, Uganda, the site of the famous 1976 raid by Israeli commandos on a hijacked airliner, Yoweri Museveni, America's second-favorite African—after Mandela—hosted a summit involving Clinton and five other heads of state, including several of the continent's so-called renaissance leaders. The summit's conclusions, the grandly named Entebbe Principles, called for "genuine transparent partnership" and "long-term, meaningful engagement" by the West, to secure peace and prosperity and to prevent the recurrence of genocide.

Three months later, Ethiopia and Eritrea, two severely impoverished dictatorships whose leaders were both charter members of the renaissance club, were at war over a dusty triangle of infertile land. When the shooting stopped, 100,000 people were dead. Two months after that, Rwanda and Uganda would invade Congo again, first aiming to knock off Kabila, by now judged an embarrassing leader whom they had been unable to control, and then taking deadly aim at each other. Six thousand high-explosive shells rained down on Kisangani, the scene of their most intense fighting, bleeding what was left of the twentieth century from the tragic city at the bend in the river. "The 'new African leaders' policy appeared to be a colossal failure," wrote Peter Rosenblum, one of the United States' best informed experts on Central Africa. "The Entebbe Principles and references to new African leaders were quietly dropped from official statements; those most closely associated with the promotion of the new leaders now say that it was little more than a turn of phrase that the press blew out of proportion."

Congo, too, was soon allowed to fade from view in Washington. No one had foreseen it, but soon the country itself would face outright disappearance.

The time for me to leave Africa had arrived. My feelings were deeply mixed, but my body and spirit were telling me to move on. The movers were due to come to our home in Abidjan to pack our things and ship them off to Hawaii, an interim step in a shift of continents, of subject matter and lifestyle—in short, of everything. I had been given a year to study Japanese at the University of Hawaii, and an exciting new posting awaited me in Tokyo. I also looked at the move as a chance to get to know my family again. My two sons had done a lot of growing during my lengthy absences over the last four years, and I was desperate to reconnect with them while there was still time.

My successor, Nori Onishi, was coming out from New York to spend a week or two with me in Abidjan for a handover before I left. With Nori scheduled to arrive a few days hence, war broke out in Congo with a startling coup de théâtre. There were deep tensions within the president's cabinet and persistent rumors of a forthcoming coup against Kabila. The so-called Katanga mafia, Kabila's kinsmen from the south of the country, were locked in an ever more public face-off against the Rwandan surrogates in the cabinet and in the security forces. That spring, there had even been a major shootout near the Palace of the Nation, in Gombé, in what everyone believed was a Tutsi-led attempt to eliminate Kabila. Central Africa buzzed with rumors that Kigali had turned into a virtual audition line for obscure

Congolese opponents of Kabila and bigwigs from the Mobutu era alike. People like Kengo wa Dondo, the former prime minister, and two of Mobutu's top generals, Kpama Baramoto Kata and Nzimbi Ngbale Kongo wa Bassa, were aggressively pushing their cases for anointment as the next president of Congo to the Rwandan leaders, who were forming a habit of colonization by remote control.

From the start of his rule, Kabila had faced a dilemma. He could be neither legitimate nor popular as long as he leaned heavily on an army and advisors borrowed from Rwanda. But after thirty-two years under Mobutu, Congo was a thoroughly ruined country; without the Rwandans and Ugandans, the writ of Kabila's government would not extend far beyond Kinshasa, and would almost certainly face a swift challenge by emboldened Congolese opponents.

Kabila, meanwhile, had run out of friends outside of Africa. Carrying the water for Rwanda for so long in the cover-up of the massacres of Hutu committed during his seven-month civil war had turned yesterday's "new leader" into an international pariah. For all of Kabila's loyal services, Rwanda had lost patience with him. The heavy investment in overthrowing Mobutu had failed to deliver on its most important goal: security on the border with Congo. In the end Kabila decided to take his chances without Rwanda. In a gambit he later defended as a preemptive strike, late in July 1998 Kabila ordered all foreign forces to leave the country immediately, and began rounding up hundreds of Tutsi in the capital. Rwanda's army initially made a great show of compliance, packing up and moving troops out with characteristic discipline. Then came the startling riposte.

On August 3, Tutsi units began seizing cities in the east of the country, places like Bukavu and Uvira that had been early targets in Kabila's own uprising less than two years before. Simultaneously, units loyal to Rwanda launched a revolt in the capital, which was quickly put down. For Kabila, the brief respite was illusory. The very next day, Tutsi units attacked Kisangani, and in an even bolder move, hijacked cargo planes to fly clear across the country from Goma in the east to Kitona, where they took control of an air force base near the mouth of the Congo River that was once used by the United States for its clandestine war in Angola.

As I flew to Kinshasa for the last time, all I could think of was how the history of Congo seemed to have been rewound, like a movie, and was now being played back again in fast forward. It had taken Kabila seven months to overthrow Mobutu, which had seemed at the time like an amazing feat. Less than a week into the new war, a rebel force controlled most of the east, and was setting itself up to march on the capital from Bas-Zaire, the province at Kinshasa's doorstep. The superlatives one tends to hear concerning Africa usually relate to misery, corruption, humanitarian crises or some form of atrocity. But given the distances involved, given Rwanda's small size and the modesty of its means, as the noose tightened on Kinshasa I thought the attack merited classification among the most audacious military offensives of a war-filled century.

The Mobutu regime once promised a "terrifying offensive," and Kabila was now threatening a "total war." When things got tough, Mobutu would lay low in Gbadolité; Kabila now holed up in Lubumbashi, his own native fief. Similarly, each man had thought that by stoking ethnic hatred he could overcome his enemies and wriggle out of difficulty. But Kabila had little more than ragged militias at his disposal, and several days into the attack the few government-controlled radio stations in the east of the country began broadcasting appeals urging people to kill Rwandan Tutsi using any tools at their disposal, from machetes to barbed wire.

My flight stopped in Lagos. Sani Abacha had recently been overthrown and replaced by a general who promised to—and later did—hand over power to an elected government. Law and order had not yet come to Lagos, though, and when a soldier boarded our flight with his automatic rifle and began demanding to see passengers' passports, and then demanding bribes, I wondered if it ever would. We landed in Kinshasa late at night, and the eighteen-mile route to the center of town was as desolate as I could remember having seen it. Congo was under attack, but as we bounded over cratered streets it was eerie not to see any soldiers in the streets. "Kabila doesn't have any soldiers," Pierre said, chuckling. As I neared my hotel, rounding the big circle near the huge Stadium of Martyrs, the first streetlights I had noticed for miles had been left on to illuminate huge billboard-style advertisements for Kabila. "Laurent Désiré Kabila, the People's Choice," read one of them. I was reminded of the old tee shirts emblazoned with the slogan "Mobutu = Solution."

Every evening, in the 80,000-seat Stadium of Martyrs I had driven past after my late-night arrival, the government managed to muster a small crowd of recruits. Many of them marched to the stadium bare chested, in small clusters, kicking up dust in the dirty streets as they chanted slogans about war and combat, without a clue as to its reality.

Late in the afternoon of August 13, the electricity went out across Kinshasa, and an air of panic coursed through the town. Talk turned to worries of another conquest, another pillage, yet more death. The information minister, Didier Mumengi, tried to explain it all away. "What we have is a technical problem," he said. "The experts are working and will have power restored shortly." It was a patent lie. The rebels had seized the Inga Dam, Africa's largest, and turned off the switch.

In the end, though, Kabila proved far more resourceful in diplomacy than he was either in defense or in governance, and for all its tactical brilliance, Rwanda, in overreaching, had provided him the escape route. Angola had been upset to see smaller East African countries like Rwanda and Uganda expanding their influence so deeply into the western reaches of Central Africa, and when Angola's leaders heard reports of old Mobutu types haunting the hotels of Kigali and Kampala, they had visions of a new safe haven for UNITA rebels on their northern border. Angola poured in troops, and soon so did a half dozen other African countries.

Kabila would survive, but it appeared likely that Congo might not.* It had not been an ordinary colony when it was run by Leopold as his own estate, and it had never truly been a nation in the independence era under Mobutu or under Kabila. At best, it had always been a personal domain, and now Congo, perhaps irreparably fissured, had many masters.

Africa had experienced more than seventy coups d'état since the end of European rule, and the very first—against Lumumba, right here in Kinshasa—was sanctioned by the CIA, but not a single one of them had led to the formation of a new state. For all of their flaws and for all of the booby traps they had produced, Africans had always regarded the borders they inherited as more or less permanent. Then came tiny Rwanda's two invasions of the gigantic land at the very heart of the continent.

It is said that at least 3.3 million people have perished in the chaos

---

*That is, Kabila survived until his murder in his presidential palace by a bodyguard on January 16, 2001.

and deprivation caused by the fighting in Congo since I was last there. Even now, hundreds of thousands of people subsist on berries and grubs, cut off from the outside world without so much as an aspirin to treat the fevers that rage in the tropics. The United Nations estimates that 600,000 of those victims are children five years old or younger—as many people as died in twenty-seven years of pretty much constant warfare in Angola. The figures are astounding.

The Congo wars, which have been called Africa's first world war, were interesting enough the first time around, when Kabila was being installed, if only for their novelty. But it seems that Bantus are not the only people addicted to spectacle, and without the garish figure of Mobutu to captivate the imagination of an outside world that makes an utter abstraction of Africa, the show quickly turned into a bore. Serving up atrocities is a business of diminishing returns, and Washington, having experimented with so-called African solutions to African problems, silently recognized its failure and vowed to stay away altogether. Since then, the forest has taken over. Smeared green and unimaginably thick across the waistline of the continent, defied only by the might of a deceptively lazy river, it muffles all cries.

By the time my successor had taken over, Kinshasa was under threat of attack, and there were no more commercial flights I could take out. Even quick runs across the Congo River to Brazzaville aboard small charter planes were becoming difficult to arrange. The saving grace for me was Rashid, a resourceful Indian businessman whose infinite connections and generosity had often rescued me. Working the collection of cell phones and two-way radios he was never without, he secured me a seat on the last Piper of the day, and promised that its fifteen-minute hop across the river would get me to Brazzaville just in time to catch an Air Afrique flight back home to Abidjan.

At the airport, we were literally held up by Kabila's security people, who shook down the pilot, the crew and the passengers for one entire sweaty hour before allowing us to take off.

I had crossed the Congo River innumerable times, aboard jet airliners, speedy, private outboard launches and rusty ferry boats, partying with Koffi Olomidé, Zaire's most popular musician. I had even crossed by dugout canoe, escaping the new Congo when its borders were still officially closed, just after Kabila had seized power, only to be arrested by the other Congo's river police, aboard a PT boat.

I had never flown out by small plane, though, and on this, my final departure from the country I had visited more than any other in Africa, I let all of the stress drain away from me as Kinshasa, colossal, shabby and now nerve-wracked, faded into the distance. After banking sharply and heading out over the river's broad expanse, the plane glided over the orderly, cultivated fields and Cartesian grid of Brazzaville.

We landed and taxied, and as if by some small miracle, the huge green Air Afrique jet, Flight RK 741 was there, just as it should have been, still parked in the middle of the airport's asphalt apron and boarding its passengers—a bit late, as usual. All I could think was that I would sleep in my own bed this night, one of my last in Africa. The Brazzaville police thought otherwise, though, and together with all of the other passengers who had flown in aboard our little plane, I was whisked away from the waiting jet toward yet another security check.

As I've said, few things are executed so energetically in Africa as what the French language so delicately calls *les formalités*. A nation may be broken and bankrupt, civil servants and soldiers may be unpaid, but a traveler can always count on having someone beckon him to check his papers—especially when he is in a hurry.

"I'm not entering this Congo," I pleaded. "I am merely here in transit. I've got to catch that plane." A sympathetic guard finally listened to me and offered to escort me to the airline's offices to get a boarding pass. When I found the airline agent, though, she was busily counting the stubs of the passengers who had already entered the Airbus. Its huge engines could be heard idling. "Le vol est fermé," she said with finality, the flight is closed, scarcely looking up. I protested that I had a first-class ticket, that I had confirmed my last-minute arrival by radio from Kinshasa, and that I knew the local director of Air Afrique. It had no impact. Determined to board the plane anyway, I ran out onto the tarmac, but the aluminum stairway was being wheeled away, and the ground personnel, their ears covered with protective gear, waved me away furiously.

I finally had to reconcile myself to the fact that I would be spending the night in Brazzaville. But it was only as I searched for a taxi amid the knots of people still milling around the terminal that I remembered that the quiet, orderly city I had once known, a place of well-dressed people and lazy cafés, was no more. It had been utterly destroyed in its own obscure "little" civil war. The Hotel Méridien was the only intact lodging left in town, so the driver I found took me straight there, warning that it was likely to be full. Indeed, the scene in the lobby wasn't encouraging. The place was swarming with stressed-out foreigners—evacuees from Kinshasa and reporters hoping to make their way there in time for the city's widely predicted fall. People were bunking up three and four to a room, but I managed to crash alone in the empty room of Robert Weiner, a CNN producer who had not yet arrived. I wanted nothing more than to call my family in Hawaii and then my office in Abidjan to say I had missed the flight. I turned on the TV and found nothing but electric snow. Brazzaville no longer had a functioning station.

I opened the curtains to capture the afternoon's final fading light, and found that the windows had been shot out so long ago that the metal frames that once held glass were rusted out. Then I picked up the phone to make a call, but got the switchboard. With incongruous cheer, the operator told me there was no longer any telephone service in Brazzaville. "If you wish to make an overseas call, though, you can come to the reception area and use our satellite phone."

I rose early after that gloomy night. My driver from the day before had come to greet me and take me back to the airport, where the scene resembled a minor riot. Brazzaville had been a major hub for Air Afrique, but very few flights landed here any longer, and officials from Kabila's Congo were sending scores of family members onward to West Africa. There were Lebanese traders jousting to get their gems to market in Antwerp. There were members of the remaining elite from here, too, people who had finally scored visas to other countries and were desperate for their wives and children to get out.

All of this meant, of course, a great opportunity for theft, and like crocodiles lying in ambush in an African riverbed awaiting the passage of migratory beasts, every uniformed corps from the Congo was heavily represented on the airport's premises.

I made it through the *formalités* on the strength of a stony expression practiced for just such occasions, and sheer moral fatigue. Three different officers, customs, army and immigration police, were fighting over the rights to the Lebanese trader who stood just before me in the dark and narrow corridor of this airport—a gauntlet, really. Someone inspected my papers and waved me on. Another demanded 2,000 CFA francs, saying it was for the "stamp tax." Yet another agent tried to order me into a small room for a pat down. "I am in transit. My money is finished," I mumbled, lying. He let me pass.

Le Roi Est Mort *(Long Live the King)*

All that remained of the Congolese state was naked extortion from the president to the lowliest government agent. But there was worse ahead. At three consecutive "customs" desks in the final, narrow, unlit corridor that led to the departure area, bags were being searched, and money was being confiscated. Those who raised too strong an objection were threatened with being sent back from whence they came. What Sony Labou Tansi had written, "This is the most sordid time there has ever been," was now manifest. Kafka translated locally meant ever more exposure to the Congolese state.

I sensed my heart racing. I was weary and stressed. There had been too many trials like these. Gentle Japan awaited me if only I could hold on, and I knew instinctively that the best approach was simply to remain cool. I must have looked unruffled, because I was never stopped.

I settled into the unenclosed departure area. There had once been a neat little first-class lounge nearby, but it was long since destroyed. Where I sat had once been the airport's observation deck. Rubble and litter were strewn all around, and there were bullet marks and blood-stains still visible on the walls, along with tatters of clothing, the remnants of a battle that had raged here for weeks.

I was sitting on a concrete ledge. Others squatted on the ground. Had it rained, I thought, as it often did for days on end in this equatorial river basin, we couldn't have been less well sheltered. As the Cameroon Airways jet I was to fly out on taxied, those of us gathered for boarding received a powerful blast from its exhaust. A skinny, enterprising waiter dressed in fading whites, a man who had invented his own job in the finest African tradition of survival, circulated among us with a tray suspended on a naked cord that hung from his neck. It contained a selection of cigarettes, soft drinks and alcohol. "I'll have a cognac, please," I said, spotting a bottle of Rémy Martin and explaining that I looked forward to a profound sleep. Without irony, he replied, "Monsieur, I do not recommend profound sleep around here."

The signal finally came, and there was a rush of people down the stairway to the tarmac. It was free seating, which meant a free-for-all. After a couple of hours in the air, we landed in Douala, the commercial capital of Cameroon, for what was billed as a three-hour layover. As in Lagos, the boarding corridors that were once used to board and deplane had long ago frozen in rust.

As delay piled upon delay, our time on the ground dragged on.

Three hours became seven. I was being treated to yet one more Central African exercise in decay. My mood was grim, and this brought to mind an earlier trip to Douala. All of the fancy lampposts that lined the grandly traced highway from the center of town to the airport had been stripped of their hardware. A collection of headless stanchions bowed in mockery of us all.

By and by I grew tired of the barren transit lounge and talked my way past immigration to the departure area, where I hoped to find some newspapers and a telephone. Finally, I thought, I would be able to reach my family.

"Is there anywhere I can make a phone call?" I asked an airport worker. "The phones have been out here for days," came the answer. "Somebody ripped out all the cables. People are poor here. This is what we do to survive."

Notes

INTRODUCTION

xvi "the global architects": John le Carré, *New York Times*, May 4, 1993.

CHAPTER ONE

Prehistory

15 "How do you think we can fight": Chinua Achebe, *Things Fall Apart* (New York: Fawcett Crest, 1984), p. 162.

16 "[Ghana] was manifestly a national state on its way": Basil Davidson, *The Black Man's Burden: Africa and the Curse of the Nation-State* (New York: Times Books, 1992), p. 76.

17 "King Coffee is too rich a neighbor": Robert B. Edgerton, *The Fall of the Ashanti Empire: The Hundred-Year War for Africa's Gold Coast* (New York: Free Press, 1995), p. 167.

18 At the end of World War II: John W. Cell, Judith M. Brown and William Roger Louis, eds., *The Oxford History of the British Empire*, vol. 4 (Oxford: Oxford University Press, 1999), p. 232.

19 "the desire—one might indeed say the need": Chinua Achebe, "An Image of Africa: Racism in Conrad's *Heart of Darkness*," *Massachusetts Review* 18 (1977).

19 "The world of the West basks": Michel-Rolph Trouillot, *Silencing the Past: Power and the Production of History* (Boston: Beacon, 1995).

19 Africa has little history worth recalling: "Obituary of Lord Dacre of Glanton, Regius Professor of History at Oxford and Master of Peterhouse, Cambridge, Who Resisted the Narrow View," *The Daily Telegraph*, Jan. 27, 2003.

19 "The prehistoric man was cursing us": Joseph Conrad, *Heart of Darkness* (New York: Penguin, 1999), p. 107.

Notes

22 But in the end: Patrick Manning, *Slavery and African Life: Occidental, Oriental and African Slave Trades* (Cambridge: Cambridge University Press, 1988).

23 "For Africans, enslavement was a threat": John Reader, *Africa: A Biography of the Continent* (London: Hamish Hamilton, 1997), pp. 437–38.

24 "Each day the traders are kidnapping our people": Adam Hochschild, *King Leopold's Ghost: A Story of Greed, Terror, and Heroism in Colonial Africa* (New York: Houghton Mifflin, 1998), p. 13.

24 "These goods exert such a great attraction": Ibid.

CHAPTER THREE

Plague

52 "Had Leopold been a different kind of man": Pagan Kennedy, *Black Livingstone: A True Tale of Adventure in the Nineteenth-Century Congo* (New York: Viking, 2002), p. 27.

53 "His political insignificance made him invisible": Ibid.

54 In little more than a generation: Hochschild, *King Leopold's Ghost*, p. 280.

58 "the claim of the stranger—the victim on the TV screen": Michael Ignatieff, *The Warrior's Honor: Ethnic War and the Modern Conscience* (New York: Holt, 1997), p. 14.

CHAPTER FOUR

The Golden Bough

72 "Your situation is rich with rewards": Sony Labou Tansi, *La Vie et Demie* (Paris: Editions du Seuil, 1979), p. 24; my translation.

73 "tomorrow with the eyes of today": Ibid., p. 10.

77 "In this country, night has the appearance of divinity": John Updike, "A Heavy World: Fury Haunts a Late Novelist's Work," *The New Yorker*, Feb. 5, 1996.

CHAPTER FIVE

Greater Liberia

102 "I started with a shotgun and three rifles": Denis Johnson, "The Small Boys' Unit: Searching for Charles Taylor in a Liberian Civil War," *Harper's*, October 2000, p. 137.

103 "Your American ambassador came": Ibid.

106 "Perhaps I made a wrong career choice": Mark Huband, *The Skull Beneath the Skin: Africa After the Cold War* (Boulder: Westview, 2001), p. 62.

CHAPTER SIX

Falling Apart

113 Here again were unmistakable echoes: Hochschild, *King Leopold's Ghost*, p. 88.

115 Abundant hydroelectric potential already existed: Jonathan Kwitney, *Endless Enemies: The Making of an Unfriendly World* (New York: Penguin, 1986), p. 23.

115 "The Domain, with its shoddy grandeur": V. S. Naipaul, *A Bend in the River* (New York: Vintage, 1989), p. 103.

CHAPTER SEVEN
Where Peacocks Roam

127 The aversion to the word "genocide": Samantha Power, "Bystanders to Genocide: Why the United States Let the Rwandan Tragedy Happen," *The Atlantic*, September 2001, p. 96.

134 The music grew ever louder: Crawford Young and Thomas Turner, *The Rise and Decline of the Zairian State* (Madison: University of Wisconsin Press, 1985), p. 153.

141 By the time most of the dust had settled: The International Rescue Committee, April 8, 2003: "The four and a half year war in the Democratic Republic of Congo has taken more lives than any other since World War II and is the deadliest documented conflict in African history, says the International Rescue Committee. A mortality study released today by the IRC estimates that since August 1998, when the war erupted, through November 2002 when the survey was completed, at least 3.3 million people died in excess of what would normally be expected during this time."

143 "Despite Rwanda's size": Philip Gourevitch, "Forsaken: Congo Seems Less a Nation Than a Battlefield for Countless African Armies," *The New Yorker*, Sept. 25, 2000, p. 56.

149 "Valuable real estate for a while": Naipaul, *A Bend in the River*, p. 27.

CHAPTER EIGHT
Castles in the Sand

152 Like General Touré before him: Robert M. Press, "Mali Elections Break New Ground," *Christian Science Monitor*, Feb. 2, 1992.

154 Washington's spending patterns were no mere abstraction: Howard W. French, "In France, Savvy Candidates for President Take a Trip to Africa," *New York Times*, Mar. 13, 1995. Speaking to a colloquium of Francophone mayors, held in Abidjan, Ivory Coast, Jacques Chirac, then mayor of Paris and a former prime minister, said: "For developing countries, multiparty politics is a political error . . . a sort of luxury that developing countries, which must concentrate their efforts on economic growth, cannot afford." Albert Bourgi, "Jacques Chirac et le sens de l'histoire," *Jeune Afrique*, no. 1523, Mar. 12, 1990, p. 18.

156 The whole process reeked of cynicism: Joseph E. Stiglitz, *Globalization and Its Discontents* (New York: Norton, 2002), p. 6.

CHAPTER NINE
Tough Love

171 Washington and its European partners were preoccupied: United States State Department, *USIA Electronic Journal*, vol. 2, no. 2 (May 1997) and the United Nations.

173 "We deployed a large marine amphibious force": Bill Berkeley, *The Graves Are Not Yet Full* (New York: Basic Books, 2001), p. 83.

173 On the ground in Liberia, American officials rejected all requests: Neil Henry, "Doctors' Group Criticizes U.S. for Not Intervening in Liberia," *Washington Post*, Aug. 16, 1990.

CHAPTER TEN

Long Knives

190 Week after week, though, the American Embassy in Kigali: Peter Rosenblum, "Irrational Exuberance: The Clinton Administration in Africa," *Current History*, May 2002.

210 Just days before, the United Nations had reported: Hrvoje Hranjski, "100,000 Refugees Are Missing in Eastern Zaire," Associated Press, Apr. 26, 1997.

210 UN Secretary-General Kofi Annan said: Ibid.

214 Che Guevara, who had come to the Congo: Piero Gleijeses, *Conflicting Missions: Havana, Washington, and Africa, 1959–1976* (Chapel Hill: University of North Carolina Press, 2002), p. 154.

215 Ultimately, Kabila forced his way: William B. Cosma, *Fizi 1967–1986: Le Maquis Kabila* (Brussels: Institut Africain-CEDAF, 1997), pp. 111–12; my translation from the French.

216 In the months immediately prior: United States Department of Defense, *Reports to Congress on U.S. Military Activities in Rwanda, 1994–August 1997*.

216 Senior officials from the American Embassy: Joseph Farah, "Did U.S. Help Zaire's Rebels?" WorldNet Daily, May 5, 1997.

222 Later I learned that Ambassador Simpson: A colorful account of Ambassador Simpson's role as catalyst and intermediary is contained in Michela Wrong, *In the Footsteps of Mr. Kurtz: Living on the Brink of Disaster in the Congo* (London: Fourth Estate, 2000), p. 276.

CHAPTER ELEVEN

Le Roi Est Mort *(Long Live the King)*

232 "Oddly, a number of recent reports": Philip Gourevitch, "The Vanishing: How Congo Became Zaire, and Zaire Became the Congo," *The New Yorker*, June 2, 1997.

232 "For weeks now, the U.N. sleuths": Philip Gourevitch, "Stonewall Kabila: Why the U.N.'s Word Is as Unreliable as the Congo Leader's," *The New Yorker*, Oct. 6, 1997. (Emphasis mine. To speak of "Kabila's forces" is to prudishly avert one's eyes from the generally acknowledged reality that the AFDL rebellion was essentially conducted by an army on loan from Rwanda.)

233 "Townspeople say they little suspected": Robert Block, "Blood Stains: Kabila's Government Is Tainted by Reports of Refugee Slaughter—Rwandan Troops That Aided Congo Leader in Victory Sought Tribal Vengeance—Deal Made or No Control?" *Wall Street Journal*, June 6, 1997.

241 "It aggressively worked to block": Samantha Power, "Bystanders to the Genocide: Why the United States Let the Rwandan Tragedy Happen," *The Atlantic*, September 2001, p. 86.

247 "He is not a politician," Kabila said: Transcribed from the author's notes, supplemented by BBC Worldwide Monitoring.

248 Three years later, long after Rwanda had turned: Philip Gourevitch, "Forsaken: Congo Seems Less a Nation Than a Battlefield for Countless African Armies," *The New Yorker,* Sept. 25, 2000, p. 54.

250 "The 'new African leaders' policy": Peter Rosenblum, "Irrational Exuberance: The Clinton Administration in Africa," *Current History,* May 2002, p. 196.

257 "This is the most sordid time": Sony Labou Tansi, *L'Anté-peuple* (Paris: Editions du Seuil, 1983), quoted from John Updike, "A Heavy World: Fury Haunts a Late Writer's Work," *The New Yorker,* Feb. 5, 1996.

Acknowledgments

Space does not allow me to thank all of the many people whose intelligence, friendliness, love and criticism helped me carry this project to fruition.

Because this book is in some sense the work of a lifetime, my thanks must first go to my parents, David and Carolyn French, and to my wife, Avouka Koffi, who, in their different ways, introduced me to the continent.

I also cannot express enough thanks to my sons, William and Henry. They put up with many long absences as small children, and yet encouraged me to persevere in the writing of this book as they developed into young men.

Robert Grossman, whose pictures illustrate my text, was a fine and steady traveling companion throughout much of the story that unfolds here. His questions often prodded me to challenge my assumptions.

Ofeibea Quist-Arcton, another colleague and frequent travel companion, did much the same. Her pluck and her grace with language, like her respect for the facts, inspired me greatly.

For whatever defects and shortcomings that are contained herein, I alone am responsible. This book has been immeasurably improved, however, by the comments and suggestions of a core group of readers, starting with Robert and Ofeibea, who began reading the earliest pages of the manuscript when I was still plagued with many doubts. Their generosity helped sustain me.

Other critical readers whose patience and thoughtfulness helped me improve this work include James French, my brother, whose love of Africa is equal to my own; Peter Rosenblum, associate projects director of Harvard Law School's Human Rights Program, whose knowledge of Central Africa is matched by his knowledge of African policy circles in Washington; and René Lemarchand, of the University of Florida, whose work on democracy and authoritarianism has always challenged conventional wisdoms about Africa. As someone who has traveled widely in Asia, but never to Africa, Stuart Isett, a close colleague in Tokyo, helped me eliminate many points of potential confusion. The suggestions of Daniel Sharfstein, my former stringer in Ghana, inspired countless refinements.

Bill Keller, who was my foreign editor at the *New York Times*, showed a rare appreciation for Africa that helped make the hardships of the road worthwhile.

Thanks also go to my editor, Jonathan Segal, whose deftness often amazed me, and to production editor Ellen Feldman, for her exemplary care for detail.

Finally, thanks to my agent, Gloria Loomis, who believed early and persisted.

Index

Howard W. French is a senior writer for the *New York Times* who has reported from six continents. After teaching English at the University of Ivory Coast in the early 1980s, he began his career as a freelance reporter covering Africa for the *Washington Post, Africa News* and numerous other publications. In 1986, French joined the *Times*, and has served as the newspaper's bureau chief for Central America and the Caribbean, West and Central Africa, and Japan and Korea. In 1997, his coverage of the fall of Mobutu Sese Seko won the Overseas Press Club of America's award for best newspaper interpretation of foreign affairs. French was born in Washington, D.C., and lives in Shanghai, China, with his wife, Avouka, and two sons.

A NOTE ON THE TYPE

This book was set in Janson, a typeface long thought to have been made by the Dutch-man Anton Janson, who was a practicing typefounder in Leipzig during the years 1668–1687. However, it has been conclusively demonstrated that these types are actu-ally the work of Nicholas Kis (1650–1702), a Hungarian, who most probably learned his trade from the master Dutch typefounder Dirk Voskens. The type is an excellent example of the influential and sturdy Dutch types that prevailed in England up to the time William Caslon (1692–1766) developed his own incomparable designs from them.

Composed by North Market Street Graphics
Lancaster, Pennsylvania

Printed and bound by Berryville Graphics
Berryville, Virginia

Designed by Soonyoung Kwon

Map by Jeffrey Ward

ML   S/04